A New Christian Manifesto
Pledging Allegiance to the Kingdom of God

Bob Ekblad

Westminster John Knox Press
LOUISVILLE • LONDON

Scripture quotations from the New Revised Standard Version of the Bible (NRSV) are copyright © 1989 by the Division of Christian Education of the National Council of the Churches of Christ in the U.S.A. and are used by permission.

Scripture quotations marked RSV are from the Revised Standard Version of the Bible, copyright © 1946, 1952, 1971, and 1973 by the Division of Christian Education of the National Council of the Churches of Christ in the U.S.A. and are used by permission.

Scripture quotations marked NIV are from *The Holy Bible, New International Version,* copyright © 1973, 1978, 1984 International Bible Society. Used by permission of Zondervan Bible Publishers.

Scripture quotations marked NASB are taken from the *New American Standard Bible,* © 1960, 1971, 1972, 1973, 1975, 1977 by The Lockman Foundation. Used by permission.

"The Scream" by Brita Miko is reprinted herein with the permission of Brita Miko.

Book design by Sharon Adams
Cover design by designpointinc.com

First edition
Published by Westminster John Knox Press
Louisville, Kentucky

This book is printed on acid-free paper that meets the American National Standards Institute Z39.48 standard. ∞

PRINTED IN THE UNITED STATES OF AMERICA

08 09 10 11 12 13 14 15 16 17 — 10 9 8 7 6 5 4 3 2 1

Library of Congress Cataloging-in-Publication Data is available at the Library of Congress, Washington, D.C.

ISBN 978-0-664-23231-3

To my beloved wife and best friend Gracie,
pure of heart and a keeper of the faith.
To my sons Isaac and Luke and my daughter Anna,
heirs of God's coming kingdom, enjoyers of its beauty and bounty.

Also from Westminster John Knox Press by Bob Ekblad

Reading the Bible with the Damned

Contents

Introduction   1

1. Born from Below   10

2. Living as Wetbacks   32

3. Stop the World   52

4. Resisting the Powers through Advocacy and Deliverance   68

5. I Pledge Allegiance to the Kingdom of God   93

6. Reentering the Promised Land   120

7. Announcing the Victory of the Cross   140

Notes   175

Acknowledgments

This project began on the beaches of Mozambique in June 2006 as I received prayer from Rolland Baker, Supresa Sithole, Jose, Francie, and other leaders of Iris Ministries. As the group prayed over me before my son Luke and I departed, Supresa suddenly began prophesying that I would write a book, that many would read. "Urgent, urgent, urgent, urgent, urgent!" he said with his thick African-Portuguese accent, and he circled me repeatedly, thrusting out his right hand toward me with each declaration. That day we flew to South Africa to visit Gerald West and Jonathan Draper. That night in Gerald West's vacation house on the coast south of Durban I awoke in the middle of the night with chapters and themes rushing through my head. This continued the following night at Jonathan and Marian Draper's home in Pietermaritzburg. So I want to offer special thanks to Supresa Sithole and Rolland and Heidi Baker, modern-day apostles of the highest order. I am also deeply thankful to Gerald West and Jonathan Draper, who have inspired me and challenged me over the years and recently regarding the themes in this book.

Without my community of beloved inmates in Skagit County Jail and my friends and colleagues at Tierra Nueva this work would not exist. Special thanks to Roger Capron, Lolito Cruz, David Calix, Amy Muia, Elizabeth Turman, Troy Terpstra, Rocio Robles, Nick Bryant, Chris Hoke, Ryann Lachowicz, Eugenio Benitez, Zack Joy, Jose Flores, Jessie Garcia, Epifania Garcia, Joe Woodbury, Tina and Scott Thomas, Rachel Beatty, Emily Martin, Salvio and Victoria Hernandez, Marcelino Santiago, and many others from our English and Spanish faith communities. Special thanks to David Calix, Elia Dominguez, and Hector Giron of Tierra Nueva in Honduras. Chris Hoke and Troy Terpstra have been especially helpful readers, ministry colleagues, and dialogue partners.

I am deeply grateful to Heidi Baker for reading through this manuscript and offering insightful and encouraging comments. Special thanks to Ron Kuyk-endall for his thoughtful critique of this manuscript and for hours of engaging discussion. I am also grateful to my brother Andy Ekblad, and to Brandon Walker, Brad Jersak, Jim Watt, John Roddam, Rich Lang, and Paul Myers for their reading of earlier versions, and for prayers and dialogue throughout the writing process. Thanks to Brita Miko for her encouragement and contribution of the brilliant poem that ends the book. I am thankful to John and Carol Arnott, for the impact of their ministry on my life and on Tierra Nueva, and for their ongoing friendship in Christ. I am forever grateful to Rosemary Lambert, Patty Stamets, Tina Thomas, and Barbara Perman, who have kept me and my family before God in their prayers. Thanks to the members of my monthly pastors prayer group, to Tom Ross, Rich DeRuiter, Steve Thompson, and Gary Short for their friendship and encouragement. Others who have contributed include Serge Jacquemus, John and Birgit Shorack, Ray Pickett and Bill and Mary Ann Nagy. Special thanks to the many people who helped on this project at Westminster John Knox, and especially to my editor Jon Berquist, whose enthusiasm and expertise have significantly enhanced this book.

Thanks to my parents Gene and Ann Ekblad; my other two brothers, Dave and Peter and sister Julie; and my children Isaac, Luke, and Anna for their constant love and support. I am deeply grateful to my wife Gracie for her love, friendship, and partnership throughout this project and our twenty-five years of marriage. Finally I thank Jesus for inspiring me throughout this writing process by his example and constant presence through the Holy Spirit, who has brought to memory Jesus' words and actions, and made Scripture after Scripture come alive freshly throughout my life and this writing process.

Introduction

"Your kingdom come, your will be done, on earth as in heaven" is prayed regularly by millions of Christians from a broad diversity of perspectives who recite the Lord's Prayer. This prayer is a demand, "your Kingdom, come! Your will be done!"—imperatives addressed to our Father in heaven, calling on heaven to break into this world here and now. What would it look like if this prayer were answered? Jesus himself announces that the kingdom of God is near. Yet he tells Pilate, "My kingdom is not of this world. If My kingdom were of this world, then My servants would be fighting, that I might not be delivered up to the Jews; but as it is, My kingdom is not of this realm" (John 18:36 NASB). What does it mean to expect the kingdom of God that is not of this world to come on earth as in heaven? How can we position ourselves to become fully engaged in announcing and experiencing God's kingdom in our lifetimes while at the same time anticipating its fulfillment after death?

In these days there is abounding confusion among Christians concerning what we can expect to see of God's presence and reign here on planet Earth and how we can bring it about. One visible division among Christians is between those who see their primary calling as proclaiming the good news of God's love in Christ to unbelievers so they will accept Jesus and receive eternal life in heaven

1

after death, and a second group who focus more on improving the lot of the poor, the excluded, and the environment in this lifetime on earth through ministries that provide relief from suffering or that emphasize sustainable development, empowerment, and human rights.

People whose primary focus is personal conversion and life after death may undervalue the importance of seeking transformation of structures that contribute to poverty, homelessness, illness, and the like. Some may focus exclusively on surviving until the "rapture," when Jesus zooms them off to heaven before all hell breaks loose on earth. Those who focus only on transforming structures of oppression may dismiss the afterlife as irrelevant or have a low expectation for the eternal to break into the present through miraculous signs and wonders that inspire faith in the unseen.

A third group includes Christians who are dedicated to helping people who do not believe in Jesus come to a place of faith and personal transformation. The highest priority for these Christians is getting people "saved" through one-on-one evangelism, proclamation, and service and miraculous "signs and wonders" that confirm the message. These sorts of Christians are often actively engaged in defending the rights of the unborn and crime victims, and of Christians' freedom to pray and worship publicly. At times they appear accommodating to wars and natural disasters, as long as they can be harnessed for the larger cause of "bringing in the harvest" through removing governments hostile to Christianity or bringing people to a place of desperation and openness. They are often criticized by the second group for naively defending violent military interventions, right-wing governments, economic systems, and laws (e.g., the death penalty) that hurt poor people and the environment. This group is increasingly involved in ministries of mercy to the poor as a way of demonstrating the love of God.

The second group tends to work for concrete changes here and now through both ministries of presence and sustainable development, and through challenging the underlying economic, political, and social class structures that contribute to poverty and oppression. They would see this as a holistic style of evangelism that shows love in concrete ways through realistically facing problems. These groups place a high value on awareness raising, organizing, protesting, racial reconciliation, victim-offender reconciliation, and institution building, and are almost exclusively focused on this world. They tend to put a low priority on evangelism, due to the high value they place on justice, conservation, inclusiveness, tolerance, and diversity. They are dedicated to human rights, economic justice, peacemaking, and protecting the environment from abuse. They often have little expectation that God will miraculously intervene to bring physical healing, deliverance, or resolution of conflict. Many of these people are burning out or are on the verge of despair in the face of ongoing wars, the AIDS epidemic, environmental degradation, and poverty. I am convinced that diverse approaches must be integrated as each group learns from the others, in order for the good news of God's love and liberation to have a maximal impact. There is an urgent need today to consider and reconsider both what we can expect to see of God's kingdom here on earth and our part in its advent.

Through his life Jesus himself reveals ways in which this prayer can be lived out to usher in heaven's realities on earth. Jesus' ministry begins at his baptism, where his identity is founded in a gesture of solidarity with sinners and in receiving love and empowerment from his Father and the Holy Spirit. This death-and-resurrection beginning must be reenacted by Christians today as a basis for a new life as Christ's body in the world—the presence of God's kingdom.

John the Baptist (Matt. 3:2) and Jesus are described in the Gospels as announcing the kingdom of God as at hand.[1] We read the Gospel narratives as illustrative of heaven becoming manifested through the ministry of the human one, Jesus of Nazareth. Matthew 4:23–24 (NASB) states Jesus' mission clearly:

> And Jesus was going about in all Galilee, teaching in their synagogues, and proclaiming the gospel of the kingdom, and healing every kind of disease and every kind of sickness among the people. And the news about him went out into all Syria; and they brought to him all who were ill, taken with various diseases and pains, demoniacs, epileptics, paralytics; and he healed them.

Jesus reveals a God who responds to people's concrete needs in their immediate lifetimes through healing the sick, casting out demons, defending the condemned, embracing the excluded sinners, feeding hungry crowds, and teaching the Scriptures to ordinary people.

We learn from the Gospel accounts that Jesus calls and works through ordinary people like Mary, fishermen, notorious sinners like Matthew the tax collector, marginalized women, and Judas his betrayer. Jesus sends out the Twelve and then the seventy-two,[2] empowering them to do his works and "greater works than these" (John 14:12 NASB).

Visions abound in Scripture of God's kingdom coming to earth. The vision of a new heaven and new earth in Isaiah 65:17–25 is mostly this-worldly and possible to realize. The imperfect verb tense shows God presently creating the new earth in a way that extends into the future—now and not yet. The vision of the new earth in Revelation 21:2–5 adds abundant detail that makes the picture even more attractive.

So how does God's kingdom come and God's will be done on earth as in heaven happen here in the midst of our broken world? How do we become effective agents of transformation of the old world into the new? I have been asking these questions since August 1982, when we founded Tierra Nueva, our current site in our struggle to see God's kingdom become visible and ultimately victorious.

Tierra Nueva started as a model farm and outreach with the objective of promoting sustainable farming and preventive healthcare among the poorest of the poor in rural Honduras. The name, Tierra Nueva or New Earth, was taken from Isaiah 65:17–25 and Revelation 21:1–5.

In Isaiah 65 the Lord declares, "For behold I am creating[3] new heavens and a new earth; and the former things shall not be remembered or come to mind. But be glad and rejoice forever in what I am creating" (vv. 17–18a NRSV). These verses jumped out at us as we cleared our land and began planting an organic-intensive farm paradise:

> No longer will there be in it an infant who lives but a few days, / Or an old man who does not live out his days; / For the youth will die at the age of one hundred. . . . And they shall build houses and inhabit them; / They shall also plant vineyards and eat their fruit. / They shall not build, and another inhabit, / They shall not plant, and another eat. . . . They shall not labor in vain, / Or bear children for calamity. . . . It will also come to pass that before they call, I will answer; and while they are still speaking, I will hear (Isa. 65:20, 21–22a, 23a, 24 NASB)

On the other hand, other verses pointed to another dimension on the other side of death.

> The wolf and the lamb shall graze together, and the lion shall eat straw like the ox. (Isa. 65:25a NASB)

> And I saw a new heaven and a new earth; for the first heaven and the first earth passed away, and there is no longer any sea. And I saw the holy city, new Jerusalem, coming down out of heaven from God, made ready as a bride adorned for her husband. And I heard a loud voice from the throne, saying, "Behold, the tabernacle of God is among men, and He shall dwell among them, and they shall be His people, and God Himself shall be among them, and He shall wipe away every tear from their eyes; and there shall no longer be any death; there shall no longer be any mourning, or crying, or pain; the first things have passed away." And He who sits on the throne said, "Behold, I am making all things new." (Rev. 21:1–5a NASB)

Isaiah 65 gave a vision of the new earth that looked as if it could be mostly realized in this life, while Revelation 21 showed a picture of a new heaven and new earth that no development program or government could bring about. We have been living in the tension between these visions.

In keeping with the vision in Isaiah 65 at Tierra Nueva, we sought to decrease infant mortality, for which Honduras had one of the highest rates in the Western Hemisphere at that time, and increase life expectancy, the lowest in the hemisphere at that time. We taught basic hygiene, encouraged people to boil their water and plant vegetable gardens, and increased basic grain production through introducing soil and water-conserving contoured terraces and establishing gravity-flow water systems. We organized agricultural committees and grain-storage cooperatives and helped people buy storage silos and land so that people could plant and benefit from the fruits of their labor. We opposed the Reagan administration's efforts to push the Honduran government to recruit more peasants for America's perceived national-security interests, so people would not bear children for calamity (Isa. 65:23).

Tierra Nueva, now an ecumenical ministry based in Burlington, Washington, includes a jail ministry; family support center for Hispanic immigrants, ex-offenders, and the homeless; Spanish and English congregations; a training center called The People's Seminary, to equip people to minister to people on the margins; and a ministry in Honduras to subsistence farmers.[4] We have encountered obstacles to real change that have humbled us and nearly destroyed us, as well as those among whom we minister.

In Central America and Mexico we have encountered complex barriers to the deceptively simple objective of helping Honduran and Mexican farmers increase production of basic grains and vegetables. Free-trade agreements privilege foreign companies and local elites, allowing North American grain farmers to sell heavily subsidized corn and beans for prices lower than peasants can produce them. Pressure from wealthy nations for poor, debtor countries to implement neoconservative belt-tightening measures to pay back loans exacerbates poverty as desperately needed social programs are cut. Consequently subsistence farmers are unable to sustain themselves in their own communities. A massive migration from Central America and Mexico to the United States has coincided with tightening security at our borders and calls for increasing enforcement to exclude undocumented workers. The failure of the United States adequately to respond to problems at home as we wage destructive and expensive wars in Afghanistan and Iraq has further pushed me and others into despair.

Here in the Northern Hemisphere, addiction to drugs like crack cocaine, heroin, methamphetamines, and alcohol has held people captive in spite of our prayers, advocacy, Bible study, and counseling. Record numbers of people are being sent off to prison in the United States during the primes of their lives, where they are further schooled in fine points of criminal life. Official legal, immigration, welfare, and healthcare systems here in the United States have each presented insurmountable obstacles to our best efforts at advocacy that have challenged our theology and practice.

Hope is possible only if the darkness of sin, death, incarceration, deportation, and war is countered by a more powerful light. Jesus' imperatives to his disciples in Matthew 10:7–8 (NASB) have deeply challenged and unsettled me: "And as you go, preach, saying, 'The kingdom of heaven is at hand.' Heal the sick, raise the dead, cleanse the lepers, cast out demons; freely you received, freely give."

Jesus' sending of his disciples as bearers of this message of an alternative world marked by life and health has always struck me as incredibly good news. Healing the sick, raising the dead, cleansing those not clean or sober, and confronting the demons of violence, hatred, and pride *radically counters* imprisonment, economic sanctions, and wars against offender countries that further sicken and kill people. Jesus' call to counter the forces of death with works that bring life has always strengthened my commitment to nonviolence and peacemaking. Yet this Scripture goes much further than I had ever known how to go.

I have sought to promote my understanding of the kingdom of God among poor Honduran peasants and immigrants, inmates, ex-offenders, mainstream churchgoers, and seminary students in Washington State. Until several years ago I did not pray regularly for the sick and had never contemplated actually raising the dead, cleansing lepers or their equivalents, or casting out demons. I taught sustainable farming and preventive health practices and helped communities install gravity-flow water projects in Honduras, read Scripture with people who consider themselves damned wherever I was ministering, stood with immigrants and the accused in court and in the fields as an advocate before prosecutors, employers, and the U.S. Border Patrol. I preached Jesus' way of nonviolence in the Sermon on the Mount and called Christians to minister among the poor and downtrodden. I have been committed to denouncing human rights abuses, unjust economic policies, U.S. interventions in Central America, Colombia, Afghanistan, and Iraq, and joined those seeking to close the notorious training center, the School of the Americas in Georgia, whose graduates include some of Latin America's most notorious human rights abusers.

I assumed that Jesus' demands to heal, raise the dead, cleanse lepers, and cast out demons were to be understood more symbolically than literally. I helped people get medical attention; counseled people struggling with addictions, considering suicide, or in deep depression; embraced the excluded; and counseled and prayed with addicts and perpetrators of domestic violence.

Love itself is propelling me into the ministry and the living presence of Jesus as I find both myself and the people among whom I minister needing a real savior here and now. I find myself moving more and more into what I am increasingly willing to call the whole ministry of Jesus. This has not been a calm, objective decision, but has come out of a growing dissatisfaction with not seeing enough transformation here and now and a longing to see the gospel as having the power truly to save, heal, liberate, deliver, and transform. Yet entering into a regular practice of Jesus' ministry leads to greater complexity and sorrow as well as a longing to see more.

Once after holding and praying for a Mexican man who wept and shouted for hours just after his thirteen-year-old son had been run over by a train, I called my wife to tell her why I was late. She floored me by asking me if I had prayed for him to be raised from the dead. After imagining how I would long for someone to pray for me if my sons or daughter were to die if they believed Jesus could in fact raise the dead, I headed back to the accident scene, my heart beating off the fear. Once the coroner had inspected the body and given the family permission to mourn over the boy, I ended up holding and praying over each of the uncles and finally the father as they wept over the dead boy. Then I was left alone on my knees before the boy, where I timidly prayed for God to raise him. Later that night I drove off for home, feeling wave after wave of the Spirit coming over me—a sign of God's strong presence, even though the boy remained dead.

Two years later, in Mozambique, I talked with a group of African leaders, two of whom had seen numerous people they'd prayed for raised from the dead—after one to eight hours of prayer. I met Francie, a South African man, who himself had been raised from the dead and completely healed of all his wounds after having been beaten to death by a mob. Francie's total healing coincided with his forgiveness and refusal to press charges against his killers upon coming back to life. The one killer who had been apprehended came to faith in Jesus in response to his victim's resurrection, pardon, and total healing.[5] He is now studying to be a pastor.

I asked this group of African leaders to lay hands on me and pray—that God would impart more of his life-giving spirit into me and our ministry. I long to see life-changing signs of God's kingdom affecting the immigrants, prisoners, Honduran peasants, theology students, and churchgoers among whom I minister.

I know that all of us have to die and anyone raised from the dead will have to die again—maybe even through martyrdom. People plotted to kill Lazarus after he was raised (John 12:10), and he most certainly ended up dying a second time. Yet when I see the joy and dynamic energy for ministry visible in my Mozambican brothers, my hunger to witness Christ's victory here and now can't help but increase. Jesus' command to raise the dead has expanded my limited notions of the possible and won me over to fighting for more life, rather than surrendering to death.

Raisings from death are hope-inspiring signs of God's victory over the powers—death being the harshest sanction the powers can level against us.[6] Signs like healing, forgiveness, winning difficult legal battles, receiving faith-inspiring revelation into people's lives and destinies, and provision of food, money, and other resources meet people's concrete and immediate needs. Even more importantly, they show that nothing can separate us from God's love and that God is victorious over the powers. In impoverished countries where corruption, death, poverty, and sickness appear to reign supreme as all-powerful deities, or are even directly associated with God, the distancing of God from sickness, death, and all opens people to recognizing God as for them and with them in a truly saving way.

If God cannot and will not do these things, then what is the point in believing in God or anything but death—since death appears to have the last word? Too often we reduce God to what we have experienced; we will not believe something that others witness to, just because we haven't seen or experienced it. I am presently desperate enough that I will go anywhere or do anything in pursuit of the gospel that has the power to save.

I expect that I will see people raised from the dead someday. I am trying to take seriously Jesus' instructions to his disciples. The only way that I will see people healed or raised or freed, however, is if I am willing to go for it with my little, very little faith, looking as foolish as I might feel. We are seeing many people healed, often of smaller things like chronic back pain, migraines, and pains in the shoulder, neck, and knees. I am starting to see apparently more difficult things: the complete recovery of a woman severely crippled by a stroke, and worn-out livers of heroin addicts and alcoholics restored to perfect health. As my love for people grows, I find myself longing for the greater things that Jesus says we can expect to see happen through us with backing from heaven. What do we stand to lose by doing this except our pride?

In addition to these sorts of signs of the presence of God's kingdom, I long to see Christians of every persuasion joining to pray and work for an end to war, torture, crime, discrimination, intolerance, indebtedness, species extinction, environmental degradation, and countless other evils afflicting our world.

Within the global body of Christ there are many ministries committed to promoting liberation, healing, and wholeness. However, the greater the darkness, the more need there is for unity between people with diverse approaches to ministry, so that the full impact of Christ's gospel can penetrate barriers to the point of breakthrough. Through my own many failures and successes I have come to a point of recognizing our need for many parts of the human family and global Christian community. We are currently experiencing a growing reconciliation in our lives and ministry here at Tierra Nueva that is coming about as a result of our desperation to see effective change. Our original ministry, which grew to include social prophetic advocacy, human rights, academic study of the Bible, contextual Bible study, pastoral counseling, and contemplative prayer, is being enriched by profound cross-pollination with the charismatic renewal movement with its focus on worship, empowerment by the Holy Spirit, inner and physical healing, deliverance, and prophetic ministry. Our evangelical and mainline Protestant background has been enriched by serious engagement with Eastern Orthodoxy, the Greek Fathers, the Cistercian tradition, and communion with contemporary Lutherans, Anglicans, Roman Catholics, Third Wave renewal people, and Pentecostals.

This cross-pollination needs to continue if we're to see God's kingdom, on earth as in heaven. In summary, this book argues that people on the margins are the most open and available to be agents of transformation. They must be valued, honored, and viewed as the front lines of ministry. They should be the highest priority for the church. Their calamities should be interpreted as signs of their high value: the enemy is attacking them, because if they are strong and healthy, they will storm the gates of hell in ways that no one else can. They should not be objects of pity, but we should be serving with them. To do this, the mainstream church must switch sides and break agreement with and allegiance to the powers (money/materialism, laws/legalism, nation/patriotism, etc.).[7] Breaking allegiance is not easy, but requires deliverance. This is because people are bound by the bigger powers that they currently worship over God. Once we begin to get free and find our place as harvesters, then we can learn to minister in ways that combine advocacy and deliverance, the social prophetic and the charismatic prophetic—and many emphases that are normally separated from each other because Christians and non-Christians are at odds with each other, divided and conquered. Jesus is into a movement of empowerment that we need to join. It involves recruiting, healing, empowering, and sending out. The victory of the cross is for now (and later). It is a death, but out of it life comes—explosive life out of death to the flesh.

This book begins with an autobiographical essay entitled "Born from Below" that describes my own recent journey, where God is mixing together the evangelical, academic, contemplative, social activist, and charismatic. The second chapter, "Living as Wetbacks," grounds a theology and practice of living "on earth as in heaven" in the baptism of Jesus. Chapter 3's "Stop the World" shows how reading Scripture with outsiders invites a breaking of allegiance with false hopes of transformation through reformation of the powers. Chapter 4's "Resisting the Powers through Advocacy and Deliverance" shows how Jesus' prophetic ministry begins with a clear-headed assault on a third-party Evil One, whom he invites us to resist as he did through deliverance and advocacy. Chapter 5's "I Pledge Allegiance to the Kingdom of God" is a call to switch sides, throwing our lot in with Jesus through loving God's person and way with *all* of our hearts, minds, and strength. Chapter 6's "Reentering the Promised Land" is a reflection on empowerment, evangelism as recruitment. Finally, chapter 7's "Announcing the Victory of the Cross" looks at how Jesus' death and resurrection was a death blow to the powers of darkness, opening the way for the kingdom to come, on earth as in heaven.

Chapter 1

Born from Below

In John 3:1–2 (NASB) a Pharisee and ruler of the Jews named Nicodemus comes to Jesus by night with a question that I can relate to: "Rabbi, we know that You have come from God as a teacher; for no one can do these signs that You do unless God is with him." Apparently Nicodemus was desperate enough to experience the authentic kingdom of God in his lifetime that he would go secretly to one considered by his own as an outsider and heretic. I too have become desperate to find good news that I do not have to be ashamed of, that truly has the power to save (Rom. 1:16). This desperation has made me willing to go anywhere and learn from nearly anyone. Being born again or "from above" has always happened as I've gone below—receiving from unlikely mediators and in unexpected places.

It is urgent that people from diverse sectors of the global body of Christ humbly learn from one other and partner when possible. God's kingdom will break in sooner and with more power to a desperate world as people serve each other in unity. This necessity becomes especially apparent when working in extreme places where breakthroughs are urgent: among the poor, persecuted, imprisoned, addicted, disabled, terminally ill; in war-torn countries, prisons, Native reservations, hospitals, and disaster areas. When the darkness and chaos of the world expose our theologies and faith practices as lacking, we, like Nicodemus, will become humbled enough to cross lines of separation. God has been calling me to receive from and partner with individuals and groups that are normally isolated from each other, birthing me into an expanding family God is bringing together as a resting place for a new movement of the Spirit committed to seeing and entering God's kingdom—on earth as in heaven. I invite you into a rich and evolving journey across well-established barriers into a borderless new country and new immigration status as empowered children of God and agents of God's coming kingdom.

After growing up in Presbyterian and Covenant churches in an affluent suburb of Seattle, I began to find my own faith and calling during travels in my early twenties to Europe, Israel, and Central America. For more than twenty-five years now I have lived and ministered among people on the margins of society in Honduras, San Francisco, and Washington State. The challenges of ministry among the poor and excluded have led me to pursue academic training in theology and biblical studies, ordination in a mainline Protestant denomination, and training in pastoral counseling. While I have seen people come to faith and experience freedom from poverty, hopelessness, addictions, and negative images of God, ministry with inmates and ex-offenders in our local Skagit County jail has humbled me, showing my lack of knowledge, experience, and spirituality. During the struggle, contemplative spiritual practices have sustained me, enriching me with the wisdom of the early church and with God's presence in the Eucharist and in the silence of monastic retreats. My attraction to men caught up in addictions to methamphetamines, crack cocaine, heroin, and alcohol increased my longing to see them experience true and lasting freedom. Desire for transformation became more and more desperate as I witnessed one beloved friend after another die or go to prison for increasingly violent crimes.

The events of September 11, 2001, impacted American people, including Christians, in a way that made it harder to see the kingdom of God here in the United States—at least in official or mainstream places. Any focus toward people on the margins appeared lost in the panic and security awareness that emerged as the United States invaded Afghanistan and later Iraq. Prayers for the perpetrators of violence were rare as people raised their flags high and prayed for the security and success of U.S. soldiers deployed to the Middle East. The inability of peace activists effectively to challenge the post-9/11 war fever and patriotism leading to the invasion of Iraq further placed me in a spiritual crisis. How could a mainstream Christian community overtly associated with the nation-state become a sheepfold for inmates, ex-offenders, and undocumented immigrants coming to faith in the jail or area migrant camps? I found myself willing to go nearly anywhere inside or "outside the camp" to receive more wisdom and empowerment that would help me bear better news.

Jesus' call to Nicodemus, "unless one is born from above, he cannot see the kingdom of God" (John 3:3 au. trans.), has taken on new dimensions as I have sought to find the kingdom of God in dark times and places. The places where I began to see the kingdom of God were quite unexpected. Each revelation served as a piece of a giant puzzle that seems to be bringing order to disparate life experiences, suggesting the birth of something new.

In response to our perception that the churches were overidentified with the national mood and the myth of redemptive violence, we at Tierra Nueva decided that we would need to start our own English-speaking worshiping community that would welcome dissenters, people struggling with addictions, ex-offenders, and others at the margins. A group of Tierra Nueva staff and volunteers began worshiping together as an English-speaking faith community in November 2003—at the height of the war in Iraq.

Our objective was to side with the people on the margins (as opposed to justifying the laws and policies of the state) as a body of Christ without borders, committed to proclaiming the good news of God's kingdom, on earth as in heaven. Three trips immediately following the beginnings of our faith community forever changed my life and ministry: Fort Benning, Georgia; Toronto; and France.

Pilgrimage #1: Fort Benning, Georgia, November 2003

In late November 2003 I attended the Society of Biblical Literature and American Academy of Religion annual meeting in Atlanta, Georgia, where nearly 10,000 professional Bible scholars and theologians gathered to listen to papers on specialized topics at a luxurious convention center.

While in Atlanta I contacted the founders of an inner-city homeless shelter called the Open Door Community. This community and founding Presbyterian pastor couple Ed Loring and Murphy Davis were famous in my circles as one of the most cutting-edge ministries to the homeless in North America. Ed Loring invited me to travel on a Sunday morning in one of two vans full of homeless people to attend the annual protest demanding the closure of the School of the Americas at Fort Benning—a military base where thousands of police and soldiers from Central America's elite units had been trained during the 1980s.

I had known about the existence of this base and opposed it during the seven years we had lived and worked in Guatemala and Honduras beginning in 1981. I knew that tens of thousands of poor peasants, labor leaders, priests, and other activists were tortured and killed by troops and intelligence agents trained at this base by American military advisors paid for by U.S. tax dollars.

There at Fort Benning I join a throng of some 10,000 protesters gathered that day from all across the U.S. and Canada. The day's event consists primarily of a peaceful march in the style of a funeral procession to commemorate Latin America's martyrs. The procession leads up to the fence at the entrance of the base between rows of mounted Georgia State Patrol and police, passing in front of the fence that some plan to climb over as an act of civil disobedience.

As we walk in orderly lines the full width of the road we hear Spanish names from a microphone on a stage. The name and age of each known individual killed by U.S.-trained troops and police are mentioned. I am surprised at how deeply I am moved. I begin to weep uncontrollably as the names and ages penetrate my heart: Ignacio Ellacuria, rector of the University of Central America and an outspoken critic of the Army—"presente"; Elba Ramos, the Jesuit's housekeeper, remembered as sensitive and intuitive—"presente"; Agustina Vigil, 25, pregnant at time of death—"presente"; child, 5, son of Dionisio Marquez—"presente"; Marto Vigil, 75, farmer, El Mazote—"presente"; Isabel Argueta, 6, El Mozote— "presente."[1]

I feel sorrow over mainstream American ignorance of our involvement in supporting oppressive regimes and pain, at the near absence of any recognition of their culpability as the protesters around me lift white crosses and call "presente" after every name. My heart is so heavy that I cry on and on as I walk toward the base. I have been despairing about the war in Iraq and the American public's general agreement about how the "war on terrorism" is being waged. What am I doing to resist our national direction?

I remember feeling this acutely when I first visited Guatemala, Honduras, and Nicaragua in 1981 and became aware of our national guilt. There I felt for the first time the shift from a God with us (Americans) to a God against us and with them in a way that forever changed my life.

I walk and cry, my head hung low, up to the fence separating the protesters from the base protectors. Scores of military police stand ready to make arrests, clusters of plastic handcuffs attached to their belts. Soldiers to my left play loud patriotic music through a megaphone. Regular announcements are blasted through speakers warning the protesters that they will be arrested if they set foot on the base.

I decide to stand against the cyclone fence as the protesters cycle past and back away to make room for the rest. I watch people place their crosses and signs in the fence and continue past me. Many tear-stained faces look gray with sorrow. I look out at the base trying to figure out what I am feeling: anger, despair, sadness, powerlessness, confusion.

"Why am I here, O Lord?" "What can we hope to achieve in this time of war?" "How can I best resist?" "What hope is there for real change when most Americans seem complacent or in agreement with nearly anything in the name of national defense?"

My prayer is interrupted by an impression that I must read Psalm 37. Curious, I pull my Bible out of my carrying case and read Psalm 37:1–2 (NRSV): "Do not fret because of the wicked; do not be envious of wrongdoers, for they will soon fade like the grass, and wither like the green herb. Trust in the LORD, and do good; so you will live in the land, and enjoy security."

As I continue to read, I begin to experience a surprising freedom to not fret, to refrain from anger, and to forsake wrath as I feel impressed by the truth of the words of this psalm:

> Refrain from anger, and forsake wrath. Do not fret—it leads only to evil. For the wicked shall be cut off, but those who wait for the LORD shall inherit the land. Yet a little while, and the wicked will be no more; though you look diligently for their place, they will not be there. (Ps. 37:8–10 NRSV)

> I have seen the wicked oppressing, and towering like a cedar of Lebanon. Again I passed by, and they were no more; though I sought them, they could not be found. (Ps. 37:35–36 NRSV)

The truth of this psalm is touching me and I feel compelled to make it my own. At the same time more questions are arising. "Who are the wicked?" I ask. As I look out through the fence, I notice that most of the soldiers are African American. "Certainly not them," I think. So many soldiers are seeking a way out of poverty, a future that beats the streets or jails and prisons.

Deep in my heart I am receiving a strong impression, almost a prophetic word: "The U.S. is on its way down as a global empire. America will fall. The time is short. These are dangerous times."

I know that America is in deep trouble. The events of 9/11 gave us an opportunity to change our way of thinking—to repent of a way of wielding power that has gained us many, many enemies. Yet we act as if we are invincible. The power of pride is an illusion. "Pride goes before destruction and a haughty spirit before a fall," I remember from my required grade-school memory verses. "Yet a little while, and the wicked will be no more; though you look diligently for their place, they will not be there. But the meek shall inherit the land and delight themselves in abundant prosperity" (Ps. 37:10–11 NRSV).

The mention of "the meek" causes me to turn away from gazing at the soldiers and the base and look at the crowd. Could they be among the meek? I wonder. I notice that many are crying. Many look hopeless. I feel drawn to read Matthew 5:1a, 2, 3–10 (NRSV):

> When Jesus saw the crowds, . . . he began to speak, and taught them, saying:
> "Blessed are the poor in spirit, for theirs is the kingdom of heaven.
> "Blessed are those who mourn, for they will be comforted.
> "Blessed are the meek, for they will inherit the earth.
> "Blessed are those who hunger and thirst for righteousness, for they will be filled.
> "Blessed are the merciful, for they will receive mercy.
> "Blessed are the pure in heart, for they will see God.
> "Blessed are the peacemakers, for they will be called children of God.
> "Blessed are those who are persecuted for righteousness' sake, for theirs is the kingdom of heaven."

I feel a sudden lifting of my sorrow and a call to minister to the protesters. "These are your people, serve them," I am thinking.

I approach a man who is weeping and point to Jesus' words in my open Bible to those who mourn: "Blessed are those who mourn, for they will be comforted." This is my place, I feel. God has called me to minister to God's people, the humble ones. At the same time I think of the soldiers across the fence, and feel compelled to return and to read another section from Jesus' Sermon on the Mount: "You have heard that it was said, 'You shall love your neighbor and hate your enemy.' But I say to you, Love your enemies and pray for those who persecute you" (Matt. 5:43–44 NRSV).

Reading this reminds me of Paul's words regarding enemies, written from prison in Romans 12:14 (NRSV): "Bless those who persecute you; bless and do not curse them."

In a moment of inspiration I point at every soldier I see and I bless them: "I bless you in the name of Jesus!" "I bless you in the name of Jesus!" "I bless you in the name of Jesus!"

I think of the seraph who flew to Isaiah holding a live coal from the altar. It feels as if once again my mouth has been touched and my guilt taken away and my sin blotted out. I've heard the call and say yes not only to comforting the meek, but also to Isaiah's call to speak to his own people a difficult message. Could Isaiah's very message be what I am to be witness to, now as mainstream America continues to live in denial as we fall under increasing debt and international disdain: "Go and say to this people: hear and hear, but do not understand; see and see, but do not perceive. Make the heart of this people fat, and their ears heavy, and shut their eyes; lest they see with their eyes, hear with their ears, and understand with their hearts, and turn and be healed" (Isa. 6:9–10 RSV).

I can see that the national blindness and deafness of Isaiah's time is now being replayed in our own. I dread the consequent fulfillment of this word in the verses that follow, which describe a more severe judgment that echoes the words of Psalm 37: "Then I said, 'For how long, O Lord?' And he answered: 'Until the cities lie ruined and without inhabitant, until the houses are left deserted and the fields ruined and ravaged, until the LORD has sent everyone far away and the land is utterly forsaken'" (6:11–12 NIV).

I hear the imperatives of Isaiah: "Cease to do evil, learn to do good; seek justice, rescue the oppressed, defend the orphan, plead for the widow (Isa. 1:16b–17 NRSV).

I think again of Psalm 37:3: "Trust in the LORD and do good; / so you will live in the land, and enjoy security" and am reminded of Romans 12:21: "Do not be overcome by evil, but overcome evil with good" (NRSV).

Is it too late for mainstream America? I wonder. As long as we are convinced that our problems are due to an abundance of wickedness that we must combat, we are in serious trouble. We need to learn to turn over the problem of the wicked to God and focus on remedying the tragic absence of good. In the absence of good, all efforts to combat evil are doomed to failure.

As our two vanloads of homeless men and shelter volunteers drive home, I talk with a black man fresh out of jail who has been estranged from his son, who is now in prison. He is afraid to reestablish contact. He doesn't want to disappoint his son again, or risk being rejected when he makes an effort to step back into relationship. I encourage him to write his son a letter. We talk with others about reading the Bible and relate it to the struggle to stay clean and sober.

They drop me off at the fancy hotel where I am staying, and I walk back into the Society of Biblical Literature and American Academy of Religion meeting. I return to the vast array of papers being presented, book tables, and scholars visiting among themselves. I am a man of unclean lips living among a people of unclean lips. Will we keep on seeing but not perceive? How long, O Lord?

Like Isaiah, the prophet Jeremiah reflects a prophetic stream announcing judgment to the people of God. God called Jeremiah to announce Judah's destruction at the hands of the Babylonians (Jer. 1:13–17). God empowered Jeremiah against the entire religious and political establishment of Judah.

> "Now, gird up your loins, and arise, and speak to them all which I command you. Do not be dismayed before them, lest I dismay you before them. Now behold, I have made you today as a fortified city, and as a pillar of iron and as walls of bronze against the whole land, to the kings of Judah, to its princes, to its priests, and to the people of the land. And they will fight against you, but they will not overcome you, for I am with you to deliver you," declares the LORD (Jer. 1:17–19 NASB).

The prophets Isaiah and Jeremiah invite a resistance alongside the oppressors on behalf of the oppressed to the point of even going down with them into exile.[2] How can I become an agent of transformation on behalf of the poor in the midst of a people committed to sanctioning, punishing, and paying back the bad guys?

Before I could answer this question, I was to see the kingdom of God in the flesh in a place "down below" my normal sights, among the economically and socially marginalized poor. God was about to show me that being born from above includes transforming encounters with God mediated by people I would not naturally receive from, because they were overly identified with the dominant culture and scandalous in my eyes: mainstream people in the charismatic renewal movement.

Pilgrimage #2: Toronto

Upon returning from the Atlanta meeting I begin preparing for a weeklong spiritual retreat I decide to take with my brother Andy, a Presbyterian pastor ministering in Fairbanks, Alaska. I had decided to step out of my comfort zone and visit Toronto Airport Christian Fellowship (TACF), home of the infamous "Toronto Blessing." This represented a major step for me, since I have been so utterly disillusioned by the American charismatic tendency to overidentify with the conservative political agenda in the United States and throughout the world and with legalistic ways of interpreting the Bible that excluded "sinners" from churches in Central America.

Verbo Church's support of Rios Montt in Guatemala in the 1980s,[3] followed by the American Christian support of the Reagan administration's contra war in Honduras as a "holy war" against communism, had caused me to doubt the Holy Spirit's involvement in many charismatic and evangelical churches. My own experience with legalistic Pentecostal churches in Honduras and earlier episodes of feeling pressured by the charismatic renewal movement in the 1970s to speak in tongues as a sign of my belonging to Jesus had further alienated me.

However, in recent years I had watched my youngest brother Peter go through a powerful conversion through repeated visits to the Toronto Airport Christian Fellowship and elsewhere.[4] Peter had struggled with addiction to cocaine and other drugs and had lost custody of his daughter to an ex-partner who appeared to be involving their young daughter in child pornography circles. Peter's conversion was at first marked by overzealous condescending, with regular comments to me like "Your church is dead" and "There is no power in your ministry." However, I watched Peter mature at an unusually rapid rate, becoming gentler and more humble as he went from renewal conference to renewal conference in Toronto and around the country.

Finally, one day while visiting in Seattle, he invited me to a Randy Clarke meeting half an hour from home. He explained how Randy Clarke was the minister who was teaching when the Spirit had fallen in Toronto eight years before. People had been so overcome by the presence of God that they had fallen to the floor. Many had experienced uproarious laughter as a manifestation of the Spirit. God continued to show up like this day after day, attracting thousands of people from all over the world to nightly meetings and regular conferences that continue today. More than five million people had visited TACF after eight years, contributing significantly to a global renewal movement marked by physical and emotional healing and a rediscovery of God as a Father who has nothing but abundant love for his children.

"Come on, Bob, be open," Peter urged. "Come and see what I've been into. You might like it."

There was no reason I could come up with to resist the invitation. As I entered the church hosting this conference, I found myself moved by worship so joyful and free that for the first time in my life I felt that maybe I could do this eternally. People from every age, social class, and ethnicity did everything—dance, sit, lie prostrate, raise their arms, bow their heads, kneel—as the worship band played one engaging song after another. At the same time I was startled and at times alarmed by bizarre cries, roars, and sights like people shaking, falling, and charging the speaker in order to receive a blessing.

On the second night of the conference, Randy Clark invited all the pastors and their spouses forward for a prayer of blessing for their lives and ministries. Gracie and I went forward along with several hundred others and joined a line across the front of a huge auditorium. The ministry team began praying for people way down to our right at the beginning of the line as the band played contemplative worship music. I watched in horror as people collapsed to the floor after receiving prayer from a ministry team that moved along the line toward Gracie and me. This was not what I had expected or desired! Yet I knew I needed as many prayers as could be offered. Rather than opt out, I decided that I would pray the Jesus prayer, "Lord Jesus Christ, Son of God, have mercy on us," as I waited, believing that Jesus would protect me from anything that he wouldn't want me to experience. When the ministry team finally reached me and began praying, I felt an incredible peace come over me, but I did not fall.

After they left, I opened my eyes and found everyone on either side of me lying on the ground, "overcome by the Spirit." Many were laughing hysterically. I rejoined my three children near the back, and immediately my second son Luke asked me if he could go up so he could receive prayer, which was then being offered to everyone present. When Randy Clark came along and prayed for Luke and me again, I looked him in the eye. His comment, "Whoa, you look like you've been hit about seven times," even though I hadn't fallen, made me feel strangely welcomed as a brother among these very different strangers. When I turned around, I immediately noticed a man convulsing dramatically before a woman who prayed for him. My first thought was that she needed help, so I came behind the man and laid my hands on his shoulders. Immediately he crumpled to his knees and began to worship, apparently touched by our combined prayers. I was moved to see pairs and circles of people praying for each other throughout the large room. This experience opened Gracie and me up to a part of the body of Christ that I had distrusted and even at times despised. Yet my prejudices about charismatics being politically right-wing was still an obstacle.

One day my brother Peter called me from TACF to tell me that one of the main speakers had called Americans to drop their national flag and raise up the flag of the kingdom of God. This surprising word was the final straw that broke down my resistance to going for myself to see whether there was something I could receive that would benefit me, my family, and our ministry. In October 2003 Gracie, the first to succumb to my brother Peter's salesmanship, decided to attend Toronto Airport Christian Fellowship's annual Catch the Fire conference. Gracie called me every evening from the conference, telling me of the amazing signs of God's presence that she was witnessing and herself experiencing. She heard the inspiring testimonies of Heidi Baker, a North American missionary to Mozambique, who had given her life to ministry to the poorest of the poor throughout the world.[5]

Heidi Baker had come to Toronto five years earlier, exhausted and thirsty for more of God, after years adopting street children off the streets of Maputu. She told of God's renewing touch and call to intimacy there at TACF that had led to greater fruitfulness in her ministry, leading to a revival among the rural poor throughout the country. Her stories caused us to trust, opening our hearts more to receiving ministry from this part of the body of Christ.

Now I was heading to Toronto to get a deeper look into a movement that I felt desperate enough to consider. I had felt a divine challenge that sounded something like this: "Bob, if you could receive from TACF one thing that would positively transform your life and ministry to the people you serve, even if there were ninety-nine features that turned you off, would you go and receive from them?"

"Yes, Lord, I will go," I remember agreeing. Much like Nicodemus, I made plans to attend the conference "by night," being careful to tell no one, to avoid embarrassment or criticism.

So on January 20, 2004, I arrived at Toronto Airport Christian Fellowship for their pastors' conference. My fears and feelings of vulnerability at opening myself up to such radical difference were somewhat eased by the sign at the entrance to the sanctuary: "Be not afraid, little children. It is the Father's good pleasure to give you the Kingdom."

The conference began with an hour or more of worship that was like nothing I had ever experienced. Several thousand pastors and leaders from all over the world sang, clapped, and danced as the worship band rocked high praises to God. Then one of the leaders (the founding pastor John Arnott) warmly welcomed all the conference participants, stressing to the Americans that not all Canadians were against them, but that many understood the need for a global police officer and were thankful to Americans for exercising this role. This "welcome" felt like a fist in the stomach, confirming my prejudices that charismatic Christians were loyal to conservative political agendas, confusing them with the kingdom of God. Since I was half-expecting to be offended in this way I decided that I would try to remain open. Later that day Carol Arnott, John's wife and cofounder of TACF, gave a talk entitled "Life or Death in the Ministry" that deeply affected me.

Carol spoke simply but compellingly about how any kind of judgment, resentment, rejection, hatred, or fear functions like a dam that blocks the flow of God's blessing to people.

"What prevents us from receiving the blessing?" she asked.

"An angry father. A controlling, dominating mother. We have buried alive many hurts that come alive in later years. We have buried these things, which must be brought to the cross. There is help, freedom, wholeness. Jesus can heal these problems," preached Carol.

She went on to describe Jesus as a man who knew he was totally loved by his Father and lived out of the security that came from a relationship with his dad. She affirmed the need to receive the Spirit of adoption as God's children so we could come into the same place of security and intimacy with the Father that Jesus experienced.

Carol insisted that to be loved we must be healed in our inner selves, and that this begins by being reconciled with our fathers and mothers. She asked the crowd, "How many of you would like to be exactly like your father or mother?" as a way of inviting any hidden resentments to surface in people's hearts. She spoke simply but compellingly about the importance of inner healing so people can be freed from performance orientation.

"If we have not been affirmed in our inner self," said Carol, "then we will try to get affirmation elsewhere: from position, degrees, relationships, whatever. There's a hurt, insecure, inner heart that makes us seek for security."

Carol went on to share familiar texts regarding forgiveness, such as Jesus' call not to judge (Matt. 7:1) and to forgive from the heart as a requirement for living a life marked by grace and not indebtedness (Matt. 18:35) and the admonition in Hebrews 12:15 to see to it that no "root of bitterness" springs up.

Carol talked about the commandment, "Honor your father and your mother," stressing how the promise that follows, "that you may live long and that it may go well with you" (Deut. 5:16 NIV), assures blessing. She went on to confess her sin of dishonoring her mother, and shared how God had freed her from resentment over a three-and-a-half-year period. She invited all of us to step into a place of grace and a refuge from the accuser, citing 1 Peter 5:8 (NRSV): "Discipline your-selves; keep alert. Like a roaring lion your adversary the devil prowls around, looking for someone to devour."

"Satan wants to bring us into justice," stated Carol. "He cannot touch us in the grace place. If you can stay in the grace of God, the enemy will not be able to get you. We want the Lord to find what is in us and deal with it so the enemy cannot find anything."

She invited anyone who felt that God was speaking to them regarding dishon-oring of their parents because of past hurts and anyone who struggled to forgive their parents completely, even if they were long dead, to come up to receive prayer.

I was hit by a longing to completely release my parents from all my judgments, so I made my way up to the front to receive prayer, so I could completely forgive my father and mother, along with 400–500 others. Carol began by inviting the Holy Spirit to come, revealing the wounds that we may have long buried. Almost immediately memories of events from my childhood surfaced. When Carol invited the Spirit to sound the depths of our hearts, removing the scar tissue so we could experience emotional healing for these old hurts, I found myself cry-ing, along with hundreds of others. Carol took us through prayers that included releasing our parent(s) into God's grace, not because they deserved it, but because of Jesus' work on the cross. I forgave my parents of any debt they had incurred toward me and asked God to forgive me for dishonoring them. As Carol led us through prayer after prayer I felt tremendous relief. When she prayed that God would pour out the Holy Spirit upon us, bringing us comfort and joy, I felt a blanket of comfort and joy flow over me. We ended by praying for the person beside us before breaking for dinner.

This session on forgiveness was only the first of a four-day conference that would change my life forever. On my way to listen to John Arnott's session on understanding manifestations of the Spirit, I asked someone standing by the door where this workshop was being held. When he responded in French, I quickly learned his name was Jean Paul and he was from Montpellier, the city in the south of France where Gracie and I had lived and studied for three years. Since he was looking for the same workshop, we ended up attending it together, and in the absence of a French translator, I translated for him.

At the end of their workshop John and Carol invited those who wanted prayer to line up around the periphery. Jean Paul and I stood together awaiting John and Carol, who moved rapidly from person to person, laying their hands on each one and saying, "Fill" or "Fire." As they moved toward us, I found my heart beat-ing wildly, and feelings ranging between terror and excitement. The next thing I knew I was on my back on the floor beside Jean Paul, overcome by an incredible peace as I "rested in the Spirit" for the first time.

That afternoon Jean Paul introduced me to Serge Jacquemus, his pastor from the Église Réformée de France, who I learned had participated in a doctoral program with me in psychoanalysis in Montpellier years before. As the days went on, I met pastors and leaders from all over the world and must have received prayer more than twenty times, either from the front or from well-trained ministry team volunteers who prayed and prophesied over people who lined up for prayer after the sessions.

Speakers regularly spoke of "the anointing," a new term for me, which signified our inclusion into Jesus' messianic ministry and the authority to carry it out through the empowerment of the Holy Spirit. They emphasized the material reality of the Holy Spirit's anointing, which like oil glistens on you, soaks in, and penetrates in a way that equips and enables for ministry.[6] This anointing comes on people through receiving an impartation from someone who is moving in "the anointing" themselves, having been baptized by the Holy Spirit or otherwise further empowered through the laying on of hands.

Speakers emphasized that the anointing is imparted in a variety of ways. In the Old Testament the Lord took the Spirit that was upon Moses and distributed it to the seventy elders, causing them to prophesy (Num. 11:25). Elisha asks his master Elijah the prophet for a double portion of his spirit, which he passionately and attentively seeks (2 Kgs. 2). For the disciples this happened when Jesus breathed on them (John 20:21) or the Spirit filled them as on the day of Pentecost in Acts 2. The anointing continues to be passed on through a myriad of ways, from the laying on of hands (1 Tim. 4:14) and hearing the word preached (Acts 10:44) to worship and soaking in God's presence.

On the final day, in the morning I went to what I thought to be an informational session with John Arnott on soaking prayer, in a building that was an old fire station. At this session I had no expectation of receiving prayer. After teaching on soaking prayer as a form of contemplative prayer, where the Spirit is welcomed to flow into people as they listen to worship music, John began to pray for the attendees to receive a special anointing for praying for others. When he came to me, he slapped his hands into my palms, saying, "Receive the full anointing of the Holy Spirit for healing, deliverance, preaching the gospel. . . ." He then placed his big hands firmly on either side of my neck under my ears, said, "Receive the Holy Spirit," and blew all over my chest and face.

The next thing I knew I was feeling like a feather in the wind and found myself fully conscious on my back on the floor. An intense, burning heat settled across my forehead just above my eyebrows, causing me to open my eyes and look up, trying to identify the source of the heat. Fluorescent lights flickered from the warehouse ceiling some thirty feet above. I felt heat radiating out of my hands and saw in my mind's eye a vision of blue flames shooting upward out of my hands. I felt a weight on me as I lay there for a while, amazed and perplexed.

Eventually I got up and made my way out, catching up with John Arnott, whom I began to talk with about my earlier upset regarding what he had said when he welcomed Americans uncritically regarding the war in Iraq. As we walked together through a parking lot in –20° F. temperatures, I shared with John that I had finally decided to come to Toronto because my brother shared that a leader had stated the need for Americans to lower the U.S. flag and raise up the flag of God's universal kingdom.

"You really came here for that reason?" John responded, causing me to realize that in fact my own thirst for more of God and desperation to see people transformed were my truest reasons for coming "by night," as Nicodemus had. I continued, though, to share how upsetting it was for me to hear him welcome America's role as global police officer.

"Our role is to be 100 percent about proclaiming the kingdom of God and not supporting the policies of governments of this world," I urged.

John said he had seen God make use of nations to stop evil dictatorships and to open the way for revivals, but finally he agreed we should be 100 percent about the work of the kingdom. He excused himself and I found my seat, feeling deeply touched by God's encounter mediated through John, vulnerable for having shared though I was minimally heard, and yet satisfied that I had been able to voice my concern.

That afternoon Serge Jacquemus invited me to accompany the Arnotts for several days in France after their speaking engagements at the annual ecumenical renewal conference Embrasse Nos Coeurs in Paris six weeks from then. He insisted that my having received my doctorate from the French Reformed graduate school in Montpellier, my membership in the contemplative spiritual community Fraternite Espirituelle Les Veilleurs and my recent induction into the spirituality there at TACF would make me a good ambassador to the French churches in need of renewal. While this invitation intrigued me, I felt far from ready to identify further with this movement. The final afternoon and evening sessions and the days that followed, however, further encouraged me to embrace these experiences as a new induction from below that would open my eyes to the works of God.

That afternoon and evening Randy Clark of Global Awakening and Colin Dye spoke on empowerment and healing, practicing their teaching by praying for people's healing based on words of knowledge that punctuated their talks. Each of the speakers that week emphasized that the gospel of Jesus must go out not in word only, but also with power. This power is received by the disciples when Jesus sends "the promise of My Father upon you" that results in their being "clothed with power from on high" (Luke 24:49 NASB). This power is the enabling of the Holy Spirit to be witnesses. After the resurrection the Spirit was given so we can produce the proof that Jesus is still alive. There must be a supernatural demonstration that Jesus is alive so that words and service will be "confirmed with the signs that follow," in such a way that not-yet-believing people will come to faith in Jesus. Each of the speakers admonished people to be so full of the Holy Spirit that we would be empowered to do the works of Jesus in ways that would break through barriers of race, religion and culture, and social class. I left feeling won over to the added value of much of this teaching received "by night" from those I had written off for years as having nothing of value to offer.[7]

The next morning, as I flew back to Vancouver on an early flight, I began to prepare for three sermons I had to do later that day. I began to read the Scriptures for the Common Lectionary for that day, which surprisingly were Isaiah 61 and Luke 4:18ff. As I read the readings I immediately stopped, shocked that these Scriptures, which had been the texts of my life, were suddenly jumping out at me in new ways:

I read through Luke 4:18–19 (NASB)'s familiar citation of Isaiah 61:1, which suddenly came alive in a new way.

> The Spirit of the Lord is upon Me,
> Because He anointed Me to preach the Gospel to the poor.
> He has sent Me to proclaim release to the captives,
> And recovery of sight to the blind,
> To set free those who are downtrodden,
> To proclaim the favorable year of the Lord.

The first line, "The Spirit of the Lord is upon Me," and "He anointed Me," was leaping off the page. Could this Spirit upon me, this anointing, be what I have in some way lacked in my ministry to people at the margins? To my left sat a Hasidic rabbi, whose side curls bobbed as he read his prayer books. I pulled out my laptop and turned to the Hebrew text of Isaiah 61. When he finished his prayers, I asked him if I could ask him a question about Isaiah 61. He agreed, and I asked him if he believed that Isaiah 61 was describing the Messiah whom his community awaited. "Yes," he said.

"When the Messiah returns, will he be the only anointed one, or do you believe that he will pass on his anointing to the Jewish people?"

"He will be the only one," replied the rabbi, revealing a significant difference from the Christian understanding of the anointing by the Spirit of all believers.

"How do you believe the prophets originally anointed the Messiahs in ancient Israel?" I asked.

"We believe they smeared oil across the forehead," the rabbi responded confidently, running his finger just over the tops of his eyebrows.

I sat stunned, wondering how this new experience of God would affect my ministry.

In the midst of my preparations for my sermon I was interrupted by a Sikh Indian man sitting beside me to my right.

"Do you believe in God?" he asked, pointing to my open Bible.

"Yes," I replied, "and how about you?"

"Well, yes, I do, but I am not very religious. Some people need God, I don't need God," he replied.

"Why do you believe in God?" he asked me.

I began to share about how I had seen God act to help people, and told the story of Eugenio, a man who had been freed from alcoholism through a process of conversion that began in jail. I told him about Alcoholics Anonymous's 12-step program, which begins with a recognition that you are incapable of stopping drinking by yourself and the affirmation that you need a higher power to free you from your addiction.

"My father drinks too much," replied the man. "When he drinks, he is very violent," he continued.

I immediately sensed that this man had witnessed his father beating his mother and commented.

"You have witnessed your father beating up on your mother when he drinks, haven't you? This was very painful for you to witness because you love your mother and father. You are worried that maybe you too will do this when you're married," I commented, surprised by my boldness.

"Yes, you are right," he responded. "I am just returning from three months with my family in India. At the beginning of my visit, my father drank. He gets violent. He feels very bad afterwards."

"Are you worried that you too may have a similar problem?" I asked, again surprised by my confidence.

"Yes, when I drink I am violent. I have a girlfriend. I am worried that I might become violent with her if I marry and keep drinking," he confessed. "But I don't need any help from God," he clarified.

"How can my father get help where he is?" he asked. "There are no AA groups where he lives."

"If you want, I would be glad to pray for you and him, that God would free you both from this problem," I offered.

"No, I don't need God," he stated emphatically.

"Well, I would be glad to pray for your father if you'd like," I backtracked.

"I would like that," he answered.

I asked him if I could place my hand on his arm as I prayed, and he agreed. As I began to pray, I felt heat pouring into this man through my hand. He immediately began to breathe heavily, almost to the point of hyperventilating. I ended my prayer and asked him how he felt.

"Very good," he said, looking surprised.

I was amazed by these first encounters after the conference. That afternoon in the jail I led Bible studies on Isaiah 61 and Luke 4:18ff., and preached at our English and Spanish services. At the close of each service I invited people to come up to be anointed with oil to remember their status as part of Jesus' messianic community.

That evening when I went to bed, I wondered whether everything would fade away, now that I was far from the intense environment of Toronto, with its incredible music leaders, ministry team members, and speakers.

In the middle of my first night home I found myself awoken by a feeling of intense energy coursing through my body. I felt as if I was plugged into the electric outlet. I awoke refreshed, but unable to think about anything except worshiping God. This continued day after day, night after night for weeks. How would this affect my ministry? I wondered.

The first week back I went to the jail for my regular Thursday Bible study, curious to see whether this retreat would in any way affect my way of operating.

Upon entering the jail's multipurpose room I immediately noticed Zack, a strapping, thirty-one-year-old Anglo man who stands 6′7″. His shaven head, mustache, mischievous face, and heavily tattooed neck and forearms make him look intimidating. About ten other Anglo guys sat around him to the right. A dozen Mexican men sat across from them to my left. After shaking hands with everyone I took a seat in the circle to begin the Bible study.

"Tonight, I don't want to impose my particular choice of a Bible study on you guys," I stated in Spanish and English, looking at each man around the circle. "Everyone is always imposing their agendas on you. I'd like to know if there's any particular question or biblical story *you* want to look at." Immediately Zack spoke up.

"These Mexicans all think I'm a racist, and maybe they're right. I do get into my fair share of fights and can be hard to live with. I just want them to know that I respect a lot of things about them and their culture—the way they value family, their willingness to work hard. I guess I'd like to learn how to get along."

The Mexicans were looking a little uncomfortable as I translated Zack's words into Spanish. There had been some tensions with Zack, so they seemed wary of his advances. I welcomed the question and then formally began the Bible study with a prayer inviting the Holy Spirit to be present as our guide and to bless each person. Thinking quickly of an appropriate text, I reached for Luke 15, about the judging attitude of the Pharisees toward Jesus for eating with tax collectors and sinners and his parable in response.

Together we read through the three stories that make up one parable, about the finding of the lost sheep, the lost coin, and the lost son. The men became noticeably more relaxed and even happy as they saw Jesus comparing God or himself to a pastor who leaves the ninety-nine compliant sheep who have their acts together to search for the one lost sheep who's in trouble—*until* he finds it! They seemed moved when we read about the woman who loses one of her precious coins and turns the house upside down. Here God does not look like the masked and heavily armed drug task force officers who scour apartments searching for illegal drugs, but like a lover looking for something precious that symbolizes *them*! Their growing amazement turned to joy as we read about the son who hits bottom partying and staggers back in humiliation, willing to do time in servitude, only to find the father running to embrace him before a confession even leaves his lips. As I wrapped up our time together by inviting people to stand for a time of prayer, something surprising happened.

Zack jumped up from his seat and ran toward me, blurting out his conviction that he thought God wanted us to pray that Fabiano's liver be healed. Fabiano, a large, heavily tattooed, Mexican man with a shaved head—the man in the room most likely to have a racial run-in with Zack—looked shocked.

"Is it true that you have a problem with your liver?" I asked. He told me that he'd been experiencing sharp pains for a while and they were getting worse and worse. "Do you mind if we pray for you?" I asked. He politely agreed.

"Don't you have a liver problem too, Zack?" I asked, knowing from a previous encounter that his seventeen years of heroin addiction had taken a heavy toll on his liver and kidneys. Zack's hands were swollen to twice their size.

"Yeah, but listen, Bob. I'm always thinking about Zack, about me and my problems. I think God wants me to focus on others, like Fabiano here."[8]

He agreed to let me pray for him too, as we gathered in a circle and held hands. I placed a hand on each man's shoulders and we prayed for God's Spirit to come to bring healing to Zack and Fabiano's livers. We prayed too for people's legal problems and families, that we'd all experience a greater thirst for God, and that God would fill us with faith, hope, and love. God's Spirit was all around us in the room. I felt it pulsing through my hands in our circuit of solidarity. There was a warmth of presence that lingered as we finished praying and said our goodbyes.

Fabiano and Zack didn't show up for the next study, but a week or so later Fabiano took his seat with a now mostly Mexican group. I asked him how he was feeling, and he told me there was no more pain in his liver. I called Zack later that day, but he said he was still feeling bad. We prayed over the phone for healing, and a few weeks later he attended our study.

"Everything seems to be better," he told me. "The doctor's tests have even come out giving me a clean bill of health." Zack told me he'd been praying for lots of people and God had been answering prayer after prayer.

I found myself unable to keep from sharing my excitement about God's new work in my life and in the jail with nearly everyone I knew in the weeks following Toronto. I felt a constant desire to worship God and to read everything I could get my hands on regarding the Holy Spirit, healing, and other topics related to renewal. Meanwhile, I made contact with Serje Jacquemus, whom I agreed to help as he hosted John and Carol Arnott.

Pilgrimage #3: France

I flew into Paris on a Saturday morning, the last day of a four-day renewal conference, Embrasse Nos Coeurs, which I envisioned as a humble group of several hundred in some old Église Réformée de France in Paris. I took the RER train to within a few blocks of the conference site and entered a modern conference center facility. Priests in monastic habits conversed outside the entrance. I joined an assortment of African immigrants and French people as we made our way into the conference. At the reception area I discovered to my surprise that I was an invited guest and speaker and was told to go to the speakers' meeting room for prayers before the morning session began. There I met Serge, who told me that I was scheduled to share my personal story in the first afternoon session, just before Carol Arnott's keynote teaching. I could not believe my ears. Not only was I feeling completely inadequate to speak alongside these people; I hadn't slept in nearly twenty-four hours and was exhausted. On my way back from lunch I ran into John Arnott, who didn't remember me. As I began to share how God had been working in my life and ministry, he placed a hand on my shoulder as we walked and said, "I thank you, Father, for your work in Bob's life. Give him more, Lord, more." I felt God's presence filling me with peace as we walked into the speakers' lounge for prayer.

Some fifty French and Swiss leaders gathered in a circle, and each person intro-duced himself or herself; then came a time of prayer for God's Spirit to come. Leaders were soon lying on the ground, resting in the Spirit. Someone approached me and pointed to a Roman Catholic priest lying beside a man in a suit and tie.

"That's a leader of the Dominicans beside the head of the Assemblies of God denomination in France," he said, smiling in astonishment.

"This is incredible; never have I seen something like this."

As we neared the end of this prayer time, the conference organizer invited Carol and me to come into the center of the group so they could lay hands on us. I could not believe how quickly I was being included as an insider. Empow-ered by this prayer, I headed out. A Roman Catholic man approached me and said, "I believe that God has showed me that you are here for more than you know. You are here to be a special blessing for France."

After nearly an hour of worship and introductions I was invited to the podium to share my story. I began in English with Serge interpreting, but was soon speak-ing for myself in French. I told of my work among the poor in Honduras and in the jails and migrant camps of Washington. I told how my entire ministry I had been inspired by Jesus' inaugural sermon in Luke 4, where he describes himself as the fulfillment of Isaiah 61. I told how the severity of people's problems had pushed me to learn from many different perspectives within the body of Christ. I shared how frustrated I had become due to my failures really to help people submerged in the darkness of heavy addictions, domestic violence, and other troubles. I told how I had been wondering why the gospel I bear did not appear to have the power truly to save. I shared how I could not accept blaming either the "sinners" or God. I told how I had seen in the Gospels that Jesus never blamed sinners for not being trans-formed. Jesus didn't give up on lost sheep, but looked for them *until they were found*. I shared how I felt like the disciples who came to Jesus wondering why they could not cast the demon out of the boy as he could. I noted how Jesus did not blame the boy but rather the disciples' practices: "This one only through prayer and fasting can be cast out" (Matt. 17:21 au. trans.). I told of my journey to Toronto and my experience of receiving the anointing through John's prayers. I told about the fire on my forehead, the Hasidic rabbi's interpretation, and the effects on all this on my life and ministry. I ended my talk telling the story of the healing of Zack's and Fabi-ano's livers and the new hope we have as God confirms our Bible studies and advo-cacy work with "signs that follow."

As I spoke I could see that John and Carol were listening intently, undoubt-edly surprised to hear such a story. I stepped down from the platform and was met by a French Jesuit priest and American missionary who offered to pray for me off to the side.

There on the side of the stage the two men prayed for me for more of the Holy Spirit. I immediately felt like a tea bag submerged in hot water and crumpled to my knees under their warm hands. As I rested there I could hear Carol speaking from the platform.

"Where is Bob?" she was asking. "Où est Bob?" said the interpreter.

I got up and made my way to my seat in the second row.

Carol spotted me and stopped her talk, inviting me to come forward. I came up to the platform as she headed down the steps with microphone in hand to meet me.

"To the one who has been faithful in little, more will be given," she said, grasping my hands in hers.

I immediately began to fall forward on top of her, until I heard her yell and found myself seconds later on my back, there in front of the stage, feeling the warm presence of God. Carol climbed back onto the stage and continued her talk, and I eventually made it back to my seat to listen to her speak on how she saw herself and other ordinary believers as like the donkey who humbly bore the presence of God into Jerusalem.

Carol spotted me returning to my seat and abruptly stopped her talk.

"Bob, where are you going?" she asked, drawing the attention of the entire assembly back to me.

"Come back up here," she commanded. "You pastors are all so busy, busy, busy. What you really need is to learn to just receive more love from God. You are too quick to get up and go. You can only give away what you have received. You need to be filled up so you are ministering from out of a fullness, out of an overflow," she continued.

Carol insisted then, as she had at other times, that in Matthew 22:37 Jesus says, "Love the Lord your God with all your heart, and with all your soul, and with all your mind." The mind comes last. She said that God told her, "Carol, I have many servants, but few lovers. Lovers will outperform servants. There is an energy from love that comes from lying down and letting yourself be loved."

"This time after I pray for you, Bob, stay down and receive," she insisted. She prayed and I went down in front of the stage. This time I stayed put, listening as God's Spirit hovered over me.

The next morning I awakened earlier than I had hoped and decided to join Serge for Sunday worship at the nearby Belleville church where he pastors. I sat near the front and at the end responded to an invitation for people called to ministry to receive prayers of empowerment for their ministries. As I headed out after the service, a man in his seventies approached me, telling me that he was a peasant from Nîmes and wanted to speak with me and pray for me.

"God wants to bring the doctors of the Word together with the prophets," he stated, and asked if he can pray for me. I was amazed that this man, who apparently knew nothing about me, had identified the two worlds that had only recently been coming together: my calling as a teacher of Scripture and "doctor of the word" and the new move toward the charismatic "prophets."

That afternoon we all took a train to Valence and headed out to do a healing service in an Église Réformée de France in the Drôme. After the service we slept in the center for Union de Prière de Charmes. Sometime in the middle of the night three vivid dreams awoke me. In the first I saw a forest fire heading up from where we were, east of the Cevennes, and from the southern part of the Cevennes, where we were heading the next day, in Saint Jean du Gard, where pastor Daniel Bourguet is based. Daniel is an Église Réformée de France pastor who has lived for the past ten years as a hermit dedicated to contemplative prayer and serves as prior of the Fraternité Espirituelle les Veilleurs. He had previously been my professor of Old Testament in Montpellier and director of my doctoral dissertation. In the second dream I saw myself laying hands on Daniel Bourguet and praying for him to receive everything I had recently been receiving from God. In the third dream a voice instructed me to tell John Arnott that he must not justify the actions or policies of powers like nation-states or he would lose the anointing. The next afternoon as we rode the train to Nîmes, I shared with John what I had received in the night, and we discussed together my concerns about Christians' support of war. I shared with him story after story of how charismatic Christians in Central America had mistakenly sided with governments guilty of committing heinous human-rights abuses.

John listened thoughtfully and responded in humility to this strong warning, "How could we know unless someone [like you] tells us?"

Later that day our delegation arrived in Nîmes, and we were picked up by people who drove us out to the Huguenot Mûsé du Desert. I asked our driver what she saw God calling the French church into. She surprised me by repeating what the old man in Paris had told me: "God is bringing the doctors of the Word together with the prophets." That same day I learned why this particular word was especially important for France, and for the global body of Christ.

The curator of the Huguenot museum gave us a tour and told us in fascinating detail about the early period when the Huguenots were worshiping underground in an arid, mountainous region of the Cevennes known by these courageous believers as the desert (the wilderness). He told about a charismatic renewal movement around 1700 centered there in the Cevennes where we were. Hundreds of uneducated peasant children between three and eighteen were having visions and prophesying in perfect French to crowds of people who met clandestinely after the French king, Louis XIV, had forbid Protestants to practice their faith.[9] He told how, as the soldiers of the king (called Dragons) stepped up their persecution, the renewal movement became militant, giving rise to an armed guerrilla resistance called the Camisards. Some of the children received and transmitted warnings through dreams and visions of attacks against the gathered believers. However, the Camisard's violent resistance was mobilized by adult prophets and some pastors who called the people to wage holy war based on supposed prophetic revelation and literal interpretation of Old Testament texts. All began to change after one of the Huguenot leaders went off to Geneva for theological training. Upon his return he prohibited this charismatic prophetic movement from operating in the Protestant churches, because the ecstatic utterances had become disconnected from a careful Christian interpretation of Scripture. The curator commented that since that time the doctors of the Word have been dominant in the Église Réformée de France and the charismatic prophets have been marginalized.

That evening after our tour of the Mûsé du Desert a group of over thirty intercessors from all over France gathered to worship and pray. I was impressed by the humility of the French intercessors as individuals proposed ways the group should pray.

"If we are to see renewal happen, we must humble ourselves before the doctors of the Word and acknowledge our arrogance and presumption, which has led them to take offense," said a woman.

Another person commented that judgments against Roman Catholics must be dropped and total forgiveness offered for the persecution of the past. A woman even stated that French Protestants must renounce their agreement with the violent beheading of King Louis XVI, which she saw as a wrong justification of violence and antiauthoritarianism which has kept people isolated and overly independent. Finally John Arnott suggested that we pray for more of the fire of the Holy Spirit.

"You are ministering in a dark and difficult place, where you need more light and more fire of God's presence," said John. "I would like to pray for your torches to be lit so you can be further empowered as firelighters," he suggested, prompting me to share my dream of the night before.

At this point I shared my dream of the forest fire that was moving from tree to tree, from the eastern part of the Cevennes, where we'd been the night before, and from the south, where we were at that moment, joining to consume the heart of French Protestant country.

People were all in agreement with this suggestion, and John invited us all to stand and began calling on the Holy Spirit to send the fire of God's presence. Immediately people began crying out, and some fell to the ground under the power of the Spirit. I felt my body overcome by a heat that was almost unbearable, which burned throughout my body for the next hour or more, as we all prayed for each other and for France, until the evening ended and I left the delegation for further visits and a retreat with my French doctor of the Word colleagues.

During the remaining seven days of my trip I met with my theologian (Docteur de la Parole) friends, sharing with them my recent experiences with the charismatic renewal movement. Some listened skeptically, critical of attitudes that I too had witnessed: self-righteousness, spiritual elitism, anti-intellectualism, fundamentalism, conservative political ideology. I attended a contemplative retreat led by Daniel Bourguet at the retreat center at "les Abeilleurs" in the Cevennes. Daniel and I had met daily to talk at length about my experiences. The chasm between himself as a doctor of the word and contemplative and the charismatic world appeared gradually to close as we talked, prayed, and worshiped together in community with the other retreatants. Daniel wisely commented, "We will see by the fruit in your life whether this is from the Holy Spirit." On the day of my departure I asked him to lay hands on me and bless me in my researching and teaching of Scripture. He humbly knelt and asked me to lay hands on him to receive whatever God had for him.

My final meeting in France was with Michel Bouttier, an Église Réformée de France professor of New Testament at Montpellier for more than twenty years and a prolific writer, then in his eighties. Michel had been one of my most respected teachers and spiritual directors for over fifteen years. I had been hesitant to share with him my recent journey, afraid of his disapproval. We met for an hour and a half in a train station in Valence, where I was able to stop on my way to Paris. As I told him about my recent journey, he sat in rapt attention, profoundly touched by the testimonies of God's intimate touch and miraculous signs. "Your stories are right in harmony with the apostolic witness in the New Testament church," he began. "I have been so thirsty for what you are experiencing. For years and years I have been working to keep the dying coals alive in my church for God to move in the ways you are describing. Pray for me!" he asked, just as my train pulled up to the *quai*. I prayed for him as we ran to get on my train.

I returned from France convinced that God is birthing something new in me that involves a coming together of disparate parts of Christ's body and the diverse witness of Scripture in service of the poor and marginalized. It is God's pleasure to see the sanctuary and the street, the monastery and the academy, the charismatic renewal movement and progressive social activists, environmentalists and evangelists, traditional liturgists and contemporary worshipers come together. I am sure that as people respond to Jesus' invitation to join him in preaching good news to the poor, we will all come to recognize our need for all the riches of our inheritance, which are currently scattered among God's people in different denominations and countries. As people see the urgent need for the kingdom of God to come in force on behalf of those who suffer, they will be increasingly willing to give up national, ethnic, partisan, and denominational allegiances in favor of "on earth as in heaven." Switching from limited allegiances to being fully identified with the whole company of Jesus includes no longer being ashamed to be seen with the different ones. Nicodemus did go on to defend Jesus, but did he go far enough? Apparently he was not willing to make the break and be fully identified with God's coming kingdom. Perhaps like most Pharisees, he was unwilling to humble himself and receive John's baptism. Unity of purpose can best happen as we return to the Jordan, to the waters of baptism, where our identity as God's sons and daughters is restored and the dividing walls are broken down. There we become freed and empowered to join Jesus in creating something new.

Chapter 2

Living as Wetbacks

I recently had a dream in which I believe God spoke to me specifically about the importance of baptismal death and rebirth as the basis for greater empowerment for fruitful ministry. In my dream I entered the narthex of a big, white megachurch and was immediately recognized and shown upcoming course offerings on reading the Bible with the poor that my hosts thought would impress me. I then walked through a hallway and immediately saw a Triqui Indian girl I recognized from the migrant labor camps running toward me barefoot, with her hands up. "What are you doing here?" I asked her, taking her up in my arms. In the next scene I entered a huge auditorium-like sanctuary and saw my wife and a coworker sitting in the back row. There were no more seats, so I headed for an overflow section in the back. Just then two white leaders approached me. "The director wants to meet you in his office tomorrow and give you an impartation," they said. I imagined an older white pastor type, seated behind a desk in an upstairs office somewhere, standing as I entered to shake my hand before praying for me. "Can't you pray for me right now?" I asked, turning and facing a tall, dark man with a long ponytail, chiseled nose, and dark face, obviously Native American, who had mysteriously appeared.

"I can," he said confidently. "Let's go back in here."

He led me into an empty Sunday school classroom and up to a wall-sized white board from which he grabbed an erasable marker. He drew me in a limp position and then himself as an Indian warrior with war paint holding me firmly, head backward, on the side of a dirt road in the wilderness somewhere. His hand was raised above him, holding what looked like a tomahawk handle that he was ready to scalp me with.

"Where is the head of the tomahawk?" I asked the man drawing the picture.

"Right here," he said, taking a big piece of black slate and attaching it to the white board at the end of the handle, forming a rustic cross.

"Now watch," he said. And the picture became a real-life scene of a white man about to be scalped by a Native brave along a road.

"Go ahead and do it!" I found myself saying, turning toward the towering Native man with his cross tomahawk raised over his head. He brought it down upon me, and I fell to the ground in darkness, only to find myself fully alive, quivering and crying at his feet. I was overwhelmed by warmth and love, and recognized him as Jesus. I awoke shaking, feeling a strong sense of the loving presence of God.

A few days later I was leading a Bible study in the jail with a group of six or seven Hispanic-looking inmates. I learned that one was an Upper Skagit Indian and assumed the rest were from Mexico. I began with a prayer that went something like this:

> Lord, I praise you for this Upper Skagit brother and for all the Native peoples of this land. I thank you that you love them and that they are the true heirs of this land white settlers have occupied as their own. Forgive us for taking what is not ours. Bless the Native peoples of this land. I praise you that you are raising up a whole new generation of warriors from out of the many Native American tribes to bring good news, healing, and liberation to their people. Bless these people and protect them in Jesus' name.

Upon completing my prayer, I invited each participant to go around. I was shocked to learn that the first four men in the circle were Native American from the Swinomish, Upper Skagit, Tulalip, and Cherokee nations. The last two were Mexicans from indigenous backgrounds. God is in the process of calling and empowering people from the exiled tribes of today's Galilees to announce and bring about the kingdom of God. If mainstream people are to participate effectively as agents of call and empowerment, we must die regularly to our natural powers and be reborn and empowered by the Spirit into our adopted identity as God's beloved children, followers of Jesus and citizens in the kingdom of heaven.

Each Gospel begins with Jesus' baptism in the Jordan River—the port of entry into the promised land. Yet Jesus' first movement as God's Son is to leave the geographical land of Israel, understood as the actual location of the kingdom of God, through this border crossing station—inviting all future followers to leave whatever has become Egypt for them in order to reenter with a new identity, a new agenda and empowerment for liberation. In order for us to see heaven's realities break into earth and be authentic announcers of the kingdom of God, we too must go into the river with Jesus, leaving behind everything from the old order of Egypt, Babylon, Rome, America (or whatever most defines our identity) under the waters of baptism so we can arise as children of our Father in heaven, members of a new family without borders, false allegiances, or divisive distinctions.

The Jordan is hardly a neutral location, nor are Jesus' point of departure at the margins of the land of Israel in Nazareth of Galilee and his destination—the desert.[1] Coming to the Jordan for baptism causes the masses who submitted to John's baptism and us as readers to remember Joshua's leading the people from the wilderness through the Jordan into the promised land. Yet Jesus' departure from the actual periphery of the promised land of Israel into the wilderness, where he is tempted for forty days, links Jesus' baptismal immersion more closely to Israel's crossing through the sea from Egypt to the wilderness of their freedom. Jesus' baptism is nothing less than an exodus event from the actual geographical promised land to another wilderness wandering and reentry into now occupied territory.

Jesus reenacts Moses' forty years in the wilderness with his forty-day fast.[2] There he resists Satan's temptations to exercise his power according to Satan's agenda. He comes back in the power of the Spirit (Luke 4:14) to face his people's own contemporary Pharaoh, officials, and taskmasters. He faces them empowered by the Spirit, preaching and performing signs and wonders at the service of his agenda, to call people from slavery to a new freedom. Throughout the Gospel narratives Jesus states that Israel's leaders have led Israel to become a false presence of the kingdom, now even occupied by the Roman army, and religious institutions (chief priest, scribes, Pharisees, Sadducees) that were failing to announce good news to the poor regarding God's coming reign. Israel had become a land of slavery, occupied land—a haunt of the powers and principalities and demons. Today's situation in America and many other nations is parallel. God is now calling people and the church as a whole to a similar departure (from the United States or any other nation, ideology, denomination, or structure that demands allegiance) through the waters of baptism.

There are big differences between John's baptism on the one hand and the children of Israel's exodus from Egypt through the sea and their entry into the promised land through the Jordan. Both Moses and Joshua led the people through the waters on dry land (Exod. 14:21–31; Josh. 3:14–17). Jesus went under water when he submitted to John's baptism of repentance for the forgiveness of sins.[3] Immediately afterward the Spirit drove him into the wilderness for forty days. What could this mean?

John's baptismal immersion[4] was a symbolic entry into the fate of the "bad guys"—Pharaoh, his army, chariots, horses and riders. Jesus' acceptance of this baptism and the entire New Testament teaching on baptism is nothing less than a call for all future followers to join in the fate of the enemies of God's kingdom, the "them" that we may deem worthy of exclusion, punishment, or death.[5]

The waters are the place of God's defeat of the enemies of the kingdom of God— the principalities and powers.[6] Waters as a symbolic location where God's enemies are destroyed is an ancient idea, clearly present in the exodus story: "Then the Lord overthrew the Egyptians in the midst of the sea. And the waters returned and covered the chariots and the horsemen, even Pharaoh's entire army that had gone into the sea after them; not even one of them remained" (Exod. 14:27–28 au. trans.).

Some of ancient Israel's original worship celebrates God's victory over Israel's (and God's) enemies, who are submerged under water, not to come up.[7]

> I will sing to the LORD, for he has triumphed gloriously;
>   horse and rider he has thrown into the sea.
> The LORD is my strength and my might,
>   and he has become my salvation;
> this is my God, and I will praise him,
>   my father's God, and I will exalt him.
> The LORD is a warrior;
>   the LORD is his name.
> Pharaoh's chariots and his army he cast into the sea;
>   his picked officers were sunk in the Red Sea.
> The floods covered them;
>   they went down into the depths like a stone.
> Your right hand, O LORD, glorious in power—
>   your right hand, O LORD, shattered the enemy,
> In the greatness of your majesty you overthrew your adversaries;
>   you sent out your fury, it consumed them like stubble.
> At the blast of your nostrils the waters piled up,
>   the floods stood up in a heap;
>   the deeps congealed in the heart of the sea.
> The enemy said, "I will pursue, I will overtake,
>   I will divide the spoil, my desire shall have its fill of them.
>   I will draw my sword, my hand shall destroy them."
> You blew with your wind, the sea covered them;
>   they sank like lead in the mighty waters.
> Who is like you, O LORD, among the gods?
>   Who is like you, majestic in holiness,
>   awesome in splendor, doing wonders?
>
> (Exod. 15:1–11 NRSV)

Jesus' acceptance of John's baptism of repentance for the forgiveness of sins may well be first and foremost an act of identificational repentance[8] with and for the death of the Egyptian firstborn and the Egyptian army in the Red Sea. Jesus' later death on the cross as God's firstborn shows Jesus' total solidarity with sinners, especially enemies of the kingdom of God. Perhaps Jesus is enacting a dual repentance. In solidarity with sinful humanity he repented for Israel and the nation's sins. As the Son of God he repented for the death of all who stood in the way of Israel, much as God repented before Moses' intercession. As a new Moses departing a later version of Egypt, Jesus embodied human intercession and divine repentance, evoking Moses' intercession in Exodus 32:12–14 (NRSV):

> "Why should the Egyptians say, 'It was with evil intent that he brought them
> out to kill them in the mountains, and to consume them from the face of

the earth'? Turn from your fierce wrath; change your mind [repent, KJV] and do not bring disaster on your people. Remember Abraham, Isaac, and Israel, your servants, how you swore to them by your own self, saying to them, 'I will multiply your descendants like the stars of heaven, and all this land that I have promised I will give to your descendants, and they shall inherit it forever.'" And the LORD changed his mind [repented, KJV] about the disaster that he planned to bring on his people.

Jesus, apologetic for forgiving and blessing enemies, is consistent with an inclusive attitude toward enemies of God's kingdom: "But love your enemies, and do good, and lend, expecting nothing in return; and your reward will be great, and you will be sons of the Most High; for He Himself is kind to ungrateful and evil men. Be merciful, just as your Father is merciful" (Luke 6:35–36 NASB).

When Jesus submitted to the death of his flesh in baptism, all that he carried from the land of Israel he was leaving that was not consistent with the kingdom of God was washed away. Descent into the waters of baptism involved a deliberate joining in solidarity with the fate of sinners. These sinners may be institutional functionaries operating like Pharaoh and his army to maintain systems at the expense of the poor and weak, or ordinary lawbreakers. This is apparently the way that Peter interpreted both the flood account and Jesus' victory over powers and principalities according to 1 Peter 3:18–22 (NASB):

> For Christ also died for sins once for all, the just for the unjust, in order that He might bring us to God, having been put to death in the flesh, but made alive in the spirit; in which also He went and made proclamation to the spirits now in prison, who once were disobedient, when the patience of God kept waiting in the days of Noah, during the construction of the ark, in which a few, that is, eight persons, were brought safely through the water. And corresponding to that, baptism now saves you—not the removal of dirt from the flesh, but an appeal to God for a good conscience—through the resurrection of Jesus Christ, who is at the right hand of God, having gone into heaven, after angels and authorities and powers had been subjected to Him.

Here we see a distinction between human beings who died in the flood, whom he went and preached to, and the angels, authorities, and powers that became subject to him through his victory. The fate of God's enemies is nothing less than death. Yet death itself is undone by Jesus' own death with and for the unrighteous. Paul writes about baptism in this way in Romans 6:3–7 (NASB):

> Or do you not know that all of us who have been baptized into Christ Jesus have been baptized into His death? Therefore we have been buried with Him through baptism into death, in order that as Christ was raised from the dead through the glory of the Father, so we too might walk in newness of life. For if we have become united with Him in the likeness of his death, certainly we shall be also in the likeness of His resurrection, knowing this, that our old self was crucified with Him, that our body of sin might be done away with, that we should no longer be slaves to sin; for he who has died is freed from sin.

All distinctions between insiders and outsiders, the saved and the damned, perpetrators and victims, the righteous and the unrighteous, clean and unclean, Israel and the nations are leveled when insiders go under water, instead of through it on dry ground. Under water we all die totally. Under water, God's chosen people join the damned. We come up dead to the flesh—that is, dead to any distinctions that would mark us as in any way superior, or worthy.

Immigrants who cross illegally over the U.S.–Mexican border are commonly called illegals or wetbacks. The term wetback was first used to describe immigrants who swam across the Rio Grande in Texas rather than going through the legal ports of entry. The notion of illegal crossing into the United States and the designation wetback is a near perfect metaphor describing the immigration status of all who are baptized in Jesus and become his followers.[9] The flesh that is put to death in baptism includes all that separates us from others, whether that be our race, nationality, social class, economic status, physical appearance, religious affiliation, IQ, education, resume, or anything else. We need to be able to confess with the apostle Paul that:

> Whatever things were gain to me, those things I have counted as loss for the sake of Christ. More than that, I count all things to be loss in view of the surpassing value of knowing Christ Jesus my Lord, for whom I have suffered the loss of all things, and count them but rubbish in order that I may gain Christ, and may be found in Him, not having a righteousness of my own derived from the Law, but that which is through faith in Christ, the righteousness which comes from God on the basis of faith, that I may know Him, and the power of His resurrection and the fellowship of His sufferings, being conformed to His death; in order that I may attain to the resurrection from the dead. (Phil. 3:7–11 NASB)

This departure from a place of power and privilege with all its entitlements is followed by a reentry to a new solidarity—which is the starting point for announcing that the kingdom of God has come close. Paul writes to the Galatians:[10] "For all of you who were baptized into Christ have clothed yourselves with Christ. There is neither Jew nor Greek, there is neither slave nor freeman, there is neither male nor female; for you are all one in Christ Jesus" (Gal. 3:27–28 NASB).

Jesus' baptism is the prototype for our own. Under the water we experience death to the flesh. The flesh, as Paul understands it, is anything that "sets its desire against the Spirit, and the Spirit against the flesh; for these are in opposition to one another, so that you may not do the things that you please" (Gal. 5:17 NASB). Paul lists the deeds of the flesh with such all-encompassing terms that every force, institutional or interior, principality, and power or sinful passion can be included. All are dealt with finally on the cross, where Jesus' baptism and our own find their ultimate fulfillment: "Now those who belong to Christ Jesus have crucified the flesh with its passions and desires. If we live by the Spirit, let us also walk by the Spirit" (Gal. 5:24–25 NASB).

Coming up out of the water, on the other side of death, we receive our new (and true) identity as God's beloved children. In the Spirit's coming upon Jesus and the Father's declaration that "this is my Son, in whom I am well pleased" we see God's recognition and declaration of Jesus' identity and our identities as sons and daughters and our inclusion into God's household, by grace. This is our true identity, the basis of our actual citizenship, which Paul writes about when he says, "For our citizenship is in heaven, from which also we eagerly wait for a Savior, the Lord Jesus Christ" (Phil. 3:20 NASB).

Our new status as God's children is not a legal status based on fulfillment of the law, but rather an "illegal status," in that we cannot achieve it through fulfilling requirements (like filling out applications, proving income, obtaining sponsors, learning the language, passing tests, and numerous other actions demanded for permanent residency status or naturalization).[11] Yet this illegal status is such only in the eyes of the powers. In God's household we have legal status based on grace. Through an amnesty of grace we have become God's children, citizens of the kingdom of God. "So then you are no longer strangers and aliens, but you are fellow citizens with the saints, and are of God's household" (Eph. 2:19 NASB).

Later this chapter we take up the question of our status and benefits as adopted children of God. First, however, let's clarify how we actually come to see and enter into the kingdom of God and into our family. We will see that we enter only by grace through God's merciful birthing of us—apart from our having fulfilled any requirements, made any right choices, or performed any act in order to receive entrance as any sort of payment or reward.

Jesus' invitation to Nicodemus to be born again, or born from above (John 3:3), is all about how we come to cross the border from being a citizen of this world into our truest identity as God's sons and daughters—citizens of the kingdom of God. In this story Jesus describes how we move into our true baptismal identity so that we too can see signs that God is with us. Seeing the kingdom of heaven on earth and being empowered to enter fully into it cannot be done through fulfilling requirements or "works."

In a recent series of four thirty-minute Bible studies in Skagit County jail, I invited a group of inmates to read John 3:1–8, the first half of that Sunday's Gospel reading in the Revised Common Lectionary. After a volunteer read the verses, I briefly introduced Nicodemus.

I described how the Pharisees were depicted in the Gospels as not accepting John's baptism (Luke 20:4–7) and as opposing Jesus.[12] Nicodemus, though, himself a Pharisee and ruler of the Jews, is impressed enough by Jesus' power demonstrated by the signs he did to come to him by night. Concrete signs of Jesus' authority and power as a son of God captured this religious performer's attention.[13]

"Rabbi, we know that you have come from God as a teacher; for no one can do these signs that you do unless God is with him (3:2)," Nicodemus said.[14]

"Why do you think Nicodemus comes to Jesus by night?" I asked.

"He was afraid of what people would think of him for being directly associated with Jesus. But he couldn't resist because he saw him doing powerful signs," someone said.

We talked briefly about how Jesus demonstrated power and authority over elements like water and over established religious and economic systems on behalf of ordinary people. He turned water into wine so wedding guests could celebrate (John 2:1–11) and drove out profiteers who took advantage of the temple for their own economic benefit (John 2:13ff.). He alluded cryptically to the ultimate sign, his crucifixion and resurrection from the dead, when he said, "Destroy this temple, and in three days I will raise it up" (John 2:19 NASB).

Jesus could see that Nicodemus wanted to enter into Jesus' kingdom, and told him how: "Truly, truly, I say to you, unless one is born again, he cannot see the kingdom of God" (3:3 NASB).

"How did Nicodemus understand what Jesus was saying to him?" I asked the men.

"He thought Jesus was actually saying that he had to go back inside his mother and be born a second time," someone commented.

We talked about how utterly impossible this would be. I asked the men if anyone remembered deciding when they would be born, and we all agreed that we have no control over our birth—it's something that happens to us when we are pushed out.

I asked the inmates how many of them had tried to start their life fresh without drugs, alcohol, or some way of being that gets them into trouble. Everyone raised their hand when I asked them if they'd tried more than once, even many times.

"I've been to treatment nine times," one man confessed.

"I've been seven times," said another.

"This will be my ninth time being deported. Every time I tell my girl that I'm not gonna drink and drive, but then I do and I end up back in here," says Israel, a Mexican man in his late twenties.

Nicodemus showed that he understood the impossibility of being born again as something he could do in order to see the kingdom of God through human effort. "How can a man be born when he is old? He cannot enter a second time into his mother's womb and be born, can he?" (John 3:4 NASB)

The inmates all agreed that Nicodemus appeared to "get it" that Jesus was telling him that something needed to happen that he could not achieve through his own efforts. This was good news to them, as many had repeatedly failed to follow through with promises to follow Jesus, go to church, or stop drinking or using drugs.

Yet Jesus' next words appeared to call them to a sort of baptismal rebirth from a posture of repentance and forgiveness of sins. Jesus' response to Nicodemus suggested that people need to come up from the cleansing waters. These words assumed that people had first entered these waters. A volunteer reread John 3:5 (NASB): "Truly, truly, I say to you, unless one is born of water and the Spirit, he cannot enter into the kingdom of God."

I asked the men what they think it means to be born of water, and most thought this was referring to baptism by water.[15] We decided that this baptism must be talking about a death and cleansing experience. Being born of water might signify surviving a purifying trial or realizing you were still alive after near death or losing everything. Maybe it was not enough to just find yourself wet, ready to start again. In fact, many of the men had experienced changes of heart and made recommitments to live a different life many times when they had gone through various crises. Turning away from destructive ways and turning toward Jesus and trying to attend a church had not been enough. I suggested that being born of the Spirit might be something that was also desperately needed, and on a regular basis. The men were intrigued and encouraged to think that there could be another dimension of faith they had been missing that could empower them to face life's challenges. These uneducated, humbled inmates could see what Jesus expected. Nicodemus, a teacher of Israel, was supposed to know (John 3:10) that we all should expect some sort of Spirit birth "from above" that is out of our control: "That which is born of flesh is flesh; and that which is born of Spirit is spirit. Do not marvel that I said to you, 'You must be born again.' The wind blows where it wishes and you hear the sound of it, but do not know where it comes from and where it is going; so is everyone who is born of the Spirit" (3:6–8 NASB).

This good news is reinforced when I invite people to turn to John 1:9–13 (NASB), where the Gospel writer describes the Word as "the true light which, coming into the world, enlightens every man." Yet, even though the world was made through him, the world did not recognize him and his own people did not receive him. People can imagine that this "true light" must in fact be subtle and even humble. Apparently it could be missed and not embraced. At the same time this light could be received, but it's not all about choice. The complexity of the next verses is comforting: "But as many as received him, to them he gave the power to become children of God, even to those who believe in his name, who were born not of blood, nor of the will of the flesh, nor of the will of man, but of God" (1:12–13 au. trans.).

"So how does new birth happen according to these verses?" I asked, knowing that people would immediately note the importance of receiving and believing.

"You have to receive the light. You have to believe in Jesus," someone said.

"Okay," I affirmed. "Attraction to and stepping into agreement with God's love and saving work for us all does seem to be important," as Jesus tells Nicodemus later in verses 3:16–17 (NASB): "For God so loved the world, that He gave His only begotten Son, that whoever believes in Him should not perish, but have eternal life. For God did not send the Son into the world to judge the world; but that the world should be saved through Him."

Knowing that the men could easily slip into a striving, effortful understanding of belief that would finally end in defeat, I turned the conversation back to the metaphor of birth. "But what about the birth, how does that happen?" I asked, inviting people to look more closely at the text.

I pointed out that birth does not happen through human reproduction, referred to by "blood." It's not about human effort, since the text specifies "nor of the will of the flesh," as Jesus was telling Nicodemus. And it's not all about making right choices, since it says "nor of the will of man." "So how does birth happen?" I asked the men.

"You got to be born of God!" someone said confidently.

"So what part do we play in this?" I asked. "Is there anything for us to do?"

I asked the men if any of them were feeling attracted to what Jesus was telling Nicodemus and the idea of birth happening to us. The men found this focus on God's taking the initiative comforting and desirable.

"It doesn't seem so difficult. It even sounds easy," someone said.

"Check this out, you guys," I said. "It says, 'To those who receive and believe in his name he gives power to become children of God.'"

I pointed out that the word for power in Greek is *dunamis,* like dynamite. "As we open ourselves to receive and move toward belief, God gives to us dynamite power to become children of God. This power is like the force that pushes us out of the birth canal. It doesn't come from us, it comes from the one who is giving birth to us," I continued.

"So if this was offered to you, would you take it?" I asked. "If you were offered a gift, would you say yes, would you want to believe life could change for you?"

Everyone appeared to be in agreement that they would in fact like to receive this gift and the power to become free children of God, as soon as possible.

I have come to understand believing God as an attraction that draws us into a life where we will see and experience more and more of the kingdom of God. When we are not attracted enough to move toward Jesus, it may be because we are not yet ready to give up other competing attractions. People continue to live under judgment until we are ready to live in the light of our new identity above the purifying baptismal waters. This is what Jesus is suggesting in John 3:18–21 (NASB):

> He who believes in Him is not judged; he who does not believe has been judged already, because he has not believed in the name of the only begotten Son of God. And this is the judgment, that the light is come into the world, and men loved the darkness rather than the light; for their deeds were evil. For everyone who does evil hates the light, and does not come to the light, lest his deeds should be exposed. But he who practices the truth comes to the light, that his deeds may be manifested as having been wrought in God.

Believing in the name of the only begotten Son of God, Jesus, brings us into a way of living that is not about striving for perfection. As we follow our attraction to the light, we will see that our actions are the fruit of God's power working in us. Our deeds are "wrought in God," and are not the result of our own work, which does not work anyway.

I invited the men who were feeling attracted to God's gift of power to become children to speak their desire to God. Nearly everyone told God in their own words, in Spanish or English, that they were open to receive and wanted to believe in his name. As I prayed I invited people to imagine themselves going down under the water and dying, entrusting themselves totally to God. I invited them to envision themselves as beneficiaries of Jesus' victory over death and all the forces that work in them to separate them from God (addictions, broken relationships, anger, greed, jealousy, their image, etc.). I invited them to envision themselves as coming up out of the water and asked anyone who desired to be filled with the Holy Spirit to put out their hands and/or open their hearts and say, "I welcome you into my life, Holy Spirit," "Te invito entrar en mi vida, Espiritu Santo." Nearly everyone opened themselves to receive God's Spirit.

At this point in the Bible study I often invite anyone who is accompanying me to go around and lay hands on each person, praying for the Spirit to come and fill them. I notice that people are often deeply moved as God touches them in different ways. Some have tears streaming down their faces. Others tell me they feel heat or feel as if they are going to fall down. Many people have experiences of physical healing.

John the Baptist understood that water baptism prepared the way for baptism in the Spirit directly by Jesus himself:

> "And I did not recognize Him, but in order that He might be manifested to Israel, I came baptizing in water." And John bore witness saying, "I have beheld the Spirit descending as a dove out of heaven; and He remained upon Him. And I did not recognize Him, but He who sent me to baptize in water said to me, 'He upon whom you see the Spirit descending and remaining upon Him, this is the one who baptizes in the Holy Spirit." (John 1:31–33 NASB)

Jesus is himself the prototype human "Son of God" who demonstrates what a life as a child of God looks like. At the same time, he is the one who baptizes in the Holy Spirit. I continue to wonder how this happens now, and fully embrace the role of the church in bringing people into this baptism. According to Matthew's Gospel, anticipating his own physical absence, Jesus gives his disciples authority to make disciples, baptizing people in the name of the Father, Son, and Holy Spirit (Matt. 28:18–20). The Roman Catholic, Eastern Orthodox, and historic Protestant churches' practice of infant baptism rightly understands baptism as God's birthing, "while we were still sinners," apart from our will, that believers can bring their children into by faith. Most of the Hispanic immigrants with whom I read Scripture in the jails and at Tierra Nueva are Roman Catholics who were baptized as infants. Almost all the mainstream people I read Scripture with in churches and seminaries are also baptized, many as infants but some as adults. Among both groups I see a lack of empowerment and authority over the powers of evil in their own personal lives and in the larger society. Rebaptizing people as Baptists or other species of evangelicals does not appear always to lead to greater empowerment or authority. I am increasingly convinced that baptism is a life-long process that involves continual death, rebirth, and filling. In Ephesians 5:18 the apostle's imperatives must be understood as continuous actions that the Greek verb tense assumes, in keeping with the continually practiced action of verses 19–20: "Do not [keep / continue to get] drunk with wine, for that is dissipation, be [keep / continue to be] filled with the Spirit, speaking to one another in psalms and hymns and spiritual songs, singing and making melody with your heart to the Lord; always giving thanks for all things in the name of our Lord Jesus Christ to God, even the Father" (Eph. 5:18–20 NASB).

The apostle Paul calls believers to a lifestyle of worship that involves continual death to the flesh and renewal of the mind:[16] "I urge you therefore, brethren, by the mercies of God, to present your bodies a living and holy sacrifice, acceptable to God, which is your spiritual service of worship. And do not be conformed to this world, but be transformed by the renewing of your mind, that you may prove what the will of God is, that which is good and acceptable and perfect" (Rom. 12:1–2 NASB).

If transformation is to happen, people's minds must be renewed. Coming to see the kingdom of God through more fully knowing God and our own true identity as God's sons and daughters through study of Scripture, prayer, worship, and continual filling by the Spirit will lead to our continual entry into the kingdom of God. The following stories from a recent visit to Tierra Nueva in Honduras show how we are beginning to see God's kingdom come and will be done, on earth as in heaven.

Angel David Calix, Tierra Nueva's forty-nine-year-old Honduran coordinator, walks from adobe house to adobe house in his village of Mal Paso, inviting people for an afternoon Bible study before darkness descends and we can no longer read. Everyone likes Angel David, a natural leader, who is involved in everything from local road and water improvement projects to Tierra Nueva's agricultural committee and the village soccer team. He has seen many of his soccer players, including his two sons, leave for the long and dangerous journey overland to the United States.

"Almost all the young men have caught the fever to go north," he tells me. "Nothing holds them back. We're in a crisis here in Honduras," he continues. "There aren't any jobs. There's no future."

As Angel David approaches houses, he places his hand on the head of every other child in the village—his God children. He blesses them with a warm smile and *Dios te bendiga*. There are no active churches in Mal Paso, which has been abandoned by both the Catholic Church and Pentecostal churches as too hard. In reality, the struggling, poor inhabitants of this dusty, sun-baked village have found Catholic teaching regarding marriage as a requirement for communion and Pentecostal legalism regarding drinking, smoking, swearing, and other prohibited behaviors seemingly impossible to comply with. Leaders like Angel David and his brother Jorge Calix have heard enough good news about God's grace to have a low tolerance for religious rules that end up excluding the majority.

"People are attracted to a Jesus with open arms," recounts Angel David to me from his cell phone in his village. "But they are traumatized by a theology of the beating. What people on the margins need is a theology of a light burden, not a theology of the heavy burden," he continues, referring to Jesus' invitation to take his easy yoke in Matthew 11:28–30.

"People hear this offer as an opportunity that includes them. The problem comes when leaders take the line that one is saved by what they do, and we forget about grace, talking only about what we do, what we have to do, what the people have to do in order to be saved," Angel David concludes.

Angel David is the closest person to a pastor for miles around Mal Paso. He himself does not attend any one church—though he will visit Catholic churches, Pentecostal churches, and nearly any place where worship happens in villages he frequents. He sees a thirst for God among many marginalized by the Catholic and evangelical churches but sees the tribalism of the different denominations as barriers to a movement of the Spirit that would really engage the more notorious sinners and people living in extreme poverty. Angel David is like one who has left religious affiliation behind after crossing over the Jordan into the wilderness.

"I am like a burro without an owner. I haven't been branded," Angel David laments about his unattachment to any particular church denomination. "I sleep wherever I want, wherever I can find a place to lie down," he continues. "Others who have a brand are not free to communicate good news that the people really need, because they are under the scrutiny of leaders with other theologies."

In Mal Paso people do gather at least once a year when I visit. They trickle into a small hermitage on a hill above the village and find seats on wooden benches we've set facing each other. A skinny, flea-bitten dog sits wagging his tail in the middle. David's brother Jorge leads us in a few songs on an out-of-tune guitar before I invite people to turn to that Sunday's lectionary text from Mark 1:21–34. We're a scraggly collection of unbranded ones, there to discover the benefits of being children of God, citizens of God's kingdom.

We talk about how Jesus began his ministry at the margins of society, in Galilee. There he preached: "The time is fulfilled, and the kingdom of God is at hand; repent and believe in the gospel" (Mark 1:15 NASB), and then immediately began calling ordinary people like fishermen to participate with him in his ministry of healing, deliverance, and proclamation.

We discuss together how early in Mark's Gospel Jesus is described as amazing the people by his teaching, "for He was teaching them as one having authority, and not as the scribes" (Mark 1:22 NASB). This authority immediately stirred up an unclean spirit from a religious insider in the synagogue, who rightly perceived Jesus as a threat: "What do we have to do with You, Jesus of Nazareth? Have You come to destroy us? I know who You are—the Holy One of God" (1:24 NASB).

Jesus in fact does want to destroy unclean spirits that inhabit churchgoers, and he rebukes the spirit with a command: "Be quiet, and come out of him!" The spirit does not come out easily; he throws the man down in convulsions and cries out with a loud voice before coming out of him (1:26). People are amazed by this and say: "What is this? A new teaching with authority!" (1:27 NASB).

We read together how Jesus then goes to Simon's mother-in-law's home. Jesus raises her up from lying sick with a fever by simply taking her hand (1:29–31). This healing is immediately followed by a sudden broadening of Jesus' ministry to include casting out demons and healing the sick of the whole city from the door of her home—outside the confines of institutional religion. "And when evening had come, after the sun had set, they began bringing to Him all who were ill and those who were demon-possessed. And the whole city had gathered at the door. And He healed many who were ill with various diseases, and cast out many demons" (1:32–34 NASB).

"Jesus had just taught people with authority, cast out an unclean spirit from a man in the synagogue, healed Simon's mother-in-law of a fever, and was now casting out demons and healing people from the entire city," I summarize. "Is there a need for any of these actions here in Mal Paso?" I ask. "Would a Jesus who did these things be welcome and attractive here?"

"Yes, it would be good. Really important," says a woman meekly.

"There are lots of people who are sick who cannot afford doctors," says someone else.

"Well, Jesus is here with us even now through the Holy Spirit," I say. "Are any of you in pain whom we could pray for right now?"

At least a third of those gathered have physical pain: back problems, knees, shoulders. Angel David and I lay hands on and pray for each one to experience God's healing presence there in Mal Paso, much as in Simon's village. Several people say they experience immediate relief from pain.

"So where did Jesus get his kind of authority to do these things?" I ask the group. After an awkward silence I invite people to read the story of Jesus' baptism, suggesting that at Jesus' baptism he receives power and authority to teach, cast out demons, and heal.

I point out that John the Baptist appeared in the wilderness preaching a baptism of repentance for the forgiveness of sins (1:4). John described one who would come after him who is much mightier. "I baptized you with water," he says, "but He will baptize you with the Holy Spirit" (1:8 NASB). Jesus is then described as coming from Nazareth in Galilee and was baptized by John: "And immediately coming up out of the water, He saw the heavens opening, and the Spirit like a dove descending upon Him; and a voice came out of the heavens: 'Thou art My beloved Son, in Thee I am well-pleased'" (Mark 1:10–11 NASB).

Jesus' coming up out of the waters of baptism there in the Jordan causes a tearing open of the heavens as the Son of God joins all the city people from Jerusalem and all the country people from Judea (1:5) who had come confessing their sins.

"What did Jesus do in order to receive the Spirit and God's favor?" I ask.

"Nothing. He just came up from the water," risks Angel David—a comment that elicits smiles from many of those gathered.

"Where was Jesus when he received the Spirit and God's approval?" I ask. "Was he in church, up by the altar, receiving the Eucharist?" I ask, knowing that most of those present are not allowed to take communion because they are living in common-law marriages or are in other ways not in compliance with the Catholic Church. The obvious answer never fails to delight people.

"He was in a river, in the Jordan," someone ventures.

I point out the obvious conclusions from the text: that Jesus had done nothing more than join the masses in a baptism of repentance for the forgiveness of sin. Before even beginning his public ministry, at his moment of greatest humility and vulnerability, the Spirit comes upon him and he is assured of his Father's favor: "Thou art My beloved Son, in Thee I am well-pleased."

Jesus receives his empowerment, his identity, his authority as God's Son when he is dripping wet at the port of entry between the wilderness and the land of Israel. God's declaring him a Son with whom he is pleased subverts any human tendency to depict favored status as a deserved reward. We end our discussion, summarizing how in baptism we, like Jesus, receive our true empowerment, identity, and authority by the Spirit, and assurance that we are beloved.

Since everyone in the room is already baptized as an infant, I ask if anyone there desires prayer to receive more empowerment from the Spirit, to become more directly involved in Jesus' ministry. All fifteen desire prayer, and David and I go from person to person, inviting the Spirit to fill and empower each one.

The next day Elia Dominguez, a Tierra Nueva promoter from Minas de Oro, and I take off to spend the day visiting women she attends to in the villages of Rio Colorado, Corralitos, El Bijao, and Las Delicias. In Rio Colorado we pray for a woman struggling with her addicted husband and their asthma-racked five-year-old son. We then pray for two teenage girls whose mother and father recount how they have been regularly fainting and experiencing dramatic seizures, followed by prolonged disorientation, that the family thinks are related to evil spirits. The first girl slips into a trancelike state as we begin to pray. After we learn that her condition began when she experienced extreme terror some fourteen months ago during a nightmare, we bind the fear and invite her to turn away from it and turn toward Jesus. Almost immediately something lifts as in Jesus' name we cast out spirits related to terror. We pray for her cousin, who also experiences freedom, and bless their family and home before we head down a steep bumpy road to Corralitos, where we park and hike up a steep path to the home of an impoverished family.

There we encounter a twenty-one-year-old girl hunched over on a bench. Her sister tells us she has been unable to walk since she stepped on a nail when she was five years old. Elia and I pray for her healing and anoint her with oil. Elia thinks she notices new hope in her face as we leave, heading to El Bijao down a steep, rutted road barely wide enough for a vehicle.

With every encounter, signs of God's kingdom become increasingly visible. In El Bijao, while visiting a woman whose husband had left her with seven children to seek work in the United States, Elia learns that a family in the hamlet above has two children suffering from dengue fever.

"Let's go pray for them, Roberto," she says.

I hesitate, afraid of getting sick at the beginning of my trip, and then remember that if it's dengue, it can be spread only by mosquitoes. My memory of reading about Jesus' healing of Peter's mother-in-law's fever the night before in Mal Paso finally mobilizes me to go for it. I hike ahead up a steep trail, accompanied by two of the woman's oldest children, to a humble home with corn husks and drying grains laid out in the sun. I introduce myself to a nearly toothless man in rags and a tattered sombrero, who bows and ushers us into the kitchen, where his wife is working. She takes us into a dark bedroom to the beds where their thirteen-year-old daughter and five-year-old son lie asleep with high fevers. I place my hand on the girl and then her brother, commanding the fever to leave in Jesus' name. The father sits at the end of his son's bed watching. I ask him whether he desires prayer for any pain or sickness. He tells me he has continual pain in his lower back that radiates down his left leg. After laying hands on him and praying, I ask him if he notices any change. He says matter-of-factly that the pain has left his back and that only his left leg is now hurting. Elia appears in the doorway, and we pray together again until he tells us with a humble grin that all the pain is gone. He enthusiastically urges his wife, who is sitting on the adjacent bed: "Tell them about your problem!" She tells us about pain in her head, neck, and spinal column and agrees to let us pray for her.

"I feel a fire going down my back," she says as she motions to the back of her head and down her neck. "There is no more pain!" she declares triumphantly.

I look over to the other bed and see that the thirteen-year-old girl is now lying with her head propped up, smiling. She says she feels better, that her fever is gone. The five-year-old is up, sitting beside his father, his fever gone. Elia and I have to leave for the next village, but can hardly contain our excitement. Two children of the neighbor woman whose husband is in the United States had witnessed this. I can tell they are moved as we head down the train giving thanks to God. I am sensing that the sixteen-year-old neighbor girl, Maria, is feeling a desire to minister like this herself, and stop briefly in the trail to ask her if she could see herself praying for the sick. She says she would really like to, and Elia and I decide to lay hands on her right there and anoint her with oil, deputizing her to work with Elia when she comes every month. She looks excited and I feel as if I'm getting a glimpse into what it must have felt like to follow Jesus. I feel as if I am experiencing myself the story in Mark 1, and can hardly wait to get to the next village to see what will happen next.

Our final visit that afternoon is to the town of Las Delicias, a remote village at the farthest reaches of Coyayagua's rugged department. There Hector Giron, a retired Tierra Nueva promoter, had organized a phenomenal Bible study with some thirty villagers that had met six nights a week for some nine years. Elia, who is originally from this village, tells me that this Bible study had been cancelled nearly two years before by the local Catholic lay leader. This is especially tragic, as the nightly gathering had nurtured this community after an especially noteworthy beginning.

Hector had approached his neighbor and brother-in-law, Elia's brother, who was dying of AIDS that he had contracted during his promiscuous life as a partying, macho truck driver. Hector had offered to read his daily lectionary readings from the Gospels to him as he lay there slowly wasting away in bed in his parents' adobe home in the center of the village. His brother-in-law at first refused but later consented. Hector read to him every afternoon, and gradually was joined by family and neighbors until the group included over thirty people, including the Catholic delegates of Word, who lead worship songs with their guitars and accordion. The meeting was held in an extremely participatory way; each person gathered in the circle was invited to make a comment on each verse before going to the next. Hector's brother-in-law had come to faith and died in great joy and peace.

The people were so moved and empowered by this experience of accompaniment and group reflection that they decided to meet six nights a week, two of which were official "celebrations of the word" led by the Catholic lay leaders. The success of Hector's Bible study eventually disgruntled Ostilio, the leading Catholic delegate of the Word, who appeared to be jealous and had prohibited villagers from attending two years before, under the pretext that Tierra Nueva was not officially Catholic and could not be trusted. Elia and I pray as we drive along the bumpy dirt road that God will help us see reconciliation and renewal in this community.

"Lord, send your angels ahead of us to open the way for reconciliation," we pray.

When we arrive, the first man we see walking up the road is Ostilio, who greets us warmly. We come into Hector's house to find him depressed and embarrassed about the Bible study having been canceled. He tells us he has not been able to work now for several years and has constant pain in his back. Encouraged by the healings we had just witnessed in El Bijao, Elia and I offer to pray for Hector, who experiences immediate relief and joy. We decide to visit some families around the village and offer to pray for the sick, instead of trying to resurrect the Bible study. Just then Ostilio comes in, inviting me and Elia to attend a special mass for the Virgin of Suyapa, a commemoration, held nationally that very day, of the Honduran manifestation of the Virgin Mary. I hesitate, wondering whether this might be a distraction from our purposes there, but then remember Mark's account we had studied the night before, of Jesus' going to the synagogues of the villages he visited (Mark 1:21). As we walk toward the service, I tell Ostilio that we'd like to go around to some houses afterward and pray for the sick.

We head up the potholed dirt road on foot, past rows of adobe houses, and are ushered into a crowed home with some fifty men, women, and children. The service begins, with songs commemorating Mary, Scripture readings, and an inspiring homily by the delegate Ostilio, who upon finishing announces that I am now going to lead the group in a service of healing. Shocked, I quickly search for a way to avoid being perceived as the gringo man of power—a role I have intensely disliked. An idea comes to me about what I can do, and I launch into a brief overview of Jesus' mission statement concerning preaching good news to the poor and all during his first sermon in Nazareth in Luke 4:16–20.

"Jesus put into practice his mission through praying for the sick, casting out demons, and proclaiming good news," I say, thinking back to the Gospel narrative in Luke 4:38–5:26, following Jesus' declaration of his fulfillment of Isaiah 61 in the synagogue of Nazareth.

"Jesus passed on this mission to his disciples in Luke 9:1ff.," I say, flashing back to the sixteen-year-old girl we had just deputized in El Bijao.

"He gave his disciples power and authority to do the same," I continue. "And it wasn't just to the original twelve, but to seventy-two other followers," I preach, referring to his village renewal strategy described in Luke 10:1ff.

"He appointed seventy-two others to pray for the sick and cast out demons, because he wanted to start a movement that would include everyone, even all of us. Jesus desires to empower all of you," I conclude, and ask whether people would like to be part of Jesus' mission.

Heads are nodding enough to encourage me to continue, and Ostilio the delegate appears to be in agreement. I invite people to pair up and pray for each other to impart the Spirit of the Lord upon their partner as they repeat Luke 4:18–19 over each other. The people obediently repeat the words of Isaiah 61:1ff. over each other as I speak them in the first person: "The Spirit of the Lord is upon *you*, because he has anointed *you* to preach the gospel to the poor. He has sent *you* to proclaim release to the captives, and recovery of sight to the blind, to set free those who are downtrodden, to proclaim the favorable year of the Lord (Luke 4:18–19). This is your holy mission."

After each person lays hands on and prays over his or her partner, I ask who in the crowd is in need of healing for physical pain or sickness. More than twenty-five people raise their hands, and I ask people to name their conditions: pain in the lower back, neck, knees, and stomach; fever; swollen hands; seizures; headaches; and toothaches were all mentioned. I then invite everyone to lay hands on each other, and I lead them in a prayer, commanding pain to leave in Jesus' name. I end by invited all the afflicted to repeat: "This healing belongs to me because I am a child of God. I receive my healing now as a free gift in Jesus' name."

I then ask people to check themselves.

"I can open and close my hands," exclaims a lady, who stands with her hands outstretched in amazement, opening and closing them and testifying that she hadn't been able to do this in weeks.

I invite people to give God a round of applause and everyone claps, a practice I first learned in this village years before.

More than fifteen people say they have experienced immediate and total healing. After each person shares how God had just healed them, the group gives rounds of applause to Jesus, who has visited them in Las Delicias in such a concrete way. We then invite anyone in need of more prayer down to a nearby home, which is soon crowded to overflowing with others from the village who have heard about the healings. Once again my mind flashes to Mark 1:32–34 (NASB):

"And when evening had come, after the sun had set, they began bringing to Him all who were ill and those who were demon-possessed. And the whole city had gathered at the door. And He healed many who were ill with various diseases, and cast out many demons."

People crowd into Elia's family home, where her brother had died of AIDS eleven years before. A woman brings us her son, whose legs are deformed and twisted under him. The child can walk only on his hands, which he uses to drag himself along.

"Can you pray for my son?" the woman asks, knowing that nothing but a miracle will free her son from being a dependent or a beggar.

I feel completely humbled, inadequate for the task. My faith waivers before the superior faith and desperation of this woman and neediness of her little boy. I invite people to gather around this boy, and we hold him and pray over him, anointing him with oil. I ask someone to keep praying for him while Elia and I pray for others: A woman who has regular seizures, a woman who suffers from insomnia and migraine headaches, an older lady with pain in her stomach. For the next hour or so Elia and I keep praying for people in pain, and many claim to experience healing. I notice that Ostilio is standing at the back and feel led to invite him to where we are in the crowded room, so we can pray for him.

Ostilio agrees to receive prayer for his face, which has been paralyzed on one side from a stroke or palsy or something that he's not sure about. He comes to us and falls to his knees and bows his head. As soon as I place a hand on his face, he begins to shake and sob. He cries out and begins to confess in a loud voice his recognition that God is calling him to humble himself before us, whom he calls his brother and sister from a different religion whom God has sent. He asks God and the community to forgive him for not accepting us and for stopping the Bible study. We hug him and pray over him. He says he feels the presence of God on his face, but we don't notice any change in his appearance. He asks us to go to his home and pray for his wife, who has just broken her leg from falling when she got out of a pickup truck. We follow him to his home and pray over his wife in their bedroom.

Elia and I drive back up the dirt road in the dark to Minas de Oro, arriving late that night. We talk about how we had witnessed many of the happenings in Mark 1 in a different order, including a version of the deliverance of the man with an impure spirit in the synagogue. Nick, a twenty-three-year-old intern with Tierra Nueva, arrives the next day and listens with some reservation to our stories. I find myself feeling both excited and foolish for daring to believe that anything extraordinary has actually taken place. Nick stays on for several weeks after I fly home and later tells me that he visited and interviewed the people we prayed for in El Bijao and Las Delicias. He tells me that people were deeply affected by our visit and claimed to continue to be pain free. He brings back pictures, recorded testimonies, and lists of people and the conditions they were healed from. He tells me that the people in Las Delicias gathered for a Bible study with him and that they all prayed for others to be healed.

I continue to be amazed that I am seeing signs of the present reality of the kingdom of God. As we pray, we find ourselves seeing and even entering God's kingdom. It appears that God's will is being done, on earth as in heaven. Yet not everyone is healed or freed from oppression. The little boy in Las Delicias still uses his arms like crutches to swing his twisted legs along. I long to see more of the ministry of Jesus being reenacted here and now. I am looking for anything in the Gospel stories that can help me make the move from the old way of thinking and operating in "this world" into a new way of being that looks more like heaven. I want to reenter into the old world that I have left and announce the kingdom of God there with Jesus, full of the Holy Spirit. How can this happen?

Mark's Gospel shows Jesus calling disciples from outside the established religious places, in Galilee, along the sea, with ordinary fishermen (Mark 1:16–20). In the synagogue he encounters a man with an impure spirit, which suggests that deliverance for religious insiders is one of Jesus' high priorities if they are to join effectively in his ministry. I feel challenged to stay in a posture of confession with Ostilio, admitting and renouncing the impure spirits of church and synagogue that keep me from going outside to the masses with the gospel of the kingdom. This best happens when we stand with people on the margins, the poor, the incarcerated, anyone who feels excluded or in any way oppressed by sin or the powers. As we encounter people on the margins, we will see clearly that which is not the kingdom of God but is impure—marked by the kingdom of darkness and under the power of the antichrist.

Chapter 3

Stop the World

Right reentry into the kingdom of God as one of God's beloved, adopted ones and citizens of heaven first necessitates departure from "the world." If we are to see God's kingdom come and will be done, on earth as in heaven, we must first recognize that what we mostly experience here on earth is not heaven, and may actually feel closer to hell for some. This recognition is more difficult for those vested with the benefits of this world: credit, capital, economic and social success, acceptance, family support, racial profile, and citizenship that offer special entitlements or any sort of privileged status. After all, Jesus did say emphatically, "Truly I say to you, it is hard for a rich man to enter the kingdom of heaven. And again I say to you, it is easier for a camel to go through the eye of a needle, than for a rich man to enter the kingdom of God" (Matt. 19:23–24 NASB).

While Jesus goes on to say that "with God all things are possible" (19:26), his words here show the difficulty of entry into God's kingdom unless people have first *left* the kingdom or systems of this world. Ministry among inmates, immigrants, and homeless people has helped me see how systems that work or are at least tolerable for people of relative privilege like myself are completely unlivable for people on the margins.[1] They have already left "the world" in a sense and are a big step closer to reentry into the kingdom of God than many mainstreamers. At the same time, many have entered other "worlds" that give them security (addictions, gang affiliation, criminal lifestyles). Crisis brought about by face-offs with family and the legal system cause many to recognize that their ways of handling anxiety and resisting the powers are leading to increased sorrow and disappointment.

Disappointment with the world may in fact be a requirement for departure and reentry. Many immigrants from Mexico who have already left their world back home experience the new world of the United States as disappointing as they struggle along with the masses of marginalized Americans to survive in El Norte. Men and women from every nationality, race, and ethnicity are daily released from jails and prisons throughout the United States owing thousands of dollars in restitution fines, court fees, and child support payments. Most have had their driver's licenses revoked until they pay their fines and complete substance-abuse treatment programs, making it difficult to get to work, should they manage to land a job. With criminal records, labels like "felon" or any sort of "sex-offender" classification, alcohol and drug problems, and lack of education, it is extremely difficult to find a job, let alone a livable income.

A recent Bible study in Skagit County jail has become a catalyst for some new understanding of the urgency of close engagement with people on the margins of our society as a basis for spiritual discernment in differentiating the true kingdom of God from that which is false.

A group of ten or so men file into the jail's multipurpose room where we do one of my Thursday evening Bible studies. For the past year or so the jail has required us to lead four thirty-minute Bible studies instead of our normal large-group bilingual gathering. This is due to overcrowding, the need to separate enemies, and the limited number of chairs. The time is so short and the needs in each group so different that I am becoming more aware of the need to be especially watchful of how the Spirit is leading, so the limited time can be most beneficial. As my companion Chris leads us in a worship song with his guitar, I look from face to face, trying to get a sense of God's leading. My eye is drawn to a boldfaced and italicized tattoo on the neck of a young Latino guy named Michael. I remember a dream I've had of a Latino gangster-looking Jesus with the names of his family (us) tattooed on his neck and chest. I start to tell this story, but then look closer at Michael's tattoo. My eyes widen as I silently read: *Fuck the World.*

"Whoa, that's a powerful tattoo," I say, and find myself adding something like, "That sounds like something Jesus would say. You sound like you could be one of his followers."

He looks surprised, and I realize I am in deeper than I am prepared for. Before I am able to think of any appropriate scriptures, I manage to ask him what he meant by "the world."

"Like the system," he says, shyly looking downward.

"So what do you mean by 'the system'?" I ask, fishing for more details.

"Everything, the whole 'f'ing system," he says, without further embellishment.

I ask him if he means the courts, the jail, things like that, and he nods.

"The prosecutors, judges, everyone that degrades others. Everybody who looks at me and says, 'That guy's a criminal.'"

Michael's description of the system reminds me of Bible studies I often do with inmates and others on the New Testament teaching about the principalities and powers. I think of the war in heaven in Revelation 12, where another Michael and his angels are fighting against the dragon and defeat them and cast them out of heaven to earth: "And the great dragon was thrown down, that ancient serpent, who is called the Devil and Satan, the deceiver of the whole world—he was thrown down to the earth, and his angels were thrown down with him" (Rev. 12:9 NRSV).

People like Michael are keenly aware that the world is under the dominion of powers and principalities. I have seen group after group of inmates and immigrants nod knowingly when we read together Ephesians 6:12 (NASB): "For our struggle is not against flesh and blood, but against the rulers, against the powers, against the world forces of this darkness, against the spiritual forces of wickedness in the heavenly places."

The Greek terms used in this verse and elsewhere in Scripture,[2] like *arche* (ruler) and *dunamis* (power), designate human rulers, nations, and institutions throughout the Greek Old Testament used by early Christians.[3] People on the margins have regular firsthand experience of spiritual oppression mediated through the structures of society, and have no trouble affirming texts like Ephesians 2:2 (NASB) that describe the world as running "according to the prince of the power of the air, of the spirit that is now working in the sons of disobedience."

I later learn that Michael has been institutionalized since he was nine years old, in and out of juvenile detention, youth centers, and more recently the county jail. His first three years in detention were for stealing car stereos, his last three for accidentally shooting a friend in the stomach when they were messing with a gun. Michael says he dropped out of school after sixth grade. He went and got his tattoo quite recently after spending seven months in jail last year while they investigated allegations of his involvement with three other young men in the rape of a girl they were partying with.

"The prosecutor knew she was lying, as they had five sworn statements that were all different," he recounts. "I had a job which I lost when they arrested me. The system doesn't give you a second chance. They keep throwing you down and don't let you up. Instead of helping you like they're supposed to, they keep you down. But that's how they make their money. They have to keep you coming back. It's a messed-up system."

Michael, like millions of young men throughout the world, has chosen sides against "the world"—understood as the entire system of demands for compliance rewarded by entitlements. It is hard to imagine that he will ever "catch up" or "measure up" in a timely enough manner to bring him across the border from the margins into anything even close to mainstream. He will never have a clean record, be able to vote, be able to travel outside the country, qualify for a mortgage, or have a pension plan. Already marked as a felon and rebel, he is a nearly fully vested member of the community of the damned.

Michael's bold tattoo impresses me. He knows he does not fit into the world. When I ask him what he means by *fuck* the world, he shrugs and says that what he means is not sexual. It is more like disregarding the demands of the world or giving in to not being able to comply[4] and being forever marked as a criminal. His resistance comes through "dissing" or ignoring the system and its demands, in response to his perception that the system is dissing him. His visible brand reveals a bold self-identification with the community of the damned, the "them" in opposition to the "us" of those who are capable of relative acceptance and success.[5] While his tattoo likely reflects some pride in this and his rebellion is not working for him or others like him, he appears to measure up to many calls in Scripture to leave, shun, or even stop the world. I affirm whatever I can in Michael, expecting the best, treating him as if his understanding and motives are fully in line with Scripture.

I wish there were time at that very moment to launch into a discussion of 1 Corinthians 15:24–27 (RSV), which shows Jesus' total "ef"ing the systems of this world that hurt Michael and so many others: "Then comes the end, when He delivers the kingdom to God the Father after destroying [read 'ef'ing] every rule and every authority and power. For he must reign until he has put all his enemies under his feet. The last enemy to be destroyed is death. For God has put all things in subjection under his feet."

"I'm serious, man, that tattoo is more in line with Jesus' teaching than you might think," I start out, stalling for time to get some direction for our remaining fifteen or twenty minutes together. "Jesus has overcome the powers of this world. He calls his followers to leave the world." I continue. "He even says if you don't hate the world you can't follow him . . . which makes you a top candidate for being one of his disciples since you're already practicing this."

Michael smiles shyly, awkward, with all eyes staring at Chris and me.

"Check out what it says here in 1 John 2:15–17," I continue, inviting someone to read this first scripture that comes close to supporting one interpretation of Michael's tattoo: "Do not love the world, nor the things in the world. If anyone loves the world, the love of the Father is not in him. For all that is in the world, the lust of the flesh and the lust of the eyes and the boastful pride of life, is not from the Father, but is from the world. And the world is passing away, and also its lusts; but the one who does the will of God abides forever" (NASB).

I can see that this first scripture has an impact, but that it is not enough to convince Michael and the others around the circle that this is actually a major theme in the Bible. I am also aware of the dangers of proof-texting or presenting texts from different parts of the Bible that reflect diverse understandings of terms like "the world." I don't ask them what they think "the things of the world," "the lust of the flesh," "the lust of the eyes," and "the boastful pride of life" might be referring to, as I know from experience that they will immediately assume this is a judgment on their desires. There is not enough time to help them see that these terms expose the vanity of the entire American Dream and the reigning "power of pride" mentality in the United States.

I am also aware of the dangers of encouraging Michael and the others in their resentment. After all, in John's Gospel we read "God so *loved the world* that He gave His only begotten son" (John 3:16 NASB). Yet I can see that the hatred of the world harbored by Michael and many others like him is compounded by the shame of mainstream people's rejection of them. This shame is usually rooted in people's experiences of rejection, abandonment, and other hurts in their core relationships with mother and father, who themselves are passing on hurts they've received from the generations that preceded them.

I invite the men to read several scriptures that show that this shame from rejection by the world is something that Jesus experienced and warned his followers they should expect. I invite people to turn to John 15:18–19 (NASB), and one of them reads: "If the world hates you, you know that it has hated Me before it hated you. If you were of the world, the world would love its own; but because you are not of the world, but I chose you out of the world, therefore the world hates you."[6]

"Maybe you are hated by the world in part because they think you stole too many of their car stereos or broke into their homes or keep breaking their rules," I suggest, inviting laughs or smiles from some of the men.

Michael expresses an awareness of this when he responds at one point by saying, "They hate me cuz of what I've done, what I do, you know?"

"But if the world hates you, you are clearly close to being in the company of Jesus. You are outside the world already, and Jesus is there with you," I suggest.

I invite people to turn to James 4:4 (NASB), which adds further weight to their being closer to God's side than they had ever thought: "You adulteresses, do you not know that friendship with the world is hostility toward God? Therefore whoever wishes to be a friend of the world makes himself an enemy of God."

I remind the men that Jesus got the death penalty because he consistently sided with the excluded sinner types rather than agreeing with the religious law enforcers. He died between two criminals[7] and invited his followers to join him in resisting, even to the point of receiving the death penalty themselves. We read about how Jesus destroyed the dividing wall, abolished hatred and the law itself by going to the cross:

> But now in Christ Jesus you who once were far off have been brought near by the blood of Christ. For he is our peace; in his flesh he has made both groups into one and has broken down the dividing wall, that is, the hostility between us. He has abolished the law with its commandments and ordinances, that he might create in himself one new humanity in place of the two, thus making peace, and might reconcile both groups to God in one body through the cross, thus putting to death that hostility through it. (Eph. 2:13–16 NRSV)

Joining him outside the world will lead to resistance that must be countered by a radical commitment to following Jesus' call to come out. We read Luke 14:26–27 (NASB): "If anyone comes to Me, and does not hate his own father and mother and wife and children and brothers and sisters, yes, and even his own life, he cannot be My disciple. Whoever does not carry his own cross and come after Me cannot be My disciple."

I am seeing clearly that only those who have been hurt by the world, who can say, "Fuck the world," can easily and fully ask for and receive a new kingdom without reservation. If they are already willing or even feel forced to be unpopular with this world's authorities, they will at least be open to newness and change. Those who have already been rejected by the world are often more ready to be recruited by Jesus to learn to see and enter the kingdom of God. I assure the men that while struggle and suffering can be expected in this world, Jesus is ultimately victorious. Our final reading is John 16:33 (NASB): "These things I have spoken to you, that in Me you may have peace. In the world you have tribulation, but take courage; I have overcome the world."[8]

We end this particular study by singing "Your Kingdom Come"—a song that repeats the first refrain of the Lord's Prayer, "Your kingdom come, your will be done," with the repeated chorus: "On earth as it is in heaven"—before gathering in a circle, holding hands, and praying for God's help and blessing.

A few weeks later I am on my way to the jail, talking to Amy, another Tierra Nueva colleague. I ask her to remember to pray for us that evening in the jail. She calls me back just as I'm pulling into the jail parking lot. "This may sound crazy, but I'll risk it. As I was praying for you just now, the name Mike came into my head. I wonder whether there may be a man named Mike who has special need of prayer."

That evening, before each of the four thirty-minute gatherings, I ask the men around the circle to say their names. There's no one named Mike. Then in the last gathering of the night Michael is there and says his name. I tell him about Amy's call, and since his name is the closest one to Mike, I ask him if he is facing any particular difficulties for which he needs special prayer.

"No, not really," he says.

When I ask him if he's sure there's nothing, he says, "Well . . . I am facing three trials." I tell him we'll have to be sure and pray for him after our songs and short Bible study.

We begin with a few songs, ending with a simple refrain that we repeat over and over, "Jesus, friend of sinners, we love you," before I invite people to read Matthew 11:19 (NASB), where Jesus tells how his contemporaries, especially religious people in the system, looked at him: "The Son of Man came eating and drinking, and they say, 'Behold a gluttonous man and a drunkard, a friend of tax-gatherers and sinners!' Yet wisdom is vindicated by her deeds."

I tell the men that the word "glutton" could easily be translated "addict." Today some people would have judged Jesus as an addict and alcoholic, a friend of criminals and others viewed as bad people. The men think it is cool that Jesus was viewed as on the side of the underdogs when he walked the earth and could be envisioned as on their side now. Since time is short, I invite people to turn to the primary text for discussion later in the chapter, Matthew 11:28–30 (NASB). Chris, a heavily bearded ex-biker with tattooed, Popeye-like bulging forearms, reads: "Come to Me, all who are weary and heavy-laden, and I will give you rest. Take My yoke upon you, and learn from Me, for I am gentle and humble in heart; and you shall find rest for your souls. For My yoke is easy and My load is light."

I briefly describe the image here, where Jesus suggests that he's like an ox or mule with a yoke who invites us to pair up with him.

"Jesus wants us to come and get help alongside him," I say. "Even though we don't know what we're doing, like a new, inexperienced ox or mule, we can come learn from Jesus, who is like an older, experienced animal who takes the lead. Jesus invites us to learn from him. He is not a harsh taskmaster or demanding, correcting drug-court judge or probation officer. He is gentle and humble in heart. Are any of you guys carrying any heavy burdens right now?" I ask.

I look from Michael to Chris and to another man to my left, and they all nod. The answer is too obviously yes to merit discussion, and I feel compelled to make it more precise.

"Were you guys carrying heavy burdens beginning at a young age, like responsibilities for your siblings or parents?" I ask, looking to Michael, hoping I'd get some clarity about how to pray for him.

"No, not me, man, I was in juvie (juvenile detention) beginning when I was nine years old," he says.

"I did," says Chris. "I've been on my own since I was eleven, and had my first kid when I was thirteen. My second kid was born before I turned sixteen."

"Michael, where you raised by your mom and dad?" I ask, trying to understand some of the roots of his delinquency.

Michael tells the group that he was raised by his grandma. His mom was on the streets, drinking all the time. His dad has been in prison all his life; he's never seen him.

"Did you worry about your mom?" I ask him.

"Yeah, of course, she's my mom," he responds—revealing an excessively heavy burden that he has carried from as far back as he can remember and that he considers normal, since it is so common among his peers on the street.

As we sit there silently for a moment, feeling the weight and the pain of what Chris and Michael have shared, I notice the air thickening around my hands, a signal that makes me aware of a gentle presence of the Holy Spirit.

"I'm feeling the presence of God with us right now," I say, and I describe to the men the details of what I am sensing. "Some people feel what I am describing, but everyone is different. Some feel heat, others tingling, many peace or joy, and many feel nothing. Are any of you feeling what might be the presence of God?" I ask, inviting people to put out their hands. (We are entering into the yoke of Christ at this point as we let the Spirit lead us.)

"Yeah, I'm definitely feeling something," says Chris. My colleagues Chris and Antonio are gently nodding, and I start to notice and mention a growing pain in my right hand that I have come to interpret as a sign that I'm supposed to pray with someone in pain.

"I'm in pain," says a man to my left who hasn't spoken until now.

When I ask him where he feels the pain, he points to his heart and tells me that his fiancée, the mother of his two young children, has just moved out of their place. I invite the others to gather around him. I ask if he can put his hand over his heart and if I can place my hand over his hand as we pray. Everyone prays over him, and he cries softly. I ask him how he's doing after we pray, and he says he felt pressure leave him and is now in peace.

I look to Michael and get an idea about how to pray.

"The system and all kinds of people have always been trying to correct you, haven't they?" I ask.

"Yeah," he says, smiling wearily.

"Has it worked?" I ask.

"No," he says.

"I'm feeling that what you really need is to be blessed. Has anyone ever blessed you?" I ask. He shakes his head and says no, never—agreeing to let us bless him.

We gather around him, and people lay hands on his shoulders. I take hold of cold, clammy hands and shake off a slight feeling of revulsion. Each of us speaks words of blessing over him. We pray about his upcoming trials and bless him with success and peace. Some of the prayers include words about how God is proud of him and wants to be closely identified with him. I find myself looking at his highly visible "Fuck the World" tattoo and thinking how amazing it is that Jesus is a true friend of sinners to the extent that he wants to include people like Michael among his coworkers.

"God wants to flow through you to others," I say. "God wants to bless others through you, because God is proud of you. You are his beloved son."

As I say this, I notice a tingling in my hands that grows to a gentle vibrating. I immediately find myself thinking that this is a sign God wants to transmit or release to Michael an already latent spiritual gift. I ask him if he is feeling anything, to see if there is any confirmation. He tells me he too is feeling tingling in his hands, and I ask him if he is open to receiving an impartation of the gift of healing, so he can lay hands on people to pray for healing and to bless people. He agrees, and I pray over his hands. I feel them turn from cold and clammy to warm and glowing. When we finish praying, I ask him how he feels about laying hands on people as we're doing.

"Yeah, man, it sure beats using these hands to beat people up and shit. I can see inviting my homies[9] to the park to chill out and barbeque," he says, smiling.

I show him in Ephesians how Jesus wants to give him more and more authority as he recognizes his true identity as one of God's sons. We read together several texts that I am convinced need to be internalized and acted upon by all of us growing up as empowered children of God. I read to Michael and the others Paul's strong affirmation about the spiritual blessings available to us: "Blessed be the God and Father of our Lord Jesus Christ, who has blessed us in Christ with every spiritual blessing in the heavenly places" (Eph. 1:3 NRSV).

We also read Ephesians 2:6–7 (NRSV) about how God has "raised us up with him and seated us with him in the heavenly places in Christ Jesus, so that in the ages to come he might show the immeasurable riches of his grace in kindness toward us in Christ Jesus."

A week later he tells me that when we prayed he felt his hands heat up and the warmth go up one of his arms. He tells me he has just agreed to a plea to take 100 months in prison rather than risk more than 300 months, should he lose his trials. He says he is excited to be part of the ministry of Jesus, beginning in prison. "Maybe I'll run into my dad there in the joint," he says. "I'm following in his footsteps," he says with a grin.

My colleague Chris leads a version of the original "Fuck the World" Bible study with a group of homeless youth that meets for a weekly Sunday morning Bible study at Seattle Vineyard. He starts by telling a sleepy and distracted group of nine young adults who live on the street about Michael in Skagit County jail and his tattoo. This gets their attention—to the point that people stop reaching for donuts.

"Do you guys ever feel that way?" Chris asks.

Yes, they can indeed relate to Michael's sentiment. They themselves feel hated by the world. They talk about being on the sidewalk, cops harassing or arresting their friends. Someone comments about how stupid it is to get dumb jobs, and how stupid a lot of stuff is.

Chris brings up what one man in a hooded sweatshirt said in the opening go-around stories of the week, how he was locked in a dumpster that he had slept in one night, trapped in there with all the garbage for the day. He laughs about it.

"Why do you think the world hates you?" he asks.

Some say it's the way they look, not playing by the rules. Others are lost for answers. After reading about how the world hates Jesus and his followers, the discussion moves in a new direction as people start catching on to the plural "you" whom Jesus addresses as they read John 15:18–19 (NASB) a few times. "If the world hates you (plural), you know that it has hated Me before it hated you."

They agree that Jesus is not talking about the redwoods or salmon, that this is not the "world" anyone feels rejected by.

A girl brings up how even if she tries to get her act together she can't just walk by and ignore her friends. She talks about how, when she worked at a coffee shop, if she obeyed the management and told her friends from the street that they could not use the bathroom that she'd be joining the "world," so to speak. Chris is impressed by how close these young men and women are, how they look out for each other on the streets, stick with each other in a remarkable solidarity. They show love to each other when the world locks them in dumpsters and rejects them. He invites them to go back and read John 15:9–17, which they do, and take note of Jesus' talk about the love between him and the Father, the one who brings them all together into one family.

"This sounds like how you guys already love each other," he tells them. "You stick together, abide in each other."

He tells me how he found himself desiring inclusion in their community of young people rejected by the world.

"If what Jesus says is true here," he tells them, "then when I read this with you guys, I feel a little jealous: I'm a 'clean white male,' as you labeled me when we first saw each other outside the building this morning."

He recounts to the group how when he first arrived and met them on the steps outside the storefront church, one of them had commented: "They're closed still, but they'll let you in, and us with you—you're a clean white male."

He tells them that this comment made him realize that the world that would not let them in early—in this case the church members—"loves me as its own."

"I'm not immediately identified by Jesus, then, as one of his own. This makes me want to be around you guys more, reading Jesus' words with people who he describes as his own, like you guys: those rejected by the world, but already chosen by him and his Father. I want to be part of that family . . . badly."

Chris describes how a number of the guys and a girl leaned forward smiling and say soft things like "Oh . . . okay, I get it," and giggle and smile at each other.

"I tell them about how hard it is to talk to folks in churches about Jesus calling us away from the ways of the world, because the world loves them as its own," recounts Chris. He encourages them, suggesting that they are already in the radical place Jesus wants more people to be in with him.

"So, if what Jesus says is true," Chris says to the group, "if this is why you don't belong to the world, would any of you be interested in acknowledging the one who chose you out of the world in the first place, to receive more of the love that the world won't give you?"

Chris recounts how he is interrupted by a number of yeahs that encourage him to continue his invitation.

"If this Father that Jesus talks about is real, are you guys open to turning from any shame or failure, from not being loved by the world or being rejected by it, and joining the family, the parent who is other than this world, who loves you? I mean, if you no longer want to be part of the world, then you can't feel rejected by it, right? We can let ourselves be received and embraced by *him* instead, and not need the world to love us.

Jesus says we can *ask for whatever we want*—more than spare change—and it will be given to us, because we're his children.

"Does anyone want more love, even love for people who pass you on the sidewalks—so that you don't fall into hating and acting like the world, the cops or the rich, like them?"

"Hands rise," recounts Chris. "We all put our hands out and ask for more."

He asks if anyone has any physical pain, and suggests that even if they feel rejected by the world, as children of God they can start right now by asking God for a tangible expression that God is not like the world, but shows love for us now.

He tells how a guy who looks like a mix of Native American, Mexican, and Irish (colored eyes, freckles) says his teeth are aching, and thinks he may have an abscess. Chris describes how he crawls across the circle and asks the man to put his hand on his own cheek and asks if he can put his hand over the man's. This causes another guy to laugh, as people express open reservations about loud, intimidating Pentecostal types who push you over when they're praying for you.

"This is a good place to talk about healing, I realize," recounts Chris, "me on the ground below all of them. I tell them that I know about all that weird stuff done in churches, but when I read the Gospels, I just see Jesus lightly touch someone [and I lightly touch this guy Isaac], and the person is healed or receives their sight. For some reason, God likes to use hands, our hands, to touch when healing. It's not weird, but pretty sweet, if you ask me."

Chris recounts how everyone smiles and agrees. Since no one is apparently feeling too awkward, he prays and asks others to put their hands on Isaac.

"His eyes are closed deeply, like he's already in another place, hearing something I'm not," says Chris. "And I feel comfortable really talking to God aloud, asking for this love to heal the teeth, to touch his son, to take away all pain right now. I get to turn and talk to others, ask if there's other stuff to pray for, but with my hand still on Isaac's cheek. Some think this is funny, but I talk about soaking, and what's the rush. Isaac nods slowly, as if he doesn't mind it continuing. He says he feels really good. Another young African American teenager says he's going into King County jail, and he's worried he'll freak out, lose it, and he's scared. All come around him as we ask God to go with him and talk to him in the cell and give him revelation and rest."

Chris asks Isaac how he feels before we all get up and go. "Huh! . . . I mean, I don't feel any pain. . . . I think I'm all right now. Wow."

"If it comes back, man, just put your own hand back on where it hurts, and ask God to keep countering the pain and healing it, as your Father," suggests Chris.

Isaac sharply nods and appears to almost look forward to it. He is loving the love that he is receiving, and he passes with no resistance from the "world" of the street into a deeper communion and fellowship of fellow strugglers in the kingdom of God. Isaac, Michael, and other are finding that Jesus is there with them in the wilderness, outside the land. This is happening as we join them in affirming in our own way the deepest and most generous interpretation of Michael's "fuck the world."

We at Tierra Nueva are hearing with increasing clarity and urgency the call to embrace the excluded, tainted ones—whatever label they are discarded under. Whether the "insiders" discard them as "illegal aliens," "felons," "homeless," "drug addicts," "habitual offender," "mentally ill," national enemies we might label "terrorists," "enemy combatants," or "Islamic extremists," Jesus calls his body to bear his shame and announce his victory to all who find themselves "outside the camp." This is in fact what we find ourselves doing, as during a series of four thirty-minute Bible studies on Hebrews 13 on a recent Thursday night in Skagit County jail.

"For the bodies of those animals whose blood is brought into the holy place by the high priest as an offering for sin, are burned outside the camp" (Heb. 13:11 NASB). "Unclean things were cast outside the Israelite camp, or outside the city of Jerusalem, to protect the rest from danger and contamination," I explain to the first group of some twenty red-uniformed inmates who sit around a circle. It was there that animal carcasses were destroyed (Lev. 16:27), lepers had to reside (Lev. 13:46), menstruating women were sent (Num. 5:2–3), and criminals were executed (Lev. 24:14, 23; Num. 15:35–36; Deut. 22:24).

"Who are those considered unclean and excludable by the insiders, by those considered worthy of staying inside in our society today?" I ask.

"*We* are," a number of them say almost immediately. "The homeless," says someone else. Others mentioned included undocumented workers, people living with AIDS, sex offenders.

"So let's see where God is located according to this scripture," I suggest, inviting a volunteer to read the next verse: "Therefore Jesus also, that He might sanctify the people through His own blood, suffered outside the gate" (Heb. 13:12 NASB).

The men were moved to see that Jesus identified himself with the ones outside the camp. We read Luke 15:1–2 (NASB), which states that "*all* the tax-gatherers and the sinners were coming near Him to listen to Him," provoking the insiders to grumble.

"So Jesus is someone who suffers with the outsiders. What else does he do according to this verse?" I ask.

We discuss how Jesus sanctified them by his blood, which means that he made unholy, rejected ones holy, righteous, or set apart—even special. I ask them if any of them have tried and failed to make themselves holy/righteous—and everyone responds that they have in fact tried and failed repeatedly.

People are moved to discover that Jesus himself makes the unclean, excluded ones righteous through his blood, shed for them. On the cross, outside the camp (John 19:20; Mark 15:20; Matt. 27:32), Jesus does what none of us can do on our own. He makes us holy, righteous, and special, through blood shed while suffering among the damned. When I ask each group whether they want to receive the gift of holiness Jesus offers them, people in each of the four groups unanimously and enthusiastically say yes.

"Well, you don't have to go very far to get Jesus' help, because, if you are already 'outside the camp,' Jesus is here with you," I say, asking someone to read the next few verses: "Hence, let us go out to Him outside the camp, bearing His reproach. For here we do not have a lasting city, but we are seeking the city which is to come" (Heb. 13:13–14 NASB).

"I am the one who has to go further than any of you, as I'm inside," I say, realizing that I'm the only one not dressed in a red jail uniform.

"No, you don't, because you're here with us," someone immediately responds, making me feel warmly included—strangely free of shame.

Jesus welcomes us all to join him outside the camp, where we find relief from striving for righteousness. Jesus has already done for all of us what we all desperately desire and need but can't do for ourselves. In so doing, he has done away with all "us-them" distinctions in a subversive act of removing all borders. This is the good news of the kingdom of God that we enthusiastically welcome and boldly announce. This message must be announced, because it comes to us through divine revelation and not through our natural perception. Those ready and willing to receive this message include many weary and disillusioned ones who still find themselves "inside the camp," as well as those who have left the camp but are now wandering aimlessly or are fighting unsustainable and losing battles.

Many mainstream people and the children of mainstreamers are already outside the camp, but have not yet identified Jesus there alongside them. Many have been driven outside the camp by their deep dissatisfaction with the status quo of church and society. Joel, a 27-year-old Caucasian raised in a "God-and-country" home, is one of a growing number of young adults who have made their way to Tierra Nueva after having renounced and in every way he knew how "ef"ed the alienating and oppressive systems of this world. Groomed to succeed inside the camp, Joel was driven outside by a deep disillusionment with the status quo of church and society. Joel describes his alienation, beginning when he was raised on military bases where his dad was a chaplain in the Army, before moving from one suburban community to another where his father pastored churches. The lack of stable community pushed him into individualism and a deep mistrust of the adult world.

In 1999, when Joel was eighteen, he spent time in inner-city Oakland with Mission Year, a Christian inner-city internship program, where he came into contact with the ghettos of America. Joel worked for two years as an intake worker for an inpatient treatment program across the street from Oakland city jail. There he witnessed firsthand men who were trying to change but were completely burdened by government requirements mediated through the bureaucracy of church-based programs. The Christian treatment program's emphasis on personal responsibility and its complete subservience to the state's myriad menial demands and bureaucratic hoops, which required people to prove they were rehabilitated, greatly disillusioned him. He saw this punitive "Christian" approach as completely ineffective, because it heaped burdens and labels on marginalized men to pressure them into compliance with a middle-class notion of what it means to function as a responsible citizen. He also worked with inner-city kids in school systems that looked more like juvenile detention centers than empowering educational facilities. In Joel's own words: "I saw lots of people dictated to by institutions that told them where they had to be at every moment. Noncompliance was punished by taking away the few freedoms that these guys had. Everything based on earning, following the rules, humiliation, and fear, all in the name of Jesus," recounts Joel.

Seeing American poverty and the hidden masses of people living in extremely difficult situations was the beginning of the unraveling of his image of America as a benevolent nation. Joel became increasingly disillusioned with the United States as a land of democracy and opportunity and freedom for everybody. He began reading about the civil rights movement and the Vietnam War and came to highly value the work of dissidents like Martin Luther King and Noam Chomsky.

After his two years in Oakland, in August 2001 Joel moved home to the Pacific Northwest, where he got a job as a caregiver of a man with compound developmental disabilities. It became increasingly difficult for Troy to join worshiping communities, as he saw many churches advocating acquiescence with the state. This became painfully apparent to him following the events of September 11, 2001—when people all seemed to be going along with what looked to him like a knee-jerk reaction, the U.S. invasion of Afghanistan. Troy's disillusionment with institutional Christianity and the United States increased. Troy got active in street protests and writing letters to congressional representatives. But his activism felt ineffective.

In 2005 Joel began listening to lectures from scholars who argue that the official explanation for the events of September 11 was deceptive. Joel became convinced that the Twin Towers were blown up by controlled demolitions and that the plane crash into the Pentagon was staged. As he looked into who was benefiting from these events and the two wars that had started, he concluded that the oil companies, defense contractors, and multinationals like Halliburton were bringing in record earnings, and the domestic population was giving unprecedented worship to the state. Were the events of 9/11 staged to justify wars to establish U.S. dominance in the oil-rich Persian Gulf and the creation of the Department of Homeland Security and other intelligence and law-enforcement agencies to turn the United States into (more of) a police state? he wondered.

"I held this opinion and found people thinking I was completely nuts," says Joel. "I began to accept the label that people were putting on me of being a conspiracy theorist who had gone off the deep end. I had been rooted in church organizations my whole life. I didn't feel like it was a place where I belonged. I started living for my own ideas and individual pleasures. I knew lots of people like me, and others who thought rock and roll was going to save us. We thought that the energy of being young and rebellious was what we needed to flow with—which was obviously futile and dissatisfying. I found myself flailing around, wondering what the hell I was supposed to be doing, and feeling paranoid about what I was learning. It's no secret that we start using drugs at this point more frequently. It's just one of a lot of ways to give the finger to the law, a way to feel an evening's worth of empowerment."

Chris, a friend of Joel's from Oakland who had been volunteering full time with Tierra Nueva for nine months, called him one day and invited him to the opening night of one of my courses, "Breaking the Chains: Biblical and Social Perspectives on Resisting Personal and Social Evil." Since Chris was now viewed as working inside a Christian ministry, Chris and Joel had fallen out of contact, due to Joel's alienation from anyone "inside the camp." Joel politely delayed responding to the invitation and unplugged his phone, settling instead for a night smoking weed and drinking in his apartment. When he thought it was too late to come, he turned his phone back on and answered a phone call from Chris, who announced that someone was arriving any moment to take him down to Tierra Nueva.

Once at Tierra Nueva, Joel says he sat back cynically to critique my talk. Joel recounts that at the end of it I had prayed a prayer that included silencing the voices of the accuser in Jesus' name.

"As soon as that prayer was prayed," recounts Joel, "I felt like the voices in my head went silent. I had been living under a cloud of self-accusation, mockery, and paranoia, which I countered by in turn judging and accusing. I was hearing voices like, 'You're an idiot. You're being watched. You're ruining your relationship with your family. You're ruining your reputation among all the people that you know. You're just acting like a fool and you need to just let this stuff go. You're pissing your life away. My life's not counting for anything.'"

That night Troy experienced God's presence in a powerful way, flooding his life with love and warmth. He moved into the building and has been volunteering at Tierra Nueva ever since. Troy describes his generation as independently minded, with a deep distrust of movements and institutions.

"People in my generation are looking for something to give our allegiance to. Something we believe in that we can give our lives to. We have a deep desire to have something to fight for. Most of my Christian teaching consisted of 'God wants you to behave yourself, so be polite and don't rock the boat.' I see the church as basically providing the state with a massive obedience program when it teaches people in this way. Whether it likes it or not, this is largely how the church is viewed by my generation. Strangely I think most of my peers who are cynical about the church really like the person of Jesus, who flipped over the tables of religious profiteers and spoke in no uncertain terms about social justice."

Joel, like Michael, has come to say "ef" the world, after experiencing extreme disappointment with things social, religious, and political. Joel is convinced that appropriate resistance must begin with fully renouncing allegiance to nation and fully switching sides to follow Jesus and working to establish the kingdom of God: on earth as in heaven.

"Clinging to my citizenship and my responsibility to these institutions was making me feel a lot of anxiety for my responsibility for things like invading Iraq and killing hundreds of thousands of people there, and our policies in Latin America that have done so much damage," says Joel.

"Activists like me are empowered by a sense of anger, fear, anxiety, and responsibility for being the oppressing Imperialist Americans," he continues. "My activism was really sad, full of anxiety and guilt. It was all about investigating atrocities. I had such a need to accuse people who I thought were evil, as a way of alleviating my own feelings of responsibility. I had no joy.

"But now I am seeing that our tails shouldn't be lit on fire by white guilt for wiping out Native Americans. I believe a thorough reading of history to expose past abuses continues to be of great importance. But I have come to believe that my motivation should be in searching for the voiceless, instead of some kind of righteous urgency to expose the crimes of my countrymen.

"I'm feeling called to renounce all allegiance to country and citizenship as part of my core identity. It's like we need to fully leave the militia in order to join another one and begin to joyfully work alongside oppressed people, whose liberation is tied up very much with ours, if Dr. King was correct. Now I believe that I can work for the betterment of this country much more effectively and joyfully by having a kingdom I can feel really good about pledging my allegiance to."[10]

Joel, like many other young people at Tierra Nueva, is feeling drawn to pledge total allegiance to the ultimate victor—Jesus. For Joel, following Jesus feels like "being invited into a camp that is more powerful than the whole military-industrial complex. It's like Jesus longs to have you be a creative, vital member of his organization, immediately promotes you to the highest rank, tells you that your creativity and imagination are vital and important, and is willing to take upon himself all of your burdens, debts, depressions, and anxieties. Jesus promises victory in the face of death and institutional hegemony. It is exciting to leave the place of disempowerment and anger. This is not about being a Christian with your head in the sand waiting for the rapture. I am now better able to engage from a place of joy and empowerment, rather than a place of anxiety and guilt . . . that is exciting to me."

I am seeing that Michael's "fuck the world" tattoo and Joel's resistance can be incorporated into the baptismal renunciations spoken at the border between the two kingdoms. If mainstream Christians are effectively to enter into the kingdom in solidarity with people on the margins, they too must revisit baptismal renunciations and affirmations, informed by the street, prison, and world(s) of today's underclass. The first requirement of reentry into the promised land, on earth as in heaven, is identifying what is *not* the kingdom of God and leaving it. Deliverance from the powers begins with an open-eyed recognition of oppression, renouncing the powers of evil in such a way that we break agreement with their legitimacy, releasing human beings through forgiveness, and replacing the old with the new, as we begin to see and enter the authentic kingdom of God.

Chapter 4

Resisting the Powers through Advocacy and Deliverance

As we contemplate following Jesus as he reenters occupied land left behind in our baptism, we may well find ourselves overwhelmed by the apparently all-powerful forces and institutions that now occupy the world, our communities, and our hearts. Making sense of the legion of spiritual and material obstacles in the way of people's entry into and survival in Jesus' company is forcing an ongoing paradigm shift as I seek the gospel that has the power to save. Whatever cosmology I end up with needs to take account of the microforces that assault people in forms such as anger, jealousy, lust, and greed, labeled by the early church fathers as "passions"[1] or "demons" and the larger macropowers such as legalism, nationalism, discrimination, and the like, labeled by social prophetic writers according to the biblical vocabulary surrounding "principalities and powers."[2] Open-eyed realism before the myriad of forces in the way of healing and transformation is showing me the need for an approach that brings together social and legal advocacy and deliverance from evil spirits, 12-step and other recovery programs emphasizing counseling and inner and physical healing. First, we must seek clarity from Scripture and people's lived experience regarding the nature of evil and effective resistance. We require today a fuller understanding of prophetic ministry that draws together true understandings of prophetism currently active in social activist/prophetic and charismatic camps.[3]

Jesus begins his ministry in the desert resisting the devil, also called Satan,[4] during a forty-day fast. In three ways the devil tempts Jesus to bring about his kingdom in keeping with the tempter's antilife agenda. Before even entering into the land to advance his kingdom, Jesus shows us there in the wilderness the basis of effective prophetic ministry: resistance to the "ruler of this world," guided by radical dependency on the Spirit and Word of God. Jesus resists and overcomes the devil's three attempts to direct Jesus' steps as the "ruler of this world" by consistently pointing to God as the master of the universe who directs him. Jesus' responses to the devil in the temptation narratives show all future disciples that discernment of and allegiance to God's voice over and against the tempter's agenda is the highest priority.

In response to the tempter's questioning of his status as Son of God and call for Jesus miraculously to turn stones to bread, Jesus affirms his total dependency on his Father and refuses to succumb to the tempter's voice or go with his own agenda by saying that humanity lives "on every word that proceeds out of the mouth of God" (Matt. 4:4 NASB).[5] The devil insists on directing Jesus' actions by getting him to prove his identity as Son of God in a spectacular, attention-getting show of jumping from the temple pinnacle into the arms of rescuing angels. Jesus calls the devil to submit to Scripture's imperatives regarding himself as the Son of God by saying: "*You* shall not tempt the Lord *your* God" (Matt. 4:7 RSV). Finally Jesus refuses the devil's call to fall down and worship him as the ruler of this world, commanding him to leave and citing Scripture to order him to submit: "*You* shall worship the Lord *your* God, and serve him only" (Matt. 4:10 NASB). The devil refuses to worship Jesus and leaves. Angels come to minister to Jesus (Matt. 4:11), in keeping with their calling to serve God and humans— showing up the devil, who wants humans subservient to him.

Jesus reenters the land as the true Son of God and returning king to undo the devil's works manifested in the antilife passions and powers occupying the land. Once back in Israel ministering, Jesus confronts demons and sickness with ease and appears to attract tax collectors, sinners, and the poor masses into his kingdom effortlessly. Jesus' successful resistance to the devil's temptations in the wilderness is followed by aggressive confrontations with invisible spiritual enemies like demons, sickness, and legalism as he announces the kingdom of God and demonstrates constant love to human beings, including his opponents.

Jesus' forty days in the wilderness is a symbolic reenactment of the judgment against the children of Israel, who were intimidated before the powers that occupied the land. After forty days of spying out the land, some of the scouts told the people:

> We came to the land to which you sent us; it flows with milk and honey, and this is its fruit. Yet the people who dwell in the land are strong, and the cities are fortified and very large; and besides, we saw the descendants of Anak there. The Amalekites dwell in the land of the Negeb; the Hittites, the Jebusites, and the Amorites dwell in the hill country; and the Canaanites dwell by the sea, and along the Jordan. . . . The land, through which we have gone, to spy it

out, is a land that devours its inhabitants; and all the people that we saw in it are men of great stature. And there we saw the Nephilim (the sons of Anak, come from the Nephilim); and we seemed to ourselves like grasshoppers, and so we seemed to them. (Num. 13:27–29, 32–33 RSV)

"Who might be today's equivalents of forces that occupy our land, threatening to enslave us?" I ask different groups in the jail, at Tierra Nueva, and elsewhere during recent Bible study on this scripture.

In the jail the men mention the courts, laws, methamphetamines, heroin, alcohol, lust, greed, the Internal Customs Enforcement (ICE), and the Department of Homeland Security. When inmates and ex-offenders consider joining Jesus' band, they often describe being assaulted by temptation and experiencing voices of mockery, accusation, and deception both in their heads and through fellow inmates, friends, and family. Others in mainstream groups mention financial institutions like mortgage lenders, credit card companies, and health insurance companies. Included in a recent list were the Bush administration, al-Qaeda, the World Bank, the U.S.–Central America Free Trade Agreement (CAFTA), the defense industry, political parties, and the advertising industry. The names listed by most groups with whom I read Scripture include everything from forces that could be classified as passions, demons, or sin to the most powerful global institutions. We read the next line of Numbers 13 that shows Caleb's bold call to move into the occupied land.

Caleb quieted the people and told them: "Let us go up at once, and occupy it; for we are well able to overcome it" (Num. 13:30 NRSV). The people were overcome by fear and intimidation before the powers and refused to go in and exercise their dominion. They cried and murmured, "Would that we had died in the land of Egypt! Or would that we had died in this wilderness! Why does the Lord bring us into this land, to fall by the sword? Our wives and our little ones will become a prey; would it not be better for us to go back to Egypt?" (Num. 14:2–3 RSV).

For every day that the spies spied out the land, the Lord gave the Israelites a year of wandering in the wilderness (Num. 14:34), until the entire congregation that gathered against the Lord in the wilderness came "to a full end" (Num. 14:35 RSV), with the exception of the weakest and most vulnerable ones: "But your little ones, who you said would become a prey, I will bring in, and they shall know the land which you have despised" (Num 14:31 RSV).

While Jesus' baptismal immersion shows solidarity with the fate of all the enemies of the kingdom of God, represented by Pharaoh and his army, his forty days in the wilderness represents a joining in the fate of the congregation of his own people, the children of Israel, who wandered and died in the wilderness. Jesus symbolically reenacts the forty-year wandering, this time confronting and vanquishing the Evil One there in the wilderness, before he even ventures to advance his victory back in the land where he announces the kingdom of God.

"Why would the Holy Spirit purposely lead Jesus into a direct confrontation with the devil?" asks Frank Hammond in his booklet *Demons and Deliverance in the Ministry of Jesus.* "He did so because Jesus had come into the world for this very confrontation: 'To this end was the Son of God manifested, that he might destroy the works of the devil'" (1 John 3:8).

Continues Hammond:

> Undoubtedly, few Christians have considered that it is God's plan that they also be in direct confrontation with the devil. Yet, just as surely as the Holy Spirit led Jesus into such an encounter, the believer will also be led to face the devil, for the believer is commissioned to do so (Mk 16:17). . . . Jesus has declared that his church will be a militant church, taking the offensive against Satan's powers: "Upon this rock I will build my church; and the gates of Hades shall not prevail against it" (Matt 16:18). Every believer in Jesus Christ is identified with his church and is called to attack "the gates of Hades."[6]

While this cosmology may seem archaic to some, my work with people struggling with addictions and mainstream people in emotional and spiritual turmoil is convincing me that our battle is not merely against flesh and blood. Take a recent Bible study on Deuteronomy 26:4–12 in the jail as an example. A volunteer read in English and then in Spanish the first few verses of the response Israelites were to speak before the Lord when they brought a basket of the first fruits of the land to the priest: "A wandering Aramean was my ancestor; he went down into Egypt and lived there as an alien, few in number, and there he became a great nation, mighty and populous. When the Egyptians treated us harshly and afflicted us, by imposing hard labor on us" . . . (Deut. 26:5–6 NRSV).

I begin the Bible study by asking a group of fifteen men how many of them have been treated harshly and afflicted by Egyptians? People smile politely, and the answer is obviously nobody.

"What forces are functioning like the Egyptians did back then, treating you harshly and oppressing you, imposing hard labor?" I specify, looking for contemporary manifestations of the ruler of this world who seeks to subjugate humans.

"Society, the system, our sins," is the first response blurted out by a young man in his early twenties who sits back reflectively, open Bible on his lap. He has fresh sores on his face and arms characteristic of addiction to methamphetamines. "Do you think?" he asks, looking slightly embarrassed by his immediate and confident answer.

I nod, encouraging him on, and ask the others, "What do you guys think?"

The men mention the courts, laws, judges, and probation officers.

"The Egyptians are like drugs, and the jail is our hard labor," suggests one of the men. Others nod their approval, and I pursue this direction and link it back into the text with another question.

"So how do drugs or alcohol treat you harshly and afflict you?" I ask.

"We thought drugs were good to us, but they were harsh. They treat us cruelly. When you're doing it, you're not happy, but you know that if you quit you'll lose your friends. You want all your friends to quit, but there's no way they're going to at the same time. So you feel trapped. If you want to get away from it, you have to lose your friends, if you can call them friends," says the young man with the sores.

The guys talk about chasing the first hit, the memory of an ecstatic rush. They tell how they felt driven to abuse their bodies, commit crimes, become impoverished.

"My addiction to meth kept me up for two weeks doing all kinds of crazy shit," a man confesses.

"A lot of people like not having to sleep, just going and going, partying day and night or doing whatever," another guys pipes in.

"When you're dealing, you want to stay up so you can make more money," says someone else.

I affirm the longing in the men for a full, energized life as a sign of a desire to be fully empowered by God's Spirit.

"The problem is, when you're no longer high, you obsess about getting money for more drugs. You'll do anything when you're desperate to feel good, like rob and steal," says a guy who says he's been doing meth for eleven straight years, supporting his habit now by dealing it to others.

I have heard men talk about this attraction to a feeling of exhilaration, boundless energy, and find the following description of the affects of methamphetamines in the Web-based Wikipedia particularly telling:

> In an interview, Stephan Jenkins, the singer in the band Third Eye Blind, said that methamphetamine makes you feel "bright and shiny." It also makes you paranoid, incoherent and both destructive and pathetically and relentlessly self-destructive. Then you will do unconscionable things in order to feel bright and shiny again. Former users have noted that they feel stupid or dull when they quit using methamphetamine. This is because the brain is adapting to a need for methamphetamine to think faster, or at what seems to be a higher level. With long-term use, abstinence often leads to slow thinking and depression, which in turn requires that the addict use more meth to "fix" it. A chronic pattern of such behavior is known colloquially as "The Vampire Life."

Men and women in the jail are fully aware of the devastating effects of an addiction in which they feel trapped and openly confess and recount their experiences.

"I was doing so much drugs that if I hadn't been arrested when I was, I'd be dead by now," a man tells the group.

"I've done all the drugs out there, since I've been at this for a while," Mark, an older, veteran drug user, states. "This meth is evil shit, way worse than anything I've ever done."

The others around the circle are nodding their heads, and I invite further comment about what they mean by "evil."

One man mentions that Hitler invented methamphetamines to energize the Nazi troops in World War II. While the Germans did not actually invent the drug, they clearly used it. The German military distributed it widely to their forces under the trade name Pervitin[7] to give them a feeling of elation and energy to go day after day in cold weather with minimal food and sleep. Adolf Hitler himself was reputedly given daily injections of methamphetamine by his personal physician Theodor Morell from 1942 until his death in 1945 as a treatment for depression and fatigue.[8] Many of the men are aware that they have likely suffered permanent damage to their brains and other organs through inhaling fumes while manufacturing meth and/or through their own prolonged personal use of this toxic drug. Today, though, a few veteran users tell me things I have never heard.

Mark tells me how, when they cook up batches of methamphetamines, each cook will put his or her own spell on their batch to increase its appeal. He says that, in batches he has made, he actually put curses on batches they even call "witches' brew" so it will affect people in distinct ways. People are confident that meth manufactured in Mexico is particularly bewitched, as *brujeria* (witchcraft) is widespread and used in ceremonies to cast spells of protection over drug traffickers. I ask five or six men who are experienced users if they notice spiritual differences between meth they buy from different sources. They look at me as if I should know the obvious.

"Yeah, I've done glass that had spirits of lust and eroticism attached to it.[9] You can definitely tell. Every batch is different, affecting you distinctly. The meth seems to almost take on the personality of the person that makes it. One real bad person made a batch with spirits of aggression and conflict. Every relationship I was in while on that drug was thrown into chaos," he tells the group.

"I want off this shit now," says a Chicano man. "Can you guys pray for me before this is over?" he requests. A lot of the other men agree that they too desire prayer for freedom from their addictions.

I agree to pray when we're through, but invite a reader to continue with the reading, and someone reads Deuteronomy 26:7–9 (NRSV): "We cried to the LORD, the God of our ancestors; the LORD heard our voice and saw our affliction, our toil, and our oppression. The LORD brought us out of Egypt with a mighty hand and an outstretched arm, with a terrifying display of power, and with signs and wonders; and he brought us into this place and gave us this land, a land flowing with milk and honey."

The men can always relate to this scripture regarding crying out, and are pleased that these verses speak so directly to their experience and need for someone to free them. While the 12-step approach begins with the recognition that an addict is unable to free himself/herself from drugs or alcohol without the help of a higher power, the court system and larger society hold people responsible to make the right choices, as if it is really only up to them to change. Deuteronomy emphasizes the need for God's direct intervention, describing God as bringing people out of Egypt "with a mighty hand and an outstretched arm, with a terrifying display of power, and with signs and wonders." The Israelites are here invited to remember the ten plagues and miraculous parting of the Red Sea before the invading Egyptian army, which is destroyed behind them once they flee through on dry ground.

"What would that look like now?" I ask the group.

No one is sure what today's equivalent of this would look like. Those in the Bible study need miraculous interventions of many kinds, but have trouble knowing how much they should ask for or expect.

We gather in a big circle for prayer, and I invite people who are ready to give God permission to free them from their addiction or any physical pain or other illnesses to identify themselves. We invite the Holy Spirit to come as defender, comforter, and healer. I often invite people who fear they have suffered serious damage to their brains or other organs to place their hands on their heads, livers, or kidneys for prayer. Nearly everyone places a hand somewhere, and we pray. I am desperate to see greater breakthrough for methamphetamine addicts in particular, which is pushing me further and further to seek greater understanding and empowerment from this gospel with the power to save.

The most familiar Christian theologies appear increasingly impoverished in their answers to the question of who to blame for cruelty, violence, chaos, and evil. The most widespread Christian explanation for chaos in the world rightly envisions God as sovereign. While some may view God as good, many view God the Father as capricious and distant. A high view of God's sovereignty often carries with it a mistakenly low view of humans. Humans are viewed on a continuum from totally depraved and rebellious, engaged in willful disobedience commonly labeled sin, to righteous and obedient ones who claim to live up to the moral standards of God and society. Many see people as exclusively responsible for evil, due to their bad choices, which are seen mainly as acts of willful disobedience. Obedience to God's requirements is viewed as the only way to benefit from God's help. Any salvation to be experienced in this life ends up being a reward for right choices, a form of "works righteousness." When evil is attributed to willfully disobedient sinners, penalties like fines, imprisonment, other sanctions, and the use of force are justified as the only realistic responses. God ends up looking like a strict father or just judge who metes out natural consequences—rewards for the righteous in the form of financial blessing and general success; punishment to the disobedient either through God's allowing sickness, calamities, and death or through himself afflicting people with disasters or making sure they get arrested.

In contrast to this explanation, others view humans as good, but victimized by unjust structures run by a rich and greedy minority of powerful people and corporations, who deprive people of basic rights to health care, education, and other opportunities. There are often unspoken assumptions regarding God, ranging from viewing him as good to merely benign or irrelevant, with little attempt to answer the big question as to why a good God would tolerate so much evil. God is ultimately viewed as either powerless to stop calamities apart from the organizing efforts of humans, or even responsible and finally untrustworthy, since evil is not being stopped. There's no room for an evil mastermind like Satan, as that is viewed as antiquated. People don't want to say that humans are bad, but get angry and depressed at the problems. Some still maintain a high view of God's sovereignty, going as far as blaming God for messing up.

"I give God an F for doing such a terrible job managing the universe," an Iranian businessman acquaintance of mine recently fired out in a discussion about the rising chaos in Iraq and Afghanistan.

Christians from conservative to liberal often agree in the end that it's all about educating and mobilizing people to make right choices. While conservatives are quick to justify punishment, violent intervention, and sanctions as not only necessary but righteous, progressives too will justify coercion and violence when all efforts at healthier communication fail. After all, regardless of one's ideology, it's hard not to see that people are messed up, prone to violence, greed, perversions, and practices that destroy human and nonhuman life. Disappointment sets in, and people start relying on control or just cynicism and despair. Anyone who doesn't get this needs only to spend time listening to the stories of people on the lower margins of any society and pay attention to what's happening around the world.

I am regularly exposed to stories of street and prison vendettas where gangsters or inmates engage in retaliatory stabbings or shootings of men from rival gangs. I hear detailed accounts of murders committed by people strung out on methamphetamines or alcohol. The most recent was recounted to me by a man who bitterly lamented his involvement with his girlfriend as the two of them killed a drunken friend by repeatedly hammering his skull with a ball-peen hammer. Many are baffled by horrific crimes of rape and murder that they have no memory of committing while inebriated. I think often of the despair, rage, and religious fervor that drive ordinary people to strap explosives to their bodies to take out other ordinary people in suicide bombings. It pains me to know that young people just out of high school now serving in the U.S. Armed Forces are having to harden their hearts enough to be able to kick down doors and train guns on ordinary Iraqis suspected as enemy combatants. The waste of life on all sides of the conflicts in the Middle East and many other places throughout the world grieves me. The indifference or paralysis of the majority of educated people before the current growth of HIV/AIDS and Malaria in Africa and elsewhere, the extinction of more and more species, and predictions of more and more flooding, drought, hurricanes, and other life-threatening effects of global warming certainly show the limits of knowing "the facts." Week after week for nearly thirteen years now I have watched young, strong, adventurous men and women in the prime of their lives head off to do years of prison with others like themselves. In prison they will almost certainly become further wounded and alienated before being released with the label "felon" or "sex offender" into an antagonistic society that offers little to no support for them to reintegrate. Regularly I pray with men whose lives and marriages are in crisis after years of addiction to Internet pornography. These examples and many others have pushed me to revamp my cosmology to make sense of the growing darkness.

I am increasingly stepping into another cosmology, with strong support in Scripture, that has a high view of both God and human beings, created in God's image, with a third-party Evil One out there messing with people and nature in ways that bring chaos, sickness, and death.[10] Sin is foreign to humans, introduced by a power antagonistic to God's purposes. Evil comes from the activities of a third party, known throughout Scripture as the Evil One, the Adversary, the powers, the accuser, the deceiver, the tempter, the enemy, the devil, Satan, and other names. The Evil One has been vanquished by Jesus on the cross. In Jesus we have all been raised to a place of authority as daughters and sons at the right hand of God. Empowered by the Holy Spirit, we exercise our authority here and now as Jesus did through announcing the kingdom of God, inviting everyone to renounce practices and mind-sets that enslave and oppress, turning and placing their total trust and allegiance in the only one who saves. God confirms our ministries with signs that follow. I am convinced that a robust and clear-eyed view of evil helps us better differentiate God's good works and people's deepest desires from the works of the Enemy, so we can invite people to choose resistance and freedom over collusion and bondage.

Throughout the New Testament the world is described as being under the power of the evil one (1 John 5:19), the ruler of the power of the air (Eph. 2:2). In Revelation 12:9 (NRSV), John of Patmos describes a war in heaven that results in the devil and his angels being cast down to earth: "The great dragon was thrown down, that ancient serpent, who is called the Devil and Satan, the deceiver of the whole world—he was thrown down to the earth, and his angels were thrown down with him."

In a recent jail Bible study we read through three texts in John's Gospel that clarify this cosmology. In the first, Jesus contrasts himself as the good shepherd, who has come to give abundant life, and the thief, who's antilife: "The thief comes only to steal and kill and destroy. I came that they may have life, and have it abundantly" (John 10:10 NRSV).

In offering this initial mug shot of the Evil One, I am fully aware that every inmate has a myriad of stories of firsthand experience of the thief's devastating work. We next turn to a scripture that shows clearly Jesus' agenda both to cast out the ruler of this world as the prime culprit responsible for evil and to save all people at the cross: "'Now is the judgment of this world; now the ruler of this world will be driven out. And I, when I am lifted up from the earth, will draw all people to myself.' He said this to indicate the kind of death he was to die" (John 12:31–33 NRSV).

I invite people to turn to the next text, John 14:30, to further illustrate John's cosmology and Jesus' response: "I will no longer talk much with you, for the ruler of this world is coming. He has no power over me" (John 14:30 NRSV).

When Jesus describes the ruler of this world as "coming," we see John's understanding that the mastermind behind Jesus' arrest, conviction, torture, and crucifixion is the Evil One, who seeks to snuff out Jesus and his kingdom of life and liberation in every way possible.

"Do any of you see signs that there is a 'thief' who robs, kills, and destroys or a power like this 'ruler of this world' who comes to you to mess with you?" I ask.

People nod and begin to share examples that include everything from strings of calamities that have marked their lives to being assaulted by temptations to engage in self-destructive behavior.

"One thing I keep seeing is that even though everything is going fine and I have no reason to stress, I will suddenly be overcome by feelings of agitation and negativity that make me want to beat on someone," confesses a Caucasian man in his early thirties.

"I'm looking at at least five years in the joint, and my attorney's doing nothing to help me get into drug court," says Dave, a Chicano man in his early twenties who says his second-degree burglary charges are all related to his addiction to methamphetamines.

The two inmates to my right ask the man a few questions to determine his eligibility for drug court. After determining that he had not yet been to prison and no violence or weapons were involved in his crimes, they assure him that there's got to be a way. I write down his name before continuing the Bible study and tell him I'll call his attorney and the people in charge of drug court and put in a good word for him.

"So we are all familiar with the work of the thief, the ruler of this world who comes to us and is up to no good," I summarize. "We can see that Jesus says this ruler of this world has no power over him—yet we know that Jesus got arrested, tortured, and killed," I add, introducing a theology of suffering that inmates and all of us need, to make sense of all the bad stuff that happens to those who seek God. Later in this book we will look at how suffering and the cross figure into an expectation of the kingdom of God coming here and now.

The final text I introduce in this particular Bible study introduces the Paraclete, whom Jesus also describes as coming to his followers to support them personally as they deal with the assaults of the ruler of this world, who also comes. I invite a volunteer to read John 16:7 (NRSV): "Nevertheless, I tell you the truth: it is to your advantage that I go away, for if I do not go away, the Advocate will not come to you; but if I go, I will send him to you."[11]

I point out how the word "Paraclete" comes from the Greek word *para,* meaning "beside" or "alongside" and *kaleo,* "to call out." I draw close to an inmate to my right and illustrate how calling out from beside could be to defend a person from an accuser, or to speak directly to the person as a comforter or helper. We discuss together how Jesus promised to send the Holy Spirit as defender, advocate, comforter, and friend whom he sends to support us in our struggles. The Paraclete, like Jesus, is not interested in accusing, judging, condemning, or sentencing us. Rather, the Paraclete, says Jesus, will convict the world "about judgment, because the ruler of this world has been condemned" (John 16:8, 11 NRSV).

"Are any of you experiencing anything that looks like the Spirit's coming to defend, comfort, or help you?" I ask the men.

People nod their heads and give examples of the Paraclete's work to build up, encourage, and console (1 Cor. 14:3).

"You two who are encouraging Dave were doing the work of the Paraclete just now as you took his side and encouraged him about getting into drug court," says Brad, a pastor friend who accompanied me that night.

The two men to my right tell about how they have been reading Scripture and praying together in their cell ever since they starting attending our weekly gatherings. They later whisper to me that that day they'd flushed down the toilet some meth that had been smuggled into the jail.

"You don't know how hard that is," they assured me. "In here there's nothing to do. It's really tempting, but we resisted," they said, with dignity in their eyes.

I ask the men if they feel a need for more of the Holy Spirit, the Paraclete, in them. Everyone wants prayer to experience more and more of God's protecting, defending, comforting presence. We end by praying for the Holy Spirit to come to fill and strengthen them. Saul, a Mixteco-speaking man from Oaxaca, complains of back pain. We pray, and after a few minutes his pain is gone. Another man cries softly as he recognizes the need to forgive his father after years of estrangement. The Paraclete keeps coming, and people in desperate need of building up, encouragement, and comfort are nearly always ready to receive.

People in crisis will nearly always welcome God's help and enjoy being mentored in discerning the often subtle ways the Spirit shows up. At the same time they find it encouraging to see that the Bible's many descriptions of sin as foreign assailant, rather than as part of their "evil nature," confirm their own experience and self-awareness. For years I have seen inmates' mouths drop open as we read together in Bible studies the apostle Paul's depiction of his struggle with the third party, sin, described eloquently as foreign and separate from humans:[12]

> For we know that the law is spiritual; but I am of the flesh, sold into slavery under sin. I do not understand my own actions. For I do not do what I want, but I do the very thing I hate. Now if I do what I do not want, I agree that the law is good. But in fact it is no longer I that do it, but sin that dwells within me. . . . For I do not do the good I want, but the evil I do not want is what I do. Now if I do what I do not want, it is no longer I that do it, but sin that dwells within me. (Rom. 7:14–17, 19–20 NRSV)

I have seen hundreds of men and women charged and convicted of all kinds of crimes recognize themselves alongside the apostle as desiring to do good but not being able, because of this third party, sin. Jorge, a sixteen-year-old Hispanic youth active in a local gang, typifies this self-assessment in a recent conversation with my Tierra Nueva colleague Chris. "I always picture myself looking at myself in the mirror, and I see it's a battle in my head between the little angel in me and the bad fool's voice. And Chris, the bad fool always wins."

Paul's realistic description and cosmology in Romans 7 offers relief from despondency before the courts' constant repetition of the dominant view, that change is all up to the individual. Romans 7 lifts the burden of personal responsibility for changing yourself. The courts say that if you've done something bad, it's always because you've chosen it and are therefore bad, responsible, and deserving of punishment. Romans offers freedom from this view. Paul understands that sin enslaves to the point that people need an outside liberator's help in order to be set free. Paul sees choosing to cry out for help from a savior, who is capable of rescuing them from forces more powerful than themselves, as perhaps the only thing our human will may be able to muster: "Wretched man that I am! Who will rescue me from this body of death? Thanks be to God through Jesus Christ our Lord!" (Rom. 7:24–25 NRSV).

As we exercise faith to choose to welcome God to come in and change our will, we become empowered by the Spirit to do God's will. Philippians 2:12–13 (NRSV) shows the relationship between human volition and God's empowerment; it reveals both a high view of God and a high view of human agency: "Therefore, my beloved, just as you have always obeyed me, not only in my presence, but much more now in my absence, work out your own salvation with fear and trembling; for it is God who is at work in you, enabling you both to will and to work for his good pleasure."

Paul describes obedience and working out one's own salvation as possible because God is at work inside us, enabling us both to desire and to accomplish God's will. Inmates, gang members, and people struggling with addictions know firsthand that working out their salvation is done in the face of a host of temptations, pressures, and powerful forces that attempt aggressively to sabotage them.

People are encouraged when Scripture confirms that they are being preyed on by invisible forces that appear more powerful than themselves, as they experience this constantly. At the same time, they are empowered by calls to resist from a God who must care for them and believe that they can overcome with God's help. Inmates are fully aware that they are being pursued by sin, much as Cain was in Genesis 4:6 (NRSV), where God tells him: "Sin is lurking at the door; its desire is for you." They feel respected by a God who believes in them enough to admonish Cain and them when God says: "You must master it" (Gen. 4:7). They know firsthand what Peter is talking about when he says, "Be on the alert. Your adversary, the devil, prowls about like a roaring lion, seeking someone to devour" (1 Peter 5:8 NASB). They are empowered by the imperative "but resist him, firm in your faith" (1 Peter 5:9a). Each of these scriptures includes both a robust view of a third-party Evil One and a high view of human agency.

After Jesus' successful confrontation of the devil in the wilderness we see his entire ministry as going after this third party, manifested in impure spirits, demons, sickness, exclusion, and legalism. When he heals someone, it is obvious that sickness is not God's will. When he casts out demons, those who were possessed are freed and the evil thing is separated from them.

In the New Testament the enemy is described in ways that help people identify when they are being preyed on. Hammond names three of the many ways the enemy attacks people: "through the channel of temptation, accusation or deception."[13] In John, Jesus describes the devil as a murderer one who "does not stand in the truth, because there is no truth in him. When he lies, he speaks according to his own nature, for he is a liar and the father of lies" (John 8:44 NRSV). As seen above in Revelation 12:9 (NASB) Satan is described as the one who "deceives the whole world,"[14] and in John 10:10 (NRSV) Jesus contrasts his own shepherding ministry with that of the thief. "The thief comes only to steal and kill and destroy. I came that they may have life, and have it abundantly." The

name "Satan" itself comes from the Greek word meaning "the accuser," a role
directly visible in Satan's coming before God to accuse Job (1:6–12; 2:1–7).

People on the margins are acutely aware that they are being preyed upon by
forces that appear to know and exploit their weaknesses. A cosmology that has
an elevated view of a third-party Evil One does not diminish people to mere pawn
status.[15] Rather, people are greatly comforted to learn that Jesus is actively pursuing them to deliver them, a picture of Jesus' ministry strongly supported by
Peter's sermon in Acts 10:37–38 (NASB): "You yourselves know the thing which
took place throughout all Judea, starting from Galilee, after the baptism which
John proclaimed. You know of Jesus of Nazareth, how God anointed Him with
the Holy Spirit and with power, and how He went about doing good, and healing all who were oppressed by the devil; for God was with Him."

Jesus crosses back into the land and heads to Galilee to take possession of his
and our inheritance as a new Joshua. Those who come out into the wilderness
around the Jordan to hear John the Baptist preach and receive his baptism of
repentance for the forgiveness of sins cannot help but remember the story of Israel
being gathered by the Jordan at Jericho, when Moses told them:

> "When you pass over the Jordan into the land of Canaan, then you shall
> drive out all the inhabitants of the land from before you, and destroy all their
> figured stones, and destroy all their molten images, and demolish all their
> high places; and you shall take possession of the land and settle in it, for I
> have given the land to you to possess it. . . . But if you do not drive out the
> inhabitants of the land from before you, then those of them whom you let
> remain shall be as pricks in your eyes and thorns in your sides, and they shall
> trouble you in the land where you dwell. And I will do to you as I thought
> to do to them." (Num. 33:51–53, 55–56 RSV)

Jesus heads back from the wilderness into the land as a new Joshua, ready to
gather a whole army of little ones[16] to join him to drive out intruders and to take
possession of the land for the kingdom of God.

The way people come to know that God is living is through the visible demonstration of acts of deliverance: "When you come to the brink of the waters of the
Jordan, you shall stand still in the Jordan. . . . Hereby you shall know that the living God is among you, and that he will without fail drive out from before you
the Canaanites, the Hittites, the Hivites" (Josh. 3:8, 10 RSV).

The language here is reminiscent of key texts in Exodus 23:27–31 and many
other passages,[17] which actually use the Greek term most used for Jesus' deliverance ministry, *ekballo*, "to cast out":

> And I will send terror before thee, and I will strike with amazement all the
> nations to which thou shalt come, and I will make all thine enemies to flee.
> And I will send hornets before thee, and thou shalt cast out [*ekballo*] the
> Amorites and the Evites, and the Chananites and the Chettites from thee. I
> will not cast them out [*ekballo*] in one year, lest the land become desolate,
> and the beasts of the field multiply against thee. By little and little I will cast
> them out [*ekballo*] from before thee, until thou shalt be increased and inherit
> the earth. (Exod. 23:27–31 LXX, Brenton)[18]

In 2 Samuel 7:23, David, recently anointed as king of Israel after many chapters of disturbing acts of violence against Philistines, Saul's followers, and others, is depicted as recognizing God as the one who casts out Israel's enemies. The Septuagint Version makes use of the Greek verb *ekballo* here, which most certainly serves as a backdrop for Jesus' ministry as a son of David: "And what other nation in the earth is as thy people Israel? Whereas God was his guide, to redeem for himself a people to make thee a name, to do mightily and nobly, so that thou shouldest cast out [*ekballo*] nations and their tabernacles from the presence of thy people, whom thou didst redeem for thyself out of Egypt" (LXX, Brenton, 410).

The language used in Numbers, Joshua, and Exodus to describe the forces that occupy the land and intimidate the children of Israel shifts in the New Testament. Consistently New Testament writers differentiate between spiritual forces antagonistic to God's reign and human beings. Forces like sickness, demons, sin, principalities, and powers are severely confronted by Jesus and the apostles much as enemies were violently attacked in the Old Testament. New Testament writers consistently call believers to forgive, love, and bless human beings who are enemies. The early church fathers interpreted the Canaanites, Hittites, and other groups as the eight mortal passions that aggressively wage war on the saints.[19] Jesus confronts the powers of darkness in the form of impure spirits, demons, sickness, and the mind-sets of religious authorities and disciples who challenge his authority. Deliverance from evil spirits and advocacy before the authorities must be combined in a rigorous resistance to both micro and macro forces that oppress. Liberation from larger institutional and spiritual powers must be announced and demonstrated, along with deliverance from the passions, demons, illness, and other powers that afflict human beings.

I regularly engage in advocacy on behalf of people experiencing accusation both from internal voices and from the powers that enforce laws. I draw from three scriptures showing Jesus' confidence that his followers have been given authority to bind destructive forces that assail people.

> I will give you the keys of the kingdom of heaven; and whatever you shall bind on earth shall have been bound in heaven, and whatever you shall loose on earth shall have been loosed in heaven. (Matt. 16:19 NASB)

> Truly I say to you, whatever you shall bind on earth shall have been bound in heaven; and whatever you loose on earth shall have been loosed in heaven. (Matt. 18:18 NASB)

> If you forgive the sins of any, their sins have been forgiven them; if you retain the sins of any, they have been retained. (John 20:23 NASB)

I and my colleagues at Tierra Nueva are discovering that we can effectively silence voices that accuse, mock, tempt, deceive, and in other ways torment people and call for the release of God's help, comfort, and illumination as we pray and advocate alongside people.

Before launching into a talk before mainstream people or a Bible study with inmates or others on the margins, I regularly ask people whether they are currently or have recently been hearing voices of accusation, mockery, or temptation. Most people respond that they have and welcome my opening prayer to bind or silence these voices. Inmates claim to experience immediate relief after I pray: "I bind and silence all voices of accusation, mockery, and deception in the name of Jesus and declare this place an accuser-free zone, a prosecutor-free zone, in the name of Jesus. We welcome the Holy Spirit, the Paraclete to pour out over us God's defending, comforting, illuminating presence in the name of Jesus." During one-on-one prayer ministry times, prayers to bind or silence voices or looks that accuse bring immediate relief, opening people to hearing or seeing God's voice and helping presence. Yet binding invisible forces must not be separated from actually physically defending people accused, condemned, exploited, or in any way tormented.

Jesus invites future followers physically to stand with the accused over and against human beings and their religious systems that join the ruler of this world to accuse and condemn people. Jesus' confrontations with the Pharisees in Mark 2:23–3:6 (NASB) and with the scribes and Pharisees in John 8:1–11 offer examples of effective advocacy on behalf of the accused.

I have led many Bible studies on Mark 2:23–3:6 with groups ranging from inmates and Honduran campesinos to mainstream churchgoers and graduate students. During a recent course on advocacy and deliverance with graduate students in theology, we begin by reading the entire text recounting Jesus' confrontation with the Pharisees over Jesus' and his disciples' picking and eating heads of grain and healing a man with a withered hand on the Sabbath.

> And it came about that He was passing through the grainfields on the Sabbath, and His disciples began to make their way along while picking the heads of grain. And the Pharisees were saying to Him, "See here, why are they doing what is not lawful on the Sabbath?" And He said to them, "Have you never read what David did when he was in need and became hungry, he and his companions: how he entered into the house of God in the time of Abiathar the high priest, and ate the consecrated bread, which is not lawful for anyone to eat except the priests, and he gave it also to those who were with him?" And He was saying to them, "The Sabbath was made for man, and not man for the Sabbath. . . ."
> And He entered again into a synagogue; and a man was there with a withered hand. And they were watching Him to see if He would heal him on the Sabbath, in order that they might accuse Him. And He said to the man with the withered hand, "Rise and come forward!" And He said to them, "Is it lawful on the Sabbath to do good or to do harm, to save a life or to kill?" But they kept silent. And after looking around at them with anger, grieved at their hardness of heart, He said to the man, "Stretch out your hand," And he stretched it out, and his hand was restored. And the Pharisees went out and immediately began taking counsel with the Herodians against Him, as to how they might destroy Him.

I invite my students to identify the characters and their actions in the two stories. In the first story, people note that Jesus' disciples pluck and eat grains of wheat on the Sabbath; the Pharisees question Jesus regarding this; Jesus defends his disciples, using the story of David and his men eating the bread of the presence in 1 Samuel 21:1ff. In so doing, Jesus indirectly identifies himself and his disciples with David and his mighty men pursued by Saul, and identifies his detractors, the Pharisees, with Saul, on his way out as God's anointed.

In the second story people observe that Jesus enters the synagogue, a man with a withered hand is there, the Pharisees are watching him in order to accuse him, Jesus commands the man to come forward and questions the Pharisees regarding the legality or illegality of doing good and saving life, doing harm and killing on the Sabbath. The Pharisees are silent. Jesus looks around with anger, is grieved at their hardness of heart, commands the man to stretch out his hand, and it is restored. The Pharisees go out to join with the Herodians to plot Jesus' destruction.

After this brief recap of what Jesus does and how the Pharisees react in each story, I ask people a question that never fails to clarify what I refer to as the dominant theology.

"If you knew God only through the words and actions of the Pharisees, what would God be like?"

I then draw a line down the middle of the white board and write "Dominant theology" on the left of the line and "Jesus' theology" on the right.

I then begin to list the attributes of the God reflected by the Pharisees as the students note them: "judging," "impersonal," "laws more important than people," "dishonest," "suspicious," "accusing," "legalistic," "not compassionate," "uncaring," "Bible used for setting rules," "out to get you," "self-righteous."

"What values are visible through the Pharisees' words and deeds?" I ask, to clarify further.

The students say that the Pharisees appear to value order, control, commitment, schedules, knowing and following the rules, and compliance. Someone notes that these theologians end up going out to conspire with the Herodians to destroy Jesus, showing that apparently they consider it legal to do harm and kill on the Sabbath. I next invite people to express Jesus' theology as it is visible in his defense of his disciples, healing of the man with the withered hand, and words to the Pharisees.

On the white board we list words and phrases describing Jesus' approach. People come up with words that starkly contrast with the dominant theology: "forgiving," "personal," "people more important than laws," "transparent," "free," "defending," "loving," "compassionate," "uses Bible for defending weak," "feeds and heals," "angry at silence," "grieves over hardness of heart." Jesus values freedom, life, love, meeting people's needs, food, forgiveness, confronting injustice; and he hates death. Jesus heals the man on the Sabbath, in contrast to the Pharisees' conspiring to kill. At this point in our Bible study, when the two theologies are most visibly opposing, I take the discussion a step further by asking who the contemporary versions of the Pharisees and accusers might be.

At first, people think of examples furthest from themselves. People mention institutions like the Internal Revenue Service (IRS), the Federal Bureau of

Investigation (FBI), child protective services (CPS), public schools, the health-care system, financial institutions. Soon, though, examples get closer to home. Courts, law-enforcement agencies, government, prisons, seminaries, boards of directors, foundations, treatment centers, administrators, and eventually ourselves are mentioned. I then ask a question that never fails to help people see themselves as to some degree in agreement with the Pharisees.

"What are the benefits of this approach?" I ask. "The Pharisees were serious, devoted believers in God," I continue. "We must be sure we understand what they and we ourselves stand to lose by stepping over to Jesus' side. What advantages are there to the Pharisees' way of thinking?"

"People pay attention to me because of my accomplishments," a woman in her second year of theological studies observes. "They love me because of what I do."

We talk about how order, rules, schedules, enforcement of sanctions, or rewards for compliance make us all productive. Others mention benefits like knowing the rules and sanctions, having your power and privilege protected, fairness, things being black and white, or at least clear.

We run out of time to talk at length about where we see contemporary versions of Jesus and what would be the advantages and disadvantages of his approach. The woman who commented on being loved for her accomplishments mentions that with Jesus you are loved for who you are and not for what you do or achieve. After a short break we look at Jesus' dealing with the woman caught in adultery in John 8, which I decide to have the class act out, as I often do in the jail and elsewhere.

Before we act out the text ourselves, I share an experience from when I was teaching in Mozambique in May 2006. There I orchestrated the acting out of this story with some 200 mostly barefoot, peasant pastors in the red dirt under a circus tent at Iris Ministries orphanage in Pemba beside the Indian Ocean.

In Mozambique I ask for volunteers to play Jesus, the scribes and Pharisees, the woman caught in adultery, and the man with whom she was caught in the act of adultery. In the first scene I invite the person playing Jesus to stand, with the others forming a big circle around him. I have the couple playing the pair caught in the act of committing adultery stand outside the circle a ways off. They sheepishly head off as people laugh and tease. A volunteer reads John 8:2–3 (NASB) to set the scene: "And early in the morning He came again into the temple, and all the people were coming to Him; and He sat down and began to teach them. And the scribes and Pharisees brought a woman caught in adultery, and having set her in the midst, they said to Him . . ."

Before sending off the men offering to act as scribes and Pharisees to apprehend the woman, I ask the participants, "Who are some of the people that get accused of sinful behavior in Mozambique?" The men mention thieves, people who commit adultery, and the poor. Nobody mentions people living with AIDS, who I am aware are particularly shunned. When I ask them about whether people dying of AIDS in their communities may be contemporary equivalents of the woman caught in adultery, many of the pastors nod slowly and look down.

At this point I give the go-ahead to those acting as scribes and Pharisees to go and catch the man playing as the woman caught in adultery, bringing her into the big circle before Jesus. "Let's see how Jesus deals with her," I say. Seven or eight men stride off, grab the adulteress under his arms, and nearly drag him into the center of the circle before a humble graying pastor playing Jesus. They try to grab the pastor playing the man, but I remind them that only the woman was brought to Jesus. I hand one of the acting Pharisees my Portuguese Bible and ask him to read the next verse that states the accusation: "'Teacher, this woman has been caught in adultery, in the very act. Now in the Law Moses commanded us to stone such women; what then do You say?' And they were saying this, testing Him, in order that they might have grounds for accusing Him" (John 8:4–6 NASB).

I ask the men whether they know if the scribes and Pharisees are right regarding the law of Moses. Nobody is sure, as most of these pastors have been Christians less than a year. Many cannot read or do not own Bibles. I ask my interpreter to read Deuteronomy 22:22 (NASB), and watch the group grow quiet and serious as they listen: "If a man is found lying with a married woman, then both of them shall die, the man who lay with the woman, and the woman; thus you shall purge the evil from Israel."

The 200 pastors are standing in the red dirt surrounding the men playing Jesus and the woman, attentively wondering where we are going from here.

"Do the scribes and Pharisees seem to be rightly enforcing this law?" I ask them. I ask the pastors where the woman's partner is, as he too is supposed to be stoned. Everyone looks outside the circle to the lone man playing the adulteress's partner, who sheepishly grins. Everyone can clearly see the injustice of the selective enforcement of the scribes and Pharisees. I ask them whether the rich and powerful are treated the same as the poor by the authorities in Mozambique. Everyone nods when a few pastors tell how people with money or position are immune from laws.

I invite the man playing the adulterer back into the circle and tell everyone to reach down and pick up an imaginary rock and hold it over their heads, ready to stone the man playing the woman there in the center of the circle before Jesus. Everyone reaches down into the red dirt and grabs and raises his imaginary rock. All eyes are on the victim, whom I begin to interview.

"What are you feeling right now?" I ask.

"Fear," he says.

Other feelings mentioned by the group include shame, aloneness, terror, and guilt. I ask the accused if he can feel all the eyes on him, and he nods.

I tell everyone to raise up their rocks higher and get ready for Jesus' verdict and ask the pastors: "So how does Jesus deal with the call of the scribes and Pharisees to enforce this Old Testament law?" My translator reads the next verse: "But Jesus stooped down, and with His finger wrote on the ground" (John 8:6 NASB).

I ask the pastor playing Jesus to stoop down and write on the ground before the accused, and he squats and begins to write. I invite everyone to notice that as

Jesus begins to write everyone's eyes are off the accused and looking at Jesus' hand and what he is writing. I ask the accused if he feels any different, and he says he feels relief. Jesus' first act of advocacy on behalf of the woman caught in adultery is to free her from the gaze of the accusers, shifting their condemning gaze onto a word not yet perceived. Jesus himself is looking down at the ground, focused on whatever he is writing with his finger, refusing the role of the accuser. We read on, and the man playing Jesus enacts the next moves. "But when they persisted in asking Him, He straightened up, and said to them, 'He who is without sin among you, let him be the first to throw a stone at her.' And again He stooped down and wrote on the ground" (John 8:7 NASB).

The man playing the pastor stands and looks at the men and repeats Jesus' words: "He who is without sin among you, let him be the first to throw a stone at her," before he squats down again and begins writing in the dirt with his finger.

I ask the men what is happening to their eyes. One pastor speaks for the group when he says, "What Jesus says makes me look away from judging the woman to my own life."

By acting out this story, everyone can clearly see that Jesus himself takes people's eyes off the woman onto himself. I point out that at the beginning of the story we are all told that the adulteress is brought to Jesus by the scribes and Pharisees "testing Him, in order that they might have grounds for accusing Him" (John 8:6 NASB). When they persist in asking him, they are looking at him. When he stands up, all eyes are on him, and when he stoops down again, eyes follow him before turning onto their own hearts. People can see that when Jesus moves from squatting to standing he exercises power and authority. Yet he does this by asking them a question that invites self-reflection, causing everyone to look at his or her own life. I note that Jesus' stooping down and writing show his refusal to take the role of the accuser, even against those surrounding the woman ready to take her life. I ask the man playing the adulteress how he is feeling at this point; he is smiling and says, "Much better." I ask my translator to read the next verse and for the pastors to enact what they hear. "And when they heard it they began to go out one by one, beginning with the older ones, and He was left alone, and the woman, where she had been, in the midst" (John 8:9 NASB).

The pastors lower their imaginary stones and step away from the circle. We pass the Portuguese Bible to Jesus, and I ask him to enact and read Jesus' final words to the woman. "And straightening up, Jesus said to her, 'Woman, where are they? Did no one condemn you?' And she said, 'No one, Lord.' And Jesus said, 'Neither do I condemn you; go your way; from now on sin no more'" (John 8:10–11 NASB).

I invite the 200 men to gather around closer to conclude our dramatic reading with some final observations. We talk about how Jesus' question to the woman invites her to see for herself that she is free from the entrapment of the accusers. Jesus exercises his power and authority as one standing before her, not to condemn but to free her. At the same time, he calls her to a new life without sin.

Then with my theology students we enact the same story and conclude as I did with the Mozambican pastors, asking people the two questions that set the dominant theology into stark contrast with Jesus' way.

"If you knew God only through the words and actions of the scribes and Pharisees, what would God be like?" "If you knew God only through Jesus' words and actions, what would God be like?"

We look at the white board with this second story in mind and add some words that contrast Jesus' way with that of the dominant theology. The God of the dominant theology appears satanic—when the actual function of the Satan as accuser is highlighted. Jesus is defender of the accused to the point of taking the accusing gaze upon himself. We conclude our class by drawing a line with chalk across the carpet from the line on the white board separating the theology of the scribes and Pharisees from that of Jesus. I invite people to stand and get on the scribes' and Pharisees' side of the line. I pray that the Holy Spirit will bring conviction to us regarding ways we come into agreement with the theology of the scribes and Pharisees. I invite people to break this agreement verbally or in their hearts with anything the Spirit brings up. People renounce attitudes and actions in the minutes that follow. I then pray that the Spirit will bring to mind anything God is calling people into. I invite people to speak out what they are feeling drawn to by Jesus.

I then invite people who are feeling drawn away from the dominant theology into Jesus' way of grace and defense physically to step over the line to the side of the white board where we've listed his way of life. My students eagerly join me as we step over the line. One woman says she feels like dancing. There's freedom in the air. In Mozambique the drums and guitars were out, and dancing and worship abounded. Jesus' advocacy for the accused before the powers that shame and condemn is desperately needed and welcomed when present. The following stories show how the ministry of the Paraclete has been enacted in the workplace and the courts as Tierra Nueva advocates stand with immigrants before the U.S. Border Patrol and federal judges in deportation proceedings. In these places we have seen God intervene to release people from impossible legal difficulties.

In 1994, when Gracie and I first moved to the Skagit Valley to begin what we then called Tierra Nueva del Norte (New Earth of the North), we immediately saw how desperately the Mexican farm workers needed advocates before the state on many fronts.

A large warehouse five blocks from our home housed a fish-processing plant that hired hundreds of undocumented immigrants. One afternoon Border Patrol agents pulled up with empty vans and squad cars, surrounding the warehouse in a surprise raid. Dozens of immigrants were arrested and deported within a few days to Tijuana, Mexico.

A pumpkin-painting operation was raided next. More than twenty federal agents surrounded a warehouse out in the middle of the farmlands, blocking all the doors and windows. A Border Patrol helicopter hovered above to alert agents standing by to people running through the fields to escape. I visit the migrant camp immediately after the raid, where immigrants shaken to tears tell me how a husband or wife is being deported, leaving children or spouses alone to pick up the pieces. People stream out of the camp in their vans for the Mexican border to pick up their loved ones anew. They are frustrated and angry at this humiliating assault, interruption of their work, and the expense of paying the $1,400 per person to the smugglers (coyotes) to bring their deported family members back across the border and up the west coast to Washington State.

The day after the raid we get a call from a grade-school principal that has two children who returned to school after finding no one at home. They have nowhere to stay, since their single mother has been deported.

"Do you know anyone who can take them until their parents return?" the principal asks.

In the camp I hear stories of abuse. A Border Patrol agent allegedly threw a young man repeatedly so hard against a van that witnesses said they saw it rocking back and forth. The warehouse workers claim to have witnessed an agent fondling a young woman he chased down and cornered to arrest. I call the Border Patrol chief to complain, and encounter defensive denials of any abuse and invitations to submit a written complaint. I contact the local newspaper, which writes up an uncritical story.

Rumors of raids and talk of abuses are rampant in all of the area's nine migrant camps. Immigrants are afraid to go to grocery stores and Laundromats, as the Border Patrol has been stopping individuals and pulling over cars to ask people for papers. The raids motivate us to start a bilingual newspaper, *Noticias Tierra Nueva—New Earth News*. Our first edition features articles documenting and denouncing raids, letters and art from immigrants in the county jail, and information on legal rights, local food banks, and a column on laws called "People's Law School." We blanket the region with 5,000 copies of our first twelve-page tabloid, which includes directions to our storefront, invitations to attend our ecumenical Spanish Bible study, and lists of daily Scripture readings. In this way Tierra Nueva becomes known among the immigrants, who enthusiastically welcome the paper and appreciate someone taking up their cause.

For months I work to organize an emergency response group, calling together church leaders, activists, farm workers, growers, and anyone else who is interested to form what we called the "Skagit-Whatcom INS Watch Group." An attorney from a regional legal services organization trains us in legal issues so that we can know how to hold Border Patrol agents accountable. An activist friend gives us trainings in nonviolence and in the use of a video camera so emergency response volunteers can effectively film Border Patrol and INS while they are conducting their enforcement operations. We organize and orient volunteer pastors willing to be on call to go to the Border Patrol's booking office in Bellingham to accompany the people while they are being fingerprinted and detained before deportation. Other volunteers are on call to visit people remaining in the migrant camps after a raid to offer support, interview witnesses, and prepare press releases. We organize several meetings with the Border Patrol and INS where farm workers, growers, and other community members can hear the official perspectives, express their disagreement, and dialogue. We present our plans regarding the watch group to the Border Patrol and INS in the presence of journalists and the aides of several regional congressional representatives.

For over a year we struggle with the Border Patrol, calling and visiting them regularly and holding them accountable through numerous editions of *New Earth News/Noticias Tierra Nueva*. We work to treat the Border Patrol agents with respect, while at the same time presenting detailed analysis in our newspaper of every enforcement action we hear about, updates on immigration law, and information on legal rights of undocumented immigrants.[20] We inform immigrants of our Skagit-Whatcom INS Watch Group, providing them with our emergency contact phone number, should there be a raid.

When I personally make the rounds delivering our paper, the people in the area migrant camps soon come to recognize me as someone they can trust. I visit the Border Patrol agents at their offices and maintain rapport. We even arrange for an entire family from Oaxaca, whose jailed son and father of four is to be deported after being arrested for a DUI, to be flown back to Mexico after the cucumber harvest, since none of the other family members can drive. One day I get a call from the assistant chief who tells me that they have decided to stop work site enforcement operations because of our pressure. This led to more than ten years of peace for farm workers in our region, which is now being threatened by renewed work site enforcement actions.

As white pastors, Gracie and I did not find it easy to win people's trust as advocates. We were automatically perceived as representatives both of the dominant culture and of the unpredictable and unsettling religious community of that time. If I were a Roman Catholic priest, I would have easier access to the people. I would at least represent something familiar and culturally comforting. However, the fact that I am not Roman Catholic made people immediately distrustful. People's experience of being pursued by a vast array of religious groups places them understandably on the defensive. Whether I am a Presbyterian, Lutheran, United Methodist, Baptist, Adventist, or a Mormon, Jehovah's Witness, or Moonie makes little difference. As a white male I am at first viewed not as a bearer of good news, but as a threat. Therefore Gracie and I work hard to win people's trust, accompanying them without conditions. From the beginning the jail has proven the best place to win people's trust and establish rapport with entire families.

Marcelino, a Triqui-speaking indigenous man in his mid-thirties from Oaxaca, faithfully came to my Thursday night and Sunday afternoon jail Bible studies. He is shy and silent during the Bible studies but appears genuinely interested, while at the same time deeply troubled. I approach him after a Bible study and hear enough of his story that I decide to talk with him at more length one on one. He speaks no English and struggles to communicate in Spanish with slow, deliberate sentences.

"They are accusing me of first-degree assault because I drew a knife on my brother. We were drinking," he tells me.

First-degree assault with a deadly weapon could mean more than ten years in prison for Marcelino, and the loss of his legal permanent residence status. Marcelino tells me with great sorrow and regret that he had nothing serious against his brother. He asks me to visit his wife, brother, and extended family in one of the migrant camps. They are unfamiliar with how the system works and need me to explain what is happening with the courts. I visit the family and find more than twenty people living together in the two-bedroom trailer. It is mid-December, and they have been out of work for a month and a half. Not only do they know nothing about the possible fate of Marcelino, but they also lack money for food and have a shortage of blankets and other basic necessities. I offer to help mediate between the family and the public defenders, who are able to work a deal to drop Marcelino's charges to third-degree assault, due to the testimony of his brother and extended family that this was an isolated incident. Marcelino and his family are extremely grateful. He was released from jail after three months, and has come faithfully ever since to our Sunday evening Bible studies at Tierra Nueva's Family Support Center.

Epifania is a woman in her forties, a single mother of five. Three of her sons have been in and out of my jail Bible studies for many years. Born in Mexico, Epifania crossed over into the United States years ago and began a life as a farm laborer, obtaining her permanent resident status under the amnesty of 1985. Her first husband hanged himself after a long struggle with alcohol. Epifania raised her children the best she could, but began dealing drugs to supplement her meager income in the fields. One day Epifania calls me from the cucumber fields, frantically recounting how the drug task force had raided her home.

"Thank God I wasn't there, Roberto."

Next thing I hear is that she has been arrested, and after the prosecutors failed to come up with enough evidence to convict her, the Immigration and Naturalization Service put a hold on her, due to a previous conviction in California for possession of cocaine with intent to deliver and possession of a firearm. Epifania is transferred to Seattle where she is detained to face deportation proceedings. I secure a pro bono attorney from Northwest Immigrant Rights Project to represent her.

After reviewing Epifania's case, the attorney calls me to discuss the impossibility of securing a cancellation of removal order. The attorney enumerates the obstacles. Under the extremely harsh amendments to the immigration act enacted in 1996, almost no relief is available to permanent residents with drug or unlawful possession of firearm charges. The federal judge assigned to Epifania's case is considered one of the most difficult and mercurial of immigration judges. Finally, Epifania's unwillingness to admit guilt in spite of overwhelming evidence against her makes it impossible for her attorney to appeal for mercy based on an honest confession.

"The only hope is if you would be willing to serve as a character witness and speak on behalf of her and her sons' and daughter's need to have their mother in the country," she tells me. "But I'm telling you even with your testimony, there is really no hope," she assures me.

"I'll come," I agree, "even though it will be challenging to come up with compelling words about her character," I remember saying.

My colleague Roger drives me down to Seattle for the hearing several weeks later, while I work on a lecture for a class I am teaching on Exodus. I am feeling the futility of advocating for Epifania, whose case is so bleak. I decide to read Roger the text I am preparing to speak on as we drive down for my 10:00 a.m. appearance:

> I am going to send an angel in front of you, to guard you on the way and to bring you to the place that I have prepared. Be attentive to him and listen to his voice; do not rebel against him, for he will not pardon your transgression; for my name is in him. But if you listen attentively to his voice and do all that I say, then I will be an enemy to your enemies and a foe to your foes. . . . I will send my terror in front of you, and will throw into confusion all the people against whom you shall come, and I will make all your enemies turn their backs to you. (Exod. 23:20–22, 27)

"Bob, maybe we should start by praying this text right now," suggests Roger.

I agree and pray: "Lord, we ask that you would send your angel ahead of us right now into the courtroom, preparing the way. Touch Epifinia so she speaks from the heart about her life. May the judge be moved with so much compassion that she orders Epifania to be released. May the prosecutor be silent. In the name of Jesus, we ask that the chains would drop off of Epifania's wrists and ankles right now, in Jesus' name."

We arrive at the INS courtroom on time for our 10:00 a.m. appearance. As we approach the metal detectors, the guard asks us why we are there. After I tell him that I am there to speak as a character witness at a trial, he responds by saying that the trial had just ended.

"How is this possible, it was supposed to continue for a minimum of four hours?" I ask. The guard tells me to talk with the attorney, who just then walks out of the courtroom.

"We won!" she announces excitedly. "Epifania poured out her heart and told about her whole life, confessed that she had sold drugs and all. The judge was deeply moved and declared to the prosecutor that she wanted to pardon her, asking if he had any response. The prosecutor was silent, offering no opposition."

"You're kidding, that's amazing!" I respond. "On our way down in the car Roger and I prayed that God would do all those things," I say.

"That's amazing. When did you pray that exactly?" she responds.

When I tell her we'd prayed around 9:40, she says this was right when all this happened, and continues to share another amazing detail.

"Another thing happened that I have never seen in all my years as a trial attorney," she continues. "The judge turned to the guards, who had brought Epifania over from detention, and said: 'Please take those handcuffs and leg chains off of this woman right now,' something that I have never seen done."

We stand around amazed together that God has answered our prayer so exactly. We feel as if we are participating directly in Jesus' work of proclaiming release to the prisoners in Luke 4:18. Epifania is released later that day, and travels up to Skagit County where she rejoins her family and gets on with her life, which we will revisit in the last chapter.

Effective advocacy for people on the margins is possible only as we step over the line from overidentifying with the system, joining in the ministry of Jesus. This move is possible only as we renounce the false security offered to us by the ruler of this world and step into a life marked by increasing allegiance to Jesus and the kingdom of God.

Chapter 5

I Pledge Allegiance to the Kingdom of God

We have seen in chapter 3 that in order to leave the land of slavery you must first hate it. This is easier to do if you have already been enslaved, deported, or in any way marginalized by the inhabitants of the land. Jesus leads the way in the "voluntary departure" of baptismal death through the original port of entry, the Jordan River. The account of Jesus' baptism shows how the Father's declaration "You are my Son, in whom I am well pleased" and the Spirit's presence upon him establishes Jesus' true identity and ours, rooting him and us in love. Jesus returns in the power of the Spirit and begins calling to himself a community of disciples who announce the kingdom of God at the farthest reaches of Israel, the territory once occupied by the ten tribes of Israel—the first to be exiled. Today Jesus is most certainly calling contemporary disciples to a similar movement: to leave behind other allegiances in favor of following after him, to join a community of those who have left "the world," and to announce and practice the kingdom of God—on earth as in heaven. Jesus will lead each of us to our own "lost sheep" and "Galilees."

It is urgent that Christians make deliberate and visible movements away from unhealthy dependencies and false allegiances, or we will remain unable effectively to join Jesus' community wholly given over to entering and announcing the authentic kingdom of God. When followers of Jesus are overly identified with their social class, nationality, church denomination, political party, ideology, or anything in addition to Jesus, both our true identity as sons and daughters of God and our witness will become impure. Whenever Christians stand with nonhuman systems over and against human beings, they will take sides against people marginalized by those systems or policies. Departing wherever has become the land of Egypt or occupied Israel for us will surely happen (and be required) when we switch sides to join the marginalized and deported, alongside Jesus. This will most naturally begin to happen and accelerate as mainstream people come to know the homeless, the incarcerated, the undocumented, the poor, and anyone marginalized "outside the camp."

Mainstream people may well see, as I have over and over, that people identify them with the rich and powerful and with oppressors.[1] People's prejudices can be simplistic, unfair, and even hurtful. I avoid becoming an apologist for myself, my race, culture, nation, or anything. Instead of justifying myself or agreeing with accusations against myself, I take note of the barriers that may keep others from receiving the best news about Jesus and the kingdom of God through me. I keep asking myself, "How can I more fully enter into Christ's baptism, so that God's love and life can flow in greater purity and generosity?"

The external, objective "facts" of our identity inevitably present obstacles for people around us who have prejudices. My first awareness of being identified with the oppressors came as I walked the streets of Quetzaltenango, Guatemala, in September of 1980. Groups of young men sneered and taunted me with "Gringo, go home," and "Yankee imperialista!" My race and nationality associated me with my government's violent campaign in 1954 to oust the democratically elected president, Jacobo Arbenz, and with its years of support for right-wing military dictators and U.S. corporations like the United Fruit Company.

The next year, in 1981, my wife Gracie and I sat among a crowd of hundreds of chanting Nicaraguans at a protest music concert in Managua, as people stood and shouted anti-American slogans, angry at the Reagan administration's attacks against their government through the dreaded CIA-organized and U.S. government–funded contras.

In 1991, at the beginning of the Gulf War, I remember feeling tensions grow as I did my weekly shopping in the Arab markets of our predominantly Muslim neighborhood in Montpellier, France. In 1994, when we were starting Tierra Nueva in Burlington, Washington, I saw fear in the faces of Mexican farm laborers as I walked through raspberry fields as they picked, at a time the U.S. Border Patrol was engaging in regular workplace enforcement actions that resulted in massive deportations. In the same way that the street youth perceived the Vineyard Church in Seattle as refusing them entry unless they were accompanied by a clean-cut white boy like Chris, today's outsiders see the church as exclusive and excluding, on the side of the dominant powers. This must change if we are effectively to reenter and with Jesus take possession of the land for the kingdom of God.

Some of the biggest challenges to total allegiance to the kingdom of God in the world today involve people's allegiance to their ethnic group, social class, nation, and religion. In America and many other nations today, the allegiance Christians pledge to the flag and homeland, legal and economic systems, confuses and weakens their identity, empowerment, and witness as citizens of the kingdom of heaven. William Stringfellow's writings speak powerfully into the current American scene.

> The task is to treat the nation within the tradition of biblical politics—to understand America biblically—not the other way around, not (to put it in an appropriately awkward way) to construe the Bible Americanly. There has been much too much of the latter in this country's public life and religious ethos. There still is. I expect such indulgences to multiply, to reach larger absurdities, to become more scandalous, to increase blasphemously as America's crisis as a nation distends. To interpret the Bible for the convenience of America, as apropos as that may seem to be to many Americans, represents a radical violence to both the character and content of the biblical message. It fosters a fatal vanity that America is a divinely favored nation and makes of it the credo of a civic religion which is directly threatened by, and, hence, which is anxious and hostile toward the biblical Word. It arrogantly misappropriates political images from the Bible and applies them to America, so that America is conceived of as Zion: as the righteous nation, as a people of superior political morality, as a country and society chosen and especially esteemed by God.[2]

Nationalism has a powerful grip on many American Christians and on Christians in many other nations, to such an extent that people are increasingly disqualifying themselves from effective ministry as announcers of God's kingdom. Many Christians assume that obedience to God includes loyal commitment to their nation and their nation's security, especially when calls to arms come from a head of state who claims to be a committed Christian. Other Christians more critical of the nation or partisan political agendas can unwittingly remain in a posture of servitude to their ethnicity and nation if they are responding to voices of accusation that identify legitimate grievances.

When followers of Jesus see themselves too much "according to the flesh" (as a citizen of their particular nation, member of a religious denomination, ethnic group, sexual orientation, or political party), they can easily fall into either justifying their ethnicity, nation, or orientation, or agreeing with accusations against themselves and seeking to right the wrongs. The Accuser, rather than the Defender, ends up setting the agenda for people's actions, unless we are continually remembering our identity as beloved son or daughter by adoption and living according to the Spirit. Whenever people live in agreement with their natural identity, they give the Accuser permission to harass them with their shortcomings according to their identity in the flesh. When our focus becomes righting the wrongs of our country or ethnic group, we step under the gaze of a judge whose demands for restitution are infinite. Voices of accusation will make sure we know that we are never doing enough. Finally, any headway we do make toward justice will end up serving the powers, magnifying the names of creatures rather than the Creator.

William Stringfellow rightly notes that "according to the Bible, the principalities are legion in species, number, variety, and name."[3] He continues:

> The very array of names and titles in biblical usage for the principalities and powers is some indication of the scope and significance of the subject for human beings. And if some of these seem quaint, transposed into contemporary language they lose quaintness and the principalities become recognizable and all too familiar: they include all institutions, all ideologies, all images, all movements, all causes, all corporations, all bureaucracies, all traditions, all methods and routines, all conglomerates, all races, all nations, all idols. Thus, the Pentagon or the Ford Motor Company or Harvard University or the Hudson Institute or Consolidated Edison or the Diners Club or the Olympics or the Methodist Church or the Teamsters Union are all principalities. So are capitalism, Maoism, humanism, Mormonism, astrology, the Puritan work ethic, science and scientism, white supremacy, patriotism plus many, many more—sports, sex, any profession or discipline, technology, money, the family—beyond any prospect of full enumeration. The principalities and powers are legion.[4]

The nation-state, government administrations, and flag fit in the category of "principalities and powers" and "creations" in biblical literature—which would place them in the category of being ruled over by humans. One of the strongest New Testament texts stating this is Colossians 1:13–16 (NASB), which describes this world and its systems as the "domain of darkness" that Jesus has delivered us from:

> For He delivered us from the domain of darkness, and transferred us to the kingdom of His beloved Son, in whom we have redemption, the forgiveness of sins. And He is the image of the invisible God, the first-born of all creation. For by Him *all things were created*, both in the heavens and on earth, visible and invisible, whether thrones or dominions or rulers or authorities—all things have been created by Him and for Him.

This scripture offers one of the New Testament's most positive understandings of the nonhuman authorities and powers as part of God's creation. The structures of society, institutions, organizations, and laws all have a legitimate role, as long as they are rightly oriented "for him" and functioning "under the dominion" or "under the feet" (Psalm 8) of human beings. According to Colossians 2:10 (NRSV) followers of Jesus "have come to fullness in him, who is the head of every ruler and authority." Our baptismal identity as "wetbacks" joined to Jesus brings us out from under the domination of the powers and into a place of freedom from rulers' and authorities' demands for total allegiance.

> When you were buried with him in baptism, you were also raised with him through faith in the power of God, who raised him from the dead. And when you were dead in trespasses and the uncircumcision of your flesh, God made you alive together with him, when he forgave us all our trespasses, erasing the record that stood against us with its legal demands. He set this aside, nailing it to the cross. He disarmed the rulers and authorities and made a public example of them, triumphing over them in it. (Col. 2:12–15 NRSV)

When humans submit to an ideology, legal system, economic or political system, government, company, denomination, or anything else over and above the Creator, human beings come under the power of the creature (or creation);[5] God's original dominion through human beings is reversed, leading to oppression of every kind. Two examples from our advocacy ministry to immigrants show different levels of subservience and freedom vis-à-vis the powers.

Once I received a call for help from the friend of a Hispanic woman in the jail, whom we will call Gloria, who was accused of third-degree child abuse. Gloria was a legal permanent resident married to a U.S. citizen. They had five young children together, all of whom were U.S. citizens. One day Gloria lost her temper and severely punished her five-year-old son, leaving visible welts on him. A day-care provider reported her to child protective services (CPS), who alerted the police. Once she was in the jail, immigration enforcement officers put an immigration hold[6] on her and scheduled her for deportation, as her crime was a deportable offense under current immigration law. I called the official who had put the hold on her and urged him to use his discretion to free this woman so she could get the counseling and parenting classes she would need. I urged him to have mercy on her for the sake of her five young children and husband.

"No, I cannot do that. If she were to beat her children again, perhaps killing one of them, then we would be responsible, we would be legally liable," he told me.

I asked him whether it would help if CPS would take responsibility for the case, agreeing with me to recommend her release. He said that if they agreed to take responsibility, he would consider removing the hold. I called and spoke with the CPS office in Gloria's region and was told by the director that their policy was not to stand with people in criminal matters but to let the law take its course. "If the woman were to hurt or kill her child, we would be responsible," he said, making it impossible to help this woman. She was deported and given a lifetime bar to reentry into the United States.

I met another man in deep trouble with the law, José, who began attending my Bible studies in 1995 in the local jail. José was a legal permanent resident married to a U.S. citizen, Becky, with whom he had four young children. José was an alcoholic, with a long criminal record of minor offenses, all related to his uncontrolled drinking. Once in jail he got really serious and reflective, participating with real brilliance and authenticity in our discussions. He grew in his newfound faith and lovingly coached other Mexican inmates. Then one day he had his fateful visit from the U.S. Border Patrol.[7] The Border Patrol agent had rightly determined that many of José's crimes were deportable offenses. An immigration hold was put on him, and he was scheduled for a deportation hearing before a federal judge as soon as he'd served his time there in the jail.

I had grown fond of José after months of weekly one-on-one pastoral visits and Bible studies and decided to advocate for him before Joe, the U.S. Border Patrol deputy who had put the immigration hold on him. Joe was a career Border Patrol agent, son of immigrants from Puerto Rico who had grown up in the New York Bronx. He had a thick New York accent in both his English and Spanish and was active in a Pentecostal church. I knew Joe well from our run-ins around Border Patrol raids the year before and called him directly to give him all my arguments for why he should use his discretion to lift José's immigration hold.

"If you only knew this man's criminal history, you would see why we have to deport him," lamented Joe.

"Maybe so," I conceded. "But if you could see what I see as he responds in Bible studies and one-on-one visits, I think you would agree that he's got a good heart and you'd release him so he could raise his children and support his wife," I responded. "Can we meet together with José, so you can know him personally and see what I mean?" I asked.

Joe agreed to meet with José and me in the jail, but insisted that I would be the one who would be agreeing with him that José was a bad apple that should be tossed out. "We'll see if he even admits to all that he's done," said Joe.

I called José and told him about our meeting, encouraging him to prepare himself for a grueling interview. "He's got your criminal record and is going to ask you about every crime you've committed, I think."

During our two-hour meeting Joe grilled José about every crime he had ever committed. José humbly confessed every crime, often breaking down and crying with no attempt to justify himself. He also gave believable and sometimes humorous reasons for the most serious offenses, like possession of stolen property. When asked why the car he was driving was full of stolen car stereos, he said that he had been drinking when some younger men under twenty-one asked him to buy some beer. They had taken him in their car to the store when the police pulled their car over. The young driver didn't have a license, and José offered to jump into the driver's seat to help him avoid a costly ticket and have his father's car impounded. When asked why he had been arrested for alluding the police, he told how he was hanging out in his car in front of the park with beer in his car. He saw the police driving toward him. When they called his name through their speakers, he freaked out because he had warrants for his arrest for not going to court. He imagined they would confiscate his car, making it impossible for his pregnant wife to get to the hospital. He reacted by driving as fast as he could back to his house. When Joe saw that José had been taken to jail to spend the night after a number of calls reporting domestic violence, José told how his mother-in-law didn't like him and would often call the police when he and Becky were just yelling at each other. I reminded Joe that in Washington State, if the police are called, one of the partners in a domestic dispute is required to spend a night in jail for a mandatory twenty-four-hour cooling-off period, even if guilt is not proved.

I could tell that Joe had warmed to José, and when he was through, I said: "So, Joe, you can see what I mean now about what a good guy José is."

Joe insisted that José was in God's hands and God would decide. I countered by insisting that José was in Joe's hand and that God had put Joe in a position where Joe had the discretion to remove the hold. Finally Joe said that the domestic violence charges made it impossible for him to remove the hold—most likely because of liability. I suggested that we call José's wife Becky right then, or go over and visit her. Joe refused at first but finally agreed. We left José in the jail and drove together to José's house, where Becky confirmed everything José had said.

"So what are you going to do?" I asked Joe. "Are you going to release him?"

"Only God knows," said Joe. "José is in God's hand."

I insisted that José was in Joe's hands and that as a Christian and as a Border Patrol agent Joe could use his authority to free José. "I'll call you tomorrow," Joe said before leaving.

The next morning Joe called me and told me José would be released later that same morning. This victory led to the conversion of José's cellmate, who had been mocking José's faith until this exciting breakthrough. José was released and returned home.

After several months, however, José was back drinking. A year or so later he ended up back in the jail with new charges. This time Joe put a hold on him that he would not remove. José was repentant and serious, growing rapidly in his faith, though he knew of his impending deportation. After doing his time he was transferred to a federal immigration detention facility, where he awaited his deportation hearing. Since José could not afford an attorney, the immigration judge allowed me to represent him in his bail hearing. His $20,000 bail was amazingly reduced to $7,500. Don, a Seattle businessman friend, called as I drove home from the detention facility in Seattle. He asked me about our ministry and then asked me if there were any particular needs he should be aware of. I told him how I had gotten José's bail reduced to $7,500, a huge amount that we had no way of obtaining.

"If you believe in this guy, I'll loan him that amount," said Don.

That same day Don wrote me a check for $7,500. The next day I bailed José out and drove him home to his family. Bart, a brilliant immigration attorney, offered to represent José for a minimal fee. For three years José had to prove his worthiness by entering an in-patient recovery center and participating in weekly 12-step meetings. Finally a federal judge granted José a cancellation of removal order. For more than seven years now José has been doing great, raising his now five children, working as a mechanic, and staying out of trouble.

Society clearly has a right and obligation to hold people accountable to laws, so disorder will not break out and life can flourish. However, when laws and policies are elevated above human beings, chaos and destruction will also result. According to Scripture, human beings are to exercise authority over creation—which includes everything nonhuman: systems, laws, policies, and every institution. Taking responsibility involves risk of failure and loss, which often requires boldness and faith and can be costly and involve sacrifice. Joe's decision to use his discretion to release José involved risk that the CPS worker in the other case was not willing to assume. Don's posting of his own $7,500 as bail for more than two years involved sacrifice and risk, as José could have taken off or committed new crimes. Yet whether one is a law-enforcement agent, soldier, social worker, teacher, or something else, disciples of Jesus are called to act from out of their identity as citizens of the kingdom of Heaven, who are beholden first to Christ and his agenda.

According to Genesis 1:26 (NASB), God said of humans: "Let Us make man in Our image, according to Our likeness; and let them rule over the fish of the sea and over the birds of the sky and over the cattle and over all the earth, and over every creeping thing that creeps on the earth." Later, in 1:28, God blessed them and said, "Be fruitful and multiply, and fill the earth, and subdue it."

The reversal of dominion is described as taking place first in the garden, when the first humans listened to the creeping thing, the serpent, rather than exercising dominion over it. They let the creature define the identity of the Creator. In coming under the subjugation of the creature or creation—in this case the nation-state—a darkening of the mind takes place that is described in Romans 1:22–26 (NASB):

> Professing to be wise, they became fools, and exchanged the glory of the incorruptible God for an image in the form of corruptible man and of birds and four-footed animals and crawling creatures. Therefore God gave them over in the lusts of their hearts to impurity, that their bodies might be dishonored among them. For they exchanged the truth of God for a lie, and worshiped and served the creature rather than the Creator, who is blessed forever. For this reason, God gave them over to *degrading passions* . . . (emphasis added)

When we agree to come under the authority of the nation-state or any institution to the extent that we serve it as the highest authority, giving over our will through choosing to obey unjust or oppressive (or any) orders, rules, and policies *over* God's voice, we too can become given over to degrading passions from which we may need deliverance. When we pledge allegiance to a flag; swear oaths of office, installation, or enlistment; or sign any kind of contract we need to be mindful of the higher calling of Spirit-guided conscience. Government functionaries like the CPS worker or Border Patrol agent had to harden their hearts against a desperate woman and her innocent and vulnerable children because of fear of liability. When we choose blind submission to the letter of the law to protect ourselves from failure and liability, there is a risk of exchanging freedom and right authority for domination and control. Right authority as children of God involves wisdom, discretion, and taking risks in the interests of love, life, and wholeness. Hardheartedness, pride, fear, hatred, aggression, desire for revenge, subservience, and nationalism are just a few of the passions visible as the beast of the nation-state is worshiped and served. I will discuss this in greater detail below.

Deliverance from National Spirits?

In books on deliverance from evil spirits, charismatic Christian authors commonly identify demons as the lowest level of evil spirits in an organized hierarchy of evil.[8] Some books include lists of demons, which authors classify according to their functions or emotions (death, suicide, murder, destruction, darkness, rage, hate, resentment, self-rejection, guilt, worry, deceit)[9] or by names such as compulsiveness, control, performance, religiosity, lust, pornography, drugs, nicotine, gluttony, anorexia, bulimia, caffeine. Some writers classify as "occult spirits" such things as Freemasonry, Christian Science, Scientology, Jehovah's Witnesses, Mormonism, Ouija boards, horoscopes, witchcraft, palmistry, or "religious spirits," and world religions like Buddhism, Islam, Hinduism, and Shintoism.[10] Absent from the lists in most charismatic Christian literature are other demons and higher-level evil spirits often experienced negatively by poor people or others on the margins of society. Nationalism, legalism, ethnocentrism, racism, and militarism are among the worst offenders, together with well-known demons like pride, fear, hatred, and greed. The oppressive spirits and others can enter into our lives when we give over our allegiance to institutions, ideologies, and other powers that are mere creatures. Authors who write on New Testament understandings of the principalities and powers from a social prophetic perspective informed by proximity to the poor identify the following (and many other) contemporary equivalents: legal system, laws, racism, U.S. dollar, economic systems and political parties (capitalism, communism, Republican Party, Democratic Party, al-Qaeda), institutions (IMF, WTO, Presbyterian Church (U.S.A.), Catholic Church, NAFTA, World Bank, Pentagon, CIA), multinational corporations (Microsoft, General Mills, Boeing), brand names (Nike, the Gap, iPod), and celebrities (Michael Jackson, Oprah, Brad Pitt, Osama bin Laden, Madonna), ethnic categories such as Caucasian, Hispanic, Semitic, or national identity (United States, France, Japan, Germany). Can higher-level spirits be attached to these powers?

Charismatic Christian literature on spiritual warfare does identify "territorial spirits" as invisible spiritual powers behind nations, territories, and organizations in ways that bridge the gulf between these perspectives.

Charles Kraft is one who identifies territorial spirits as spiritual forces that are associated directly with nation states.

> The territory over which spirit beings wield their authority seems to be defined by humans. It is humans who work out the boundaries over which they will have authority. These human boundaries seem to be honored in the spirit world. The fact that the territories of Persia (Daniel 10:13, 20) and Greece (Daniel 10:21), over which satanic principalities held sway, are labeled by human territorial names points in that direction.[11]

Kraft notes that there are likely spiritual powers that exercise authority by promoting their agendas: "There seem to be cosmic-level spirits with authority over organizations, institutions and activities. Probably there are cosmic-level spirits whose job it is to promote pornography [and other social evils] and [to] encourage organizations devoted to such sins."[12]

Absent from Kraft's list (but in full alignment with them) are forces like nationalism, militarism, racism, environmental degradation, gluttony, greed, ethnic pride, usury, and other sins identified by social prophetic voices. Yet Kraft is clear when he describes how people give power to the powers: "In order for spirit beings to have authority over territories and organizations, they must have legal right. Such rights *are given them* through the allegiance, dedication and behavior of the humans who now use and have used the territories and organizations in the past" (148).

Kraft's astute observation regarding people giving power to spirit beings tied to territories or organizations is in keeping with two key texts from 1 Corinthians regarding idolatry. In 1 Corinthians 8 Paul addresses the question of whether the Christians in Corinth should eat things sacrificed to idols:

> We know that there is no such thing as an idol in the world, and that there is no God but one. For even if there are so-called gods whether in heaven or on earth, *as indeed there are many gods and many lords*, yet for us there is but one God, the Father, from whom are all things, and we exist for him; and one Lord, Jesus Christ, through whom are all things, and we exist through him. (1 Cor. 8:4b–6 NASB, emphasis added)

Here Paul refuses to acknowledge the power of the idol. At the same time, though, he recognizes the spiritual dimension of idols, or "creations" as among many "so-called gods," as "indeed there are many gods and many lords." He goes on to show that the empowerment of these idols or "gods" comes because humans give them power through the ignorance that there is in fact only one God: "However not all men have this knowledge; but some, being accustomed to the idol until now, eat food as if it were sacrificed to an idol; and their conscience being weak is defiled" (1 Cor. 8:7 NASB).

Later in 1 Corinthians 10 Paul urges believers to "flee from idolatry" (v. 14). Once again he refuses to acknowledge that idols are anything. Yet at the same time he recognizes that people open our hearts to evil spirits when we sacrifice, worship, or pledge allegiance to things that are not God: "What do I mean then? That a thing sacrificed to idols is anything, or an idol is anything? No, but I say that the things which the Gentiles sacrifice, they sacrifice to demons, and not to God; and I do not want you to become sharers in demons" (vv. 19–21).

Paul urges Christians to avoid unhealthy attachments to idols occasioned even through merely eating food sacrificed to them. "For us there is but one God," he insists in 1 Corinthians 8:6. This is so we will remain free from demonic oppression.

When human beings give their allegiance or sacrifice to organizations (whether they be a nation, corporation, denomination, or anything), these man-made things can function as idols, opening people up to the demonic. Paul warned Christians living in Rome, at the heart of the global empire of his time, that even those who profess to be wise can become fools: "Exchanging the glory of the incorruptible God for an image in the form of corruptible man and of birds and four-footed animals and crawling creatures" (Rom. 1:23).

Idolatrous subservience to idols, creatures, and creation puts us at risk of exchanging the truth of God for a lie, worshiping the creature rather than the creator. The result as we saw above is that people can be given over to degrading passions.

The categories Paul uses in Romans 1:23 must be read as inclusive of all the forces in the cosmos that he insists in Philippians 2:10–11 will bow the knee and confess Jesus as Lord, referred to as "those who are in heaven, and on the earth, and under the earth." Paul's reference to "birds" in Romans 1:23 is a direct reference to Genesis 1:28's "birds of the air." "Birds" were understood to represent the many spiritual forces "of the air" that snatch away or rob what humans have planted or in any way achieved. "Four-footed animals" refer to forces here on earth that are sometimes more specifically referring to the economy when they are more specifically identified as "sheep and oxen" (Ps. 8:7) and forces that prey on or are able to wreak havoc on humans when referred to as "beasts of the field" (Ps. 8:7). These may well include forces of nature, institutions, and diseases. Finally "crawling creatures" appears to refer to lower-level demonic powers associated with the Evil One, who first appears on the scene in Genesis 3:1 (NASB) as a tempter described as "more crafty than any beast of the field."

Paul's description of God giving them over to "the lusts of their hearts to impurity" (Rom. 1:24 NASB) is reminiscent of the "impure spirits" that Jesus and the disciples cast out in Mark's Gospel, which clearly include "Legion" (Mark 5:9)—a term indicating number and strength that at the same time links the Gerasene demoniac's evil spirits to the Roman occupation of Israel. Being given over to "lusts" or to "degrading passions" is one way of describing being demonized or afflicted by evil spirits.

One way to discern the signs of demonization or of being given over to degrading passions is to compare the visible attitudes and actions in oneself to the fruit of the Spirit and in the deeds of the flesh in Galatians 5:19–21 (NRSV): "Now the works of the flesh are obvious: fornication, impurity, licentiousness, *idolatry*, sorcery, *enmities, strife, jealousy, anger, quarrels, dissensions, factions,* envy, drunkenness, carousing, and things like these. I am warning you, as I warned you before: those who do such things will not inherit the kingdom of God" (emphasis added).

Many Christians have wrongly assumed that this list of deeds is referring to more individual and personal "sins" or exclusively to interpersonal relations. Divisions between social activist and charismatic and evangelical groups can be seen in which of the "deeds of the flesh" each group chooses to highlight. Yet idolatry, enmities, and strife are certainly present in people's hearts as a nation contemplates or engages in war, as are "outbursts of anger, disputes, dissensions and factions" (v. 20 NASB). What might be some other signs of demonization through allegiance to or unhealthy attachment to territorial spirits?[13]

Signs of Demonization

In reaction to September 11, 2001, many Americans have intensified their allegiance to nation, political party, and national leaders. I have identified the following list of attitudes as symptomatic of "deeds of the flesh" or "degrading passions" that many Americans appear to have been "delivered over to."

Anxiety, fear, and paranoia have been visible in the post–9/11 North American scene. Anger, rage, and hatred have also surfaced. In response to terrorist attacks Americans rallied behind the flag in an unprecedented way. Bumper stickers like "The Power of Pride" appeared in our region, elevating the most notorious of the eight mortal passions identified as sins by the early church fathers to the level of a virtue. Calls for retaliation and vengeance abounded as people rallied behind leaders who demanded nearly blind allegiance. Other signs of demonization by the national spirit include these:

- Succumbing to the violence of war as "the only," "necessary," or "rational" solution
- Hatred for enemies and despising opponents; disdain for people of different faiths or political persuasions
- Glee over retributive acts and enemy death counts
- Toleration or celebration of the loss of human life "sacrificed" for a political agenda, ideology, way of life, or something deemed a "higher good"
- War fever and fascination with weaponry and destruction
- Silence before injustice (Abu Ghraib and Guatánamo Bay prisoner scandals)
- Silence before oppression (surveillance, torture, raids, mass arrests)
- Support of acts of punishment or vengeance (striking the Taliban; invasion of Iraq; justification of torture)
- Nationalism; praying for our leaders, people, and troops and not theirs
- Willingness to tolerate extreme expenditures for war
- Being comforted by flags over dead soldiers
- Inability to hear criticism of government policies; unwillingness to entertain serious critiques of Iraq war; impasse between Republicans and Democrats—no real open dialogue but rather entrenchment and demonizing of the other
- Blindness to the signs (no weapons of mass destruction found)
- Believing deception; uncritical acceptance of false explanations; blind trust in and allegiance to leaders
- Disregard for the teaching of Jesus regarding love, love of enemy

"Deeds of the flesh" become visible through comparing with the "fruit of the Spirit": "But the fruit of the Spirit is love, joy, peace, patience, kindness, goodness, faithfulness, gentleness, self-control; against such things there is no law" (Gal. 5:22 NASB).

When we compare 1 Corinthians 13 to the dominant attitudes, we can see the distance between God's ways and ours: "Love is patient, love is kind, and is not jealous; love does not brag and is not arrogant, does not act unbecomingly; it does not seek its own, is not provoked, does not take into account a wrong suffered, does not rejoice in unrighteousness, but rejoices with the truth; bears all things, believes all things, hopes all things, endures all things, love never fails" (1 Cor. 13:4–8a NASB).

As we compare reigning attitudes toward national and personal enemies to New Testament descriptions of love, it becomes clear how far we are from experiencing the fullness of the kingdom of God and close we are to experiencing the negative consequences about which Paul warns the Galatians: "I forewarn you just as I have forewarned you that those who practice such things shall not inherit the kingdom of God" (Gal. 5:21 NASB).

Reentry into the land, the kingdom of God, requires awareness of how the counterfeit kingdom becomes established in our hearts.

Entry Points for the Demonic

Writers on deliverance ministry describe numerous entry points for evil spirits that appear to apply equally to territorial spirits. According to these writers, demons are given legal rights through areas in our lives where we have given them an "open door." The four most commonly identified open doors include ancestral sins and inherited curses, soul ties, ungodly beliefs, and physical and/or psychological trauma. These categories represent open doors or footholds that must be effectively identified and shut or removed through a dialogical process involving recognition, repentance, and renunciation or breaking agreement.

The first category, described as "ancestral sins and inherited curses," includes spiritual oppression that is discerned as coming down through the generations of father and mother to affect an individual. Spiritual oppression is commonly rooted in past generations and passed on from generation to generation. Alcoholism, anxiety disorders, depression, a propensity to domestic violence, and countless physical conditions ranging from heart disease and diabetes to breast and prostate cancer are often recognized as inherited conditions. However, idolatrous practices and the allegiances of our ancestors to religion, political party, and nation can also have an adverse effect on descendants.

Descendants of slaveholders or settlers involved in displacing or massacring Native Americans bear the guilt and likely the curses pronounced against them. Pride and self-justification combine to establish attitudes of superiority and entitlement common in nationalism. I have witnessed descendants of Scandinavian settlers become enraged when their right to land confiscated from the Native tribes in the Skagit Valley of Washington was brought up. They justified ownership by describing the years of work clearing what is now prime farmland of trees and stumps. Many anglers who themselves are descendants of settlers who benefited from free or inexpensive land offered to homesteaders become infuriated by Indians' special treaty-guaranteed fishing rights. Experienced practitioners of deliverance ministry insist that ancestral sins and inherited curses must be identified, confessed, and renounced, and curses must be broken, in order to close these doors to the demonic.

The second category described as soul ties or relationship bonds involves ties to ancestral sins and inherited curses through unhealthy unions. The term "soul tie" or "soul bond" designates a bond established between one person and another human, object, or spiritual power. Soul ties can be positive[14] and negative.[15]

> Ungodly soul ties stemming from covenant or contractual relationships pass sin energy down through the family line. Soul ties are the result of covenant relationships. Covenants are contracts which may be written, verbal, or understood. . . . When you enter into a covenant with another person or with God, a soul tie develops which allows the life, energies, and provisions of the two to be shared.[16]

Another common sign that a soul tie is unhealthy is the effort of one partner in the relationship "to dominate, manipulate, or control another. If violence, fear, or abuse becomes part of the soul tie, it is ungodly."[17] In deliverance literature, teaching on soul ties is nearly always limited to interpersonal relationships.[18] Yet it is obvious that ties to nation, race, and ideology can be highly destructive when humans unite their wills with evil forces like Nazism or ethnic cleansing, or when believers are kept from their universal mission (Gen. 12:1–4) through narrow allegiances.

In every nation, unhealthy soul ties are established between citizens and their homeland that need to be identified and broken. At the same time, any positive aspects of soul ties between people and their communities, cities, and nations should be identified and affirmed. This should be done regularly as followers of Jesus discern God's call on their lives amid other competing demands. Otherwise, people will blindly come into agreement with agendas that are foreign or antagonistic to the kingdom of God.

Healthy and destructive soul ties are established and regularly reinforced between Americans and the principalities of the United States through frequent pledging of allegiance to the flag. In the majority of grade schools, middle schools, and high schools throughout the United States the school day begins with a corporate pledging of allegiance to the flag. Before public sporting events and meetings of weekly social groups like the Rotary or Kiwanis clubs, Boy Scouts, Girl Scouts, and 4-H clubs and at many other events, people habitually pledge allegiance. People commonly stand, face the flag, reverently place their right hand over their heart, and recite the pledge: "I pledge allegiance to the flag of the United States of America, and to the republic for which it stands, one nation under God, indivisible, with liberty and justice for all."

During World Word II, Japanese Americans living in internment camps were required to stand before the attorney general and swear the following oath of allegiance to the United States of America:

> I, the undersigned, do solemnly swear that I will support and defend the constitution of the United States of America against all enemies, foreign and domestic; that I will bear true faith and allegiance to the same; that I do hereby forswear and repudiate any other allegiance which I knowingly or unknowingly

may have held here to fore; and that I take these obligations freely, without any mental reservation whatsoever or purpose of evasion, so help me God.

When permanent residents become citizens now, they are required to recite an oath of renunciation and allegiance.[19] This shows a sensitivity to the need for people to formally leave behind, to the point of renouncing them, foreign allegiances, understood as soul ties, before entering into citizenship through taking vows of allegiance. The requirement to break past allegiances to another nation may well reflect a legitimate demand by a nation receiving a new citizen. Disciples of Jesus certainly cannot repudiate their allegiance to the kingdom of God in favor of allegiance to nation, and should use great discernment in making any pledge or oath. Yet the current law reads that "A person who has applied for naturalization shall, in order to be and before being admitted to citizenship, take in a public ceremony before the Attorney General or a court with jurisdiction under section 310(b) an oath:

1. *to support* the Constitution of the United States;
2. *to renounce* and *abjure absolutely*[20] and entirely all allegiance and fidelity to any foreign prince, potentate, state, or sovereignty of whom or which the applicant was before a subject or citizen;
3. *to support and defend* the Constitution and the laws of the United States against all enemies, foreign and domestic;
4. *to bear true faith and allegiance* to the same; and
5a. *to bear arms on behalf of* the United States when required by the law, or
5b. *to perform noncombatant service* in the Armed Forces of the United States when required by the law, or [to do an alternative form of service defined in a long, detailed section that follows]."

Men and women who enlist in the U.S. Armed Forces are required to swear the following oath of enlistment.

> I, _____, do solemnly swear (or affirm) that I will support and defend the Constitution of the United States against all enemies, foreign and domestic; that I will bear true faith and allegiance to the same; and that I will obey the orders of the President of the United States and the orders of the officers appointed over me, according to regulations and the Uniform Code of Military Justice. So help me God.

Other ways that people reinforce soul ties to the nation are through taxation, voting, attending partisan political rallies, giving campaign contributions, and agreeing with nationalist rhetoric.[21]

The first step in closing doors to unclean spirits through unhealthy attachments to individuals, institutions, objects, or any spiritual force is to invite the Holy Spirit to reveal attachments that provide footholds for spiritual control or oppression. The Spirit is the guide that leads us to the truth (John 14:16–17, 26) and brings conviction regarding sin (John 16:8–9). Once we are aware of our own participation in joining with spirits that are not of God, the second step is to confess our involvement. This should be followed by a deliberate turning away from our involvement through renouncing unhealthy attachments. The following prayer can be used to sever effectively destructive aspects of soul ties with anything, including ethnic or territorial spirits associated with our nation or ideologies: "In the name of the Father, Son, and Holy Spirit, I supernaturally break all the ungodly bondages that have been established between me and _____. I ask you, Lord, to cleanse me from every negative impact and influence it has had on my life. I ask you, Father, to place the cross of Jesus between me and _____ to stop the flow of everything ungodly between the two of us. Amen."[22]

Writers on deliverance ministry describe the third category of open doors to the demonic as "ungodly beliefs." Another name for this is simply bad theology.

We all need help to identify and break our agreement with accusations or lies about ourselves, others, and God. We need to turn away from distorted understandings of self, others, and God and replace these with truer affirmations. Changing our images of God, self, and others is a primary objective of my Scripture reading in *Reading the Bible with the Damned*.

Pledging allegiance to the flag or to the constitution of any country or obedience to commanding officers could easily fit into the biblical category of idolatry, which is prohibited by the first commandment in Exodus 20 and the Shema of Deuteronomy 6. Throughout the Bible there are calls to total allegiance to God, which often include overt renunciations of other gods or reigning powers. These powers are named with a diverse vocabulary (gods, idols, likenesses, etc.). Exodus 20:2–5a (NASB) reads, "I am the LORD your God, who brought you out of the land of Egypt, out of the house of slavery. You shall have *no other gods* before Me. You shall not make for yourself an idol, or any likeness of what is in heaven above or on the earth beneath or in the water under the earth. You shall not worship them or serve them" (emphasis added).

God ordered ancient Israel to "have no other gods" in a way that parallels the United States' requirement for citizens to renounce other allegiances. As the Israelites are about to go over to inherit/possess the promised land (Deut. 6:1), God calls her to wholehearted allegiance in the Shema: "Hear, O Israel! The LORD is our God, the LORD is one! And you shall love the LORD your God with all your heart and with all your soul and with all your might" (Deut. 6:4–5 NASB).

These words were considered of such importance that they were to be remembered and recited continuously.

> And these words, which I am commanding you today, shall be on your heart; and you shall teach them diligently to your sons and shall talk of them when you sit in your house and when you walk by the way and when you lie down and when you rise up. And you shall bind them as a sign on your hand and they shall be as frontals on your forehead. And you shall write them on the doorposts of your house and on your gates. (Deut. 6:6–9 NASB)

The people are warned that when they come into the land they must be careful not to forget who brought them there: "Then watch yourself, lest you forget the LORD who brought you from the land of Egypt, out of the house of slavery. You shall fear only the LORD your God; and you shall worship Him and swear by His name. You shall not follow other gods, any of the gods of the peoples who surround you, for the LORD your God in the midst of you is a jealous God" (Deut. 6:12–15a NASB).

Jesus taught that purity of vision was essential and called people away from orientation toward the reigning gods of his time, including mammon:

> The lamp of the body is the eye; if therefore your eye is clear, your whole body will be full of light. But if your eye is bad, your whole body will be full of darkness. If therefore the light that is in you is darkness, how great is the darkness! No one can serve two masters; for either he will hate the one and love the other, or he will hold to one and despise the other. You cannot serve God and mammon. (Matt. 6:22–24 NASB)

Jesus calls disciples, "Seek first His kingdom and His righteousness; and all these things [of this world] will be added to you" (Matt. 6:33 NASB).

The belief that Germany, America, France, Japan, or any nation is superior or "number one" is false and is countered throughout the Scriptures. All nations are viewed as insignificant, according to Isaiah 40:15, 17 (NASB): "Behold, the nations are like a drop from a bucket, and are regarded as a speck of dust on the scales; behold, He lifts up the islands like fine dust. . . . All the nations are as nothing before Him, they are regarded by Him as less than nothing and meaningless."

The nation of Israel, God's chosen people, was certainly not spared from God's judgment of the nations. While Israel herself was languishing in exile in Babylon after her own leaders were dethroned, the prophet Isaiah provided a scathing glance that included every nation in his sight: "He it is who reduces rulers to nothing, who makes the judges of the earth meaningless. Scarcely have they been planted, scarcely have they been sown, scarcely has their stock taken root in the earth, but He merely blows on them, and they wither, and the storm carries them away like stubble" (Isa. 40:23–24 NASB).

Throughout Scripture God is described as reigning over all of the nations, as in Psalm 47:8–9 (NIV), "God reigns over the nations. . . . The kings of the earth belong to God," and Jeremiah 10:7, which affirms that God is the King of the nations. "Dominion belongs to the LORD and he rules over the nations," affirms the psalmist in Psalm 22:28 (NIV). "He changes times and seasons; he sets up kings and deposes them" (Dan. 2:21 NIV). "The LORD foils the plans of the nations; he thwarts the purposes of the peoples. But the plans of the LORD stand firm forever, the purposes of his heart through all generations" (Ps. 33:10–11 NIV).

In Revelation 18 we see one of the strongest statements regarding the impossibility of redeeming the all-powerful nation-state, referred to here as Babylon.

> Fallen, fallen is Babylon the great! It has become a dwelling place of demons, a haunt of every foul spirit, a haunt of every foul bird, a haunt of every foul

and hateful beast. For all the nations have drunk of the wine of the wrath of her fornication, and the kings of the earth have committed fornication with her, and the merchants of the earth have grown rich from the power of her luxury. (Rev. 18:2–3 NRSV)

In apparent contrast to this, the apostle Paul's admonitions to be subject to governing authorities in Romans 13:1–6 (NRSV) is often cited by those who see government as exercising legitimate authority at a higher level over believers and nonbelievers alike. This text is also used as a justification of state violence like the death penalty, law-enforcement activities, war, and national defense.

Let every person be subject to the governing authorities; for there is no authority except from God, and those authorities that exist have been instituted by God. Therefore whoever resists authority resists what God has appointed, and those who resist will incur judgment. For rulers are not a terror to good conduct, but to bad. Do you wish to have no fear of the authority? Then do what is good, and you will receive its approval; for it is God's servant for your good. But if you do what is wrong, you should be afraid, for the authority does not bear the sword in vain! It is the servant of God to execute wrath on the wrongdoer. Therefore one must be subject, not only because of wrath but also because of conscience. For the same reason you also pay taxes, for the authorities are God's servants, busy with this very thing.

This scripture certainly supports the need for believers to submit whenever possible to civil authorities. Governments do have a legitimate role to provide security and maintain order in society. However, Romans 13 must be read carefully first in its own literary context, as well as in the context of the entire witness of Scripture and teachings on prophetic ministry.

The apostle Paul appealed to his rights as a Roman citizen, demanding that functionaries treat him according to the law. At the same time he spent many years of his life incarcerated, experiencing both protection from his Jewish enemies and unjust detention. When reading Romans 13:1ff. immediately following Romans 12:9ff., one sees that governing authorities were also viewed as persecutors and enemies. Paul has just called believers to "bless those who persecute you; bless and do not curse them" (Rom. 12:14 NRSV). Living in subjugation to governing authorities does not mean joining or applauding them in their use of violence and control. Rather it means engaging them from the perspective of those who are not conformed to this world, but being transformed by the renewing of our minds (Rom. 12:2). I do not believe that Romans 13 should be used to justify Christians agreeing with or participating in state violence, war, or law-enforcement activities as "the way of Jesus." While the state has a legitimate right to wield the sword, disciples of Jesus are first and foremost citizens of a kingdom not of this world. Christians may choose to serve in government, law-enforcement agencies, and the military and can have a powerful impact as they act in ways that show they are beholden to a suffering Messiah. Their roles will be complicated and made difficult by the higher call of Jesus and allegiance to the kingdom of God, which may well require them to disobey in ways leading to persecution, demotion, court martial, and even martyrdom. Jesus' way of dealing with evil is articulated clearly in the verses immediately preceding Romans 13 and must not be reduced to only the way we deal with personal enemies. Paul rightly understands Jesus' Sermon on the Mount as the grid through which followers of Jesus live their whole lives.

> Do not repay anyone evil for evil, but take thought for what is noble in the sight of all. If it is possible, so far as it depends on you, live peaceably with all. Beloved, never avenge yourselves, but leave room for the wrath of God, for it is written, "Vengeance is mine, I will repay, says the Lord." No, "if your enemies are hungry, feed them; if they are thirsty, give them something to drink; for by doing this you will heap burning coals on their heads." Do not be overcome by evil, but overcome evil with good. (Rom. 12:17–21 NRSV)

In 1 Peter 2:13–14 (NRSV) there is another strong call to submit to authorities, which is often not read together with the verses that precede and follow: "For the Lord's sake accept the authority of every human institution, whether of the emperor as supreme, or of governors, as sent by him to punish those who do wrong and to praise those who do right."

This call must be read in the context of Peter's clear articulation to his readers in 1 Peter 2:9 that "you are a chosen race, a royal priesthood, a holy nation, God's own people." Peter identifies his readers in 2:11 as "aliens and exiles" whom he calls to conduct themselves honorably among the Gentiles "so that, though they malign you as evildoers, they may see your honorable deeds and glorify God when he comes to judge" (2:12 NRSV). Peter's call to believers to accept the authority of secular government is a call respectfully to submit when possible to the rightful use of governmental authority. It is not, however, a call to patriotic loyalty or blind obedience. Peter is addressing marginalized, maligned people, calling them both to avoid unnecessary trouble and more importantly to show honor and love to people, including their enemies: "For it is God's will that by doing right you should silence the ignorance of the foolish. As servants of God, live as free people, yet do not use your freedom as a pretext for evil. Honor everyone. Love the family of believers. Fear God. Honor the emperor" (2:15–17).

Throughout the Bible the authority of leaders is acknowledged and usually respected.[23] At the same time, God's people are called to resist when reigning powers are at odds with the priorities of God's kingdom. Resistance to or disobedience of governing authorities is visible when kings are secular, as in the case of Pharaoh, Nebuchadnezzar, and Darius. YHWH sends Moses before Pharaoh to demand that he let his people leave Egypt.

The book of Daniel contains important teaching for people living as exiles in the midst of empire. Daniel maintained faith in YHWH in the midst of Babylon in ways that required him not to do the equivalent of pledging allegiance to the Babylonian flag.

In the first incident, Nebuchadnezzar set up a golden image, inviting all the functionaries to come to a dedication of the image. All were required to fall down and worship the golden image at the sound of the music (Dan. 3:5). Anyone not falling down and worshiping was to be thrown into the furnace of blazing fire (Dan. 3:6). Shadrach, Meshach, and Abednego disregarded the king; "they do not serve your gods or worship the golden image which you have set up" (Dan. 3:12 NASB). When given a final opportunity to save their lives by showing their allegiance to the image of gold, they said, "Let it be known to you, O king, that we are not going to serve your gods or worship the golden image that you have set up" (Dan. 3:18 NASB). When Nebuchadnezzar saw how they were delivered from the flames, he said, "Blessed be the God of Shadrach, Meshach, and Abednego, who has sent his angel and delivered his servants who trusted in him. They disobeyed the king's command and yielded up their bodies rather than serve and worship any god except their own God" (Dan. 3:28 NRSV).

The king acknowledged God, saying, "How great are his signs, how mighty his wonders! His kingdom is an everlasting kingdom, and his sovereignty is from generation to generation" (Dan. 4:3 NRSV).

The commissioners, one of which was Daniel, were placed over the kingdom. Two commissioners were jealous of Daniel's special favor. They established a law "that anyone who makes a petition to any god or man" beside the king during thirty days would be thrown into the lions' den. The law was established in a way that made it unchangeable. The text shows Daniel practicing civil disobedience: "Although Daniel knew that the document had been signed, he continued to go to his house, which had windows in its upper room toward Jerusalem, and to get down on his knees three times a day to pray to his God and praise him, just as he had done previously" (Dan. 6:10 NRSV).

The commissioners came and found Daniel making petition and supplication before his God (Dan. 6:11), and they denounced him—forcing the king to enforce the law by having Daniel thrown into the lions' den.[24] When King Darius saw that God had sent his angel to shut the mouths of the lions, he came to agree that Daniel's God was sovereign over all the nations, including his own, to the point that he decreed "that in all the dominion of my kingdom men are to fear and tremble before the God of Daniel: "For he is the living God, enduring for ever. His kingdom shall never be destroyed, and his dominion has no end. He delivers and rescues, he works signs and wonders in heaven and on earth; for he has saved Daniel from the power of the lions" (Dan. 6:26–27 NRSV).

In the book of Daniel there are no illusions that change is brought about by subservience to governments with the belief that they will be reformed into effective agents of God. Rather, they are viewed as inherently destructive and finite, heading toward destruction. In Daniel's dream in Daniel 7 he sees four great beasts coming out of the sea, representing four kings (7:17) who were devouring, dominating, and crushing—each one apparently worse than the other (7:3ff.). Daniel keeps looking and sees thrones set up and the Ancient of Days taking his seat, surrounded by myriads upon myriads (7:10). The fourth and worst beast is destroyed by fire (7:11) and the other beasts lose their dominion after their appointed time runs out (7:12). Then "One like a Son of Man" comes to the Ancient of Days (7:13 NASB), who gives him "dominion, glory and a kingdom, that all the peoples, nations, and men of every language might serve Him. His dominion is an everlasting dominion which will not pass away; and His kingdom is one which will not be destroyed" (7:14 NASB). In Daniel's vision it is "the holy ones of the Most High" who are given the kingdom (7:18 NRSV). The fourth beast is described as dominating the earth and persecuting the saints until God judges it: "And his dominion shall be taken away, to be consumed and totally destroyed. The kingship and dominion and the greatness of the kingdoms under the whole heaven shall be given to the people of the holy ones of the Most High; their kingdom shall be an everlasting kingdom, and all dominions will serve and obey them" (7:26 NRSV).

Resistance to governing authorities was also encouraged when they were God's official "anointed ones." The prophets were the ones who anointed Israel's kings (1 Sam. 10:1; 16:13) and called them to faithfulness to the highest purposes of God's kingdom as described in the Torah and Prophets. The prophets often directly confronted the kings (1 Sam. 15:10; 2 Sam. 12:1ff.).

When Israel's first king, Saul, was anointed, having a king was viewed as a rejection of God and was associated with serving other gods. YHWH said to Samuel, "They have not rejected you, but they have rejected me from being king over them. Just as they have done to me, from the day I brought them up out of Egypt to this day, forsaking me and serving other gods" (1 Sam. 8:7b–8 NRSV).

Samuel warned the people that a king would draft their young into armies and service (1 Sam. 8:11–14) and oppress them with taxes (1 Sam. 8:15–17) until they cried out. The Lord would leave them to suffer the consequences of their own "democratic" choice: "And in that day you will cry out because of your king, whom you have chosen for yourselves; but the LORD will not answer you in that day" (1 Sam. 8:18 NRSV).

When Samuel enthroned Saul, he clearly repeated that their choice to submit to a government like the surrounding nations represented a rejection of God: "But today you have rejected your God, who saves you from all your calamities and your distresses; and you have said, 'No! but set a king over us!'" (1 Sam. 10:19 NRSV).

Samuel also insisted that, even though they rejected YHWH as their king and chose a human king to reign over them, whom he even anointed as a messiah, people must still serve and listen to God's voice.

> But when you saw that King Nahash of the Ammonites came against you, you said to me, "No, but a king shall reign over us," though the LORD your God was your king. See, here is the king whom you have chosen, for whom you have asked; see, the LORD has set a king over you. If you will fear the LORD and serve him and heed his voice and not rebel against the commandment of the LORD, and if both you and the king who reigns over you will follow the LORD your God, it will be well; but if you will not heed the voice of the LORD, but rebel against the commandment of the LORD, then the hand of the LORD will be against you and your king. (1 Sam. 12:12–15 NRSV)

When Israel first came under the authority of anointed kings, they were admonished to pledge total allegiance to God over anything else, serving God with all their hearts: "Do not be afraid; you have done all this evil, yet do not turn aside from following the LORD, but serve the LORD, with all your heart; and do not turn aside after useless things that cannot profit or save, for they are useless. . . . Only fear the LORD, and serve him faithfully with all your heart; for consider what great things he has done for you" (1 Sam. 12:20, 24 NRSV).

Israel's prophets are continually described as confronting and resisting and announcing judgment against kings whom God called them to anoint as messiahs. Samuel confronted Saul for his disobedience to YHWH and announced God's rejection of him as king (1 Sam. 13:11–14; 15:1–35). The prophet Nathan confronted David for his adultery with Bathsheba and the murder of Uriah (2 Sam. 12). Amos was accused of conspiracy for speaking words of judgment against King Jeroboam (Amos 7:10–11). The prophet Hanani announced judgment against King Baasha (1 Kgs. 16:1–4). YHWH sent Elijah to confront King Ahab for stealing Naboth's land and murdering him, announcing judgment (1 Kgs. 21:17–26). Micaiah predicted King Ahab's defeat and death if he should go to war against Syria (1 Kgs. 22:1–23). Elijah confronted King Ahaziah for consulting Beelzebub, the god of Ekron, and announced his death (2 Kgs. 1:1–17). Jeremiah continually confronted the kings of Judah (Jer. 23:1ff.), announcing their demise (Jer. 29:17; 32:1ff.). He called them to submit to their enemies, the Babylonians (Jer. 27:12ff.; 38:17), to the point that he was repeatedly imprisoned (38:6).

This prophetic role continued in the New Testament with John the Baptist, who was imprisoned and beheaded for confronting King Herod (Mark 6:14–32). According to Matthew's Gospel, Jesus' birth as king of the Jews was perceived as a threat to King Herod, who slaughtered Bethlehem's male children (Matt. 2:1–16). Jesus himself regularly confronted the religious leaders of his day, who functioned as the modern-day equivalents of governing officials and law enforcers (Mark 7:1–13; Luke 11:37–54). He refused to be subject to the law as they understood it. He publicly confronted the law enforcers through blatantly breaking laws regarding the Sabbath in his numerous healings.[25] Jesus disrupted the social order by transgressing purity rules that separated clean from unclean (Luke 17:11ff.), sinners from the righteous,[26] Jews from Samaritans (John 4). Jesus stood with people over and against the law on numerous occasions (John 8).

The prophetic role was universalized with the coming of the Holy Spirit upon believers at Pentecost in Acts 2. There Peter cites Joel 2:28–32: "In the last days it will be, God declares, that I will pour out my Spirit upon all flesh, and your sons and your daughters shall prophesy, and our young men shall see visions, and your old men shall dream dreams. Even upon my slaves, both men and women, in those days I will pour out my Spirit; and they shall prophesy" (Acts 2:17–18 NRSV).

The apostles consistently obeyed God over human authorities. This is evident in the immediate aftermath of Pentecost, when the authorities reacted to the healing of the paralytic at the temple gate recorded in Acts 3. In Acts 4:5, rulers, elders, and scribes came together and prohibited Peter and John from proclaiming Jesus to the people (Acts 4:18). These leaders were Jewish religious leaders who exercised authority over civil and religious matters in Roman-occupied Israel.

"But Peter and John answered and said to them, 'Whether it is right in the sight of God to give heed to you rather than to God, you be the judge; for we cannot stop speaking what we have seen and heard" (Acts 4:19–20 NASB).

Later, after the high priest arrested the apostles and ordered them to not teach in Jesus' name, Peter and the apostles answered, "We must obey God rather than men" (Acts 5:29 NASB). While Paul himself did not overtly resist civil authorities, everywhere he went people resisted him to the point of beating and imprisoning him. This is in keeping with the biblical witness, which consistently shows the apostles at odds with the authorities (Acts 12:1ff.; 17:5–9) or deliberately disobeying religious and civil rulers.

Writers on deliverance ministry rightly teach that ungodly beliefs (unhealthy theology) need to be identified, renounced, and then replaced by godly beliefs (healthy theology). While there are many shifts needed in all of our thinking, I propose embracing the following three: Jesus' teaching on the kingdom of God, his commitment to the cross as the only way to combat evil, and his commitment to nonviolent love of human enemies. Some of these topics will be dealt with in more detail in later chapters.

Jesus himself proclaimed the kingdom of God or the kingdom of heaven (Matt. 3:17) from the beginning to the end of his earthly ministry, and not merely the advancement of the nation of Israel. Jesus taught that when you see the abomination of desolation being set up in Jerusalem, you should not declare holy war but flee to the mountains (Mark 13:14; Matt. 24:15).

Jesus consistently taught love of human enemies: "You have heard that it was said, 'You shall love your neighbor and hate your enemy.' But I say to you, Love your enemies and pray for those who persecute you, so that you may be children of your Father in heaven. . . . For if you love those who love you, what reward do you have? Do not even the tax collectors do the same?" (Matt. 5:43–46 NRSV).

Some point out that John the Baptist did not tell Roman soldiers to abandon the military, and Jesus did not call the Roman centurion who approached him to leave his profession as a soldier. Those who use these texts to support Christians' use of violence as members of the armed forces misuse Scripture. Modern equivalents of Roman soldiers and centurions of first-century Palestine would be occupying British soldiers in colonial America, American soldiers in Iraq, or any enemy force of occupation. A Roman centurion executioner was even given the honor of being the first to confess Jesus as Son of God as he saw the way Jesus died (nonviolently) in both Matthew and Mark (Matt. 27:54; Mark 15:39), and declared him innocent in Luke's account (Luke 23:47).

Jesus' view of nation-states was that they would be at each other's throats: "nation will rise against nation, and kingdom against kingdom" (Mark 13:8 NRSV). He warned his disciples to be on their guard, expecting persecution from authorities: "For they will hand you over to councils; and you will be beaten in synagogues; and you will stand before governors and kings because of me, as a testimony to them" (Mark 13:9).

Jesus' main concern was that persecuted believers would be a testimony to the authorities, for "the gospel must first be preached to all the nations" (Mark 13:10 NASB). Paul's and Peter's writings regarding obedience to authorities must be read in the light of Jesus' willingness to face the cross—the final consequence of his ministry of announcing the kingdom of God.

Jesus consistently faced persecution through submitting to his enemies. He walked ahead of his disciples toward his passion in Jerusalem (Mark 10:32), fully conscious that he would be betrayed, condemned, mocked, tortured, and executed by his human enemies. Jesus was confident in his Father's deliverance as the one who would raise up on the third day (Matt. 20:17–19). Jesus refused to let his disciples defend him with violence at his arrest, saying, "Put your sword back into its place; for all who take the sword will perish by the sword. Do you think that I cannot appeal to my Father, and he will at once send me more than twelve legions of angels?" (Matt. 26:52b–53).

Jesus showed a way of being the Messiah that involved beating the power of evil through the superior force of love. Jesus expected disciples to recognize his way of being a suffering Messiah as legitimate and the only way a disciple of Jesus could rightly read the Old Testament. The just-resurrected Jesus on the road to Emmaus met disciples who were disappointed that Jesus did not meet their expectations as the awaited Messiah. Jesus strongly rebuked them for not seeing that redemptive suffering in the way of the bearer of the anointing: "'Oh, how foolish you are, and slow of heart to believe all that the prophets have declared! Was it not necessary that the Messiah should suffer these things and then enter into his glory?' Then beginning with Moses and all the prophets, he interpreted to them the things about himself in all the scriptures" (Luke 24:25–27 NRSV).

Paul rightly understood Jesus' commitment to nonviolence when he wrote, "Do not be overcome by evil, but overcome evil with good" (Rom. 12:20 NRSV).

The final category of open doors to the demonic is commonly called "physical and/or spiritual trauma." The "national spirit U.S.A." could conceivably become established in a person through trauma ranging from attacks on U.S. soil, such as the Japanese invasion at Pearl Harbor or the terrorist attacks in New York on September 11, 2001, or participation in a war by a person or a family member or ancestor. A terrorist attack or the trauma of being physically or psychologically wounded in war opens doors to fear, shame, guilt, anger, resentment, and other negative spirits.

In the United States, Americans are regularly invited throughout the year to commemorate national and personal traumas related to war on Veteran's Day, Fourth of July, Memorial Day, and September 11, when Americans are encouraged to "never forget." It is not difficult to see how these holidays can strengthen allegiances to the national spirit U.S.A. or to institutions like the U.S. Armed Forces, the presidency, the American dream, or other nonhuman entities. Commemorations of wars, invasions, terrorist attacks, and veterans punctuate the year like an ecclesiastical liturgical calendar (Advent, Christmas, Easter, Pentecost), functioning like civil rites or even "worship" celebrations that can end up strengthening spirits like national pride, hatred of national enemies, and superiority, to the point that unhealthy ties to the spirit of the nation become entrenched. Bondage to a national spirit is especially strengthened through remembering traumatic events that involved the shedding of blood.

When life is sacrificed and blood is shed on behalf of nation, ethnic group, political party, family, or any organization, ties become especially strong. In the same way that human sacrifice and the spilling of blood bonded aboriginal peoples to their deities, satanic ritual abuse victims to their covens, and soldiers to their fallen comrades, celebrating veterans' sacrifices of their lives during national commemorations links citizens to the nation. Whenever there are fatalities in war, blood sacrifice is offered to an ideology or principle.[27] For America, these idols include U.S. national security, U.S. democracy for the Middle East or any other region, freedom of religion, uninterrupted oil supply. Demonic bonds are likewise established to ideologies, ethnicities, religions, denominations, corporations, or any other organization through the human sacrifice. The value of the cause must be celebrated in order to justify and provide meaning to the loss of people's life by war, accidents, or disease. Martyrdom strengthens people's bonding to the larger cause, whether they are youth gang members, radical Islamic suicide bombers, Taliban or al-Qaeda combatants, Guatemalan or Salvadoran guerrillas, or U.S. Marine Corps soldiers, or self-sacrificing members of religious sects. The draping of the caskets of U.S. soldiers in the American flag before burial is one of the most visible manifestations of how death for a power strengthens allegiance to something less than God.

Before healing can happen, traumas that have opened the doors for excessive devotion to nation, gang, ethnic group, or religion must first be identified. The Holy Spirit will reveal losses and hurts that function as open doors to spiritual oppression, guiding the healing process in whatever ways are necessary. Inner healing of physical and emotional trauma must certainly include a period of grieving. Mourning the losses brings cleaning of our heart. Recognition of our own harmful responses to trauma should be followed by confession and receiving God's forgiveness. Turning away from our own destructive actions and attitudes often includes forgiving people who have sinned against us, and even blessing them. Lamentation is a genre of prayer throughout Scripture that must be recovered and practiced to help us rightly face devastating losses that may appear meaningless.

Deliverance from Territorial Spirits

In order for deliverance from national, ethnic, religious, or other territorial spirits to be effective, it is important to identify all powers elevated above God. One of the roles of the prophet in Scripture is to bring to light, to speak the truth, to expose the lie.[28] Jesus taught, "What is spoken to you in the darkness, speak in the light" (Matt. 10:27 au. trans.). This must be done in response to God's voice and word. The Lord's call to Isaiah regarding people's blindness and Isaiah's own conversion experience shows us that it is hard and even impossible to recognize your need for deliverance due to blindness and deafness. In Isaiah 6 God describes judgment as a necessary stage that brings people to a place of repentance. "How long, O Lord?" he asks. "Until cities lie waste without inhabitant," responds the Lord (Isa. 6:11 NRSV).

If people are willing to recognize, renounce, and turn away from false allegiances, deliverance can be easy and permanent. This process involves identifying and countering unhealthy practices.[29] Breaking agreement with unhealthy beliefs, allegiances, and actual commitments is a deliberate process requiring thoughtful analysis and spiritual discernment. Once idolatrous commitments have been identified, they must be broken in order to reverse their power.[30]

One of the most powerful ways to break unhealthy attachments to a national, territorial, or any other spirit not of God is through ancient Christian baptismal affirmations. The early church's baptismal rite included three renunciations and three corresponding affirmations that broke past allegiances and replaced them with positive commitments. In solidarity with the early church practice of facing the west, the location of the sun's descent into darkness, I invite groups to stand and join in repeating the three ancient renunciations:

> Do you renounce Satan and all the spiritual forces of wickedness that rebel against God?[31]

> Do you renounce the evil powers of this world which corrupt and destroy the creatures of God?

> Do you renounce all sinful desires that draw you from the love of God?

After vocalizing these three renunciations, I invite groups to face the east, the location of the rising sun, and pledge their allegiance only to God: Father, Son, and Holy Spirit.

> Do you turn to Jesus Christ and accept him as your Savior?

> Do you put your whole trust in his grace and love?

> Do you promise to follow and obey him as your Lord?

Baptismal renunciations are in keeping with the voice from heaven in Revelation 18:4–5 that calls the faithful out of Babylon.

> "Come out of her, my people, so that you do not take part in her sins, and so that you do not share in her plagues; for her sins are heaped high as heaven, and God has remembered her iniquities. Render to her as she herself has rendered, and repay her double for her deeds; mix a double draught for her in the cup she mixed. As she glorified herself and lived luxuriously, so give her a like measure of torment and grief. Since in her heart she says,

'I rule as a queen; I am no widow, and I will never see grief,' therefore her plagues will come in a single day—pestilence and mourning and famine—and she will be burned with fire; for mighty is the Lord God who judges her." (Rev. 18:4–8 NRSV)

As followers of Jesus Christ join Abram and Sarai in leaving nation, ethnicity, and family to become "strangers and aliens," we will become increasingly eligible for and effective at ministry to people on the margins of any society. Departure from false securities is possible only as we respond to God's call to go "to a place that I will show you" (Gen. 12:1 au. trans.). Leaving nation, ethnicity, and family is essential in order for us to experience God's abundant blessing (Gen. 12:2) and protection (Gen. 12:3) and effectively to become people of blessing who are integral parts of the *you* in God's promise: "in *you* all the families of the earth shall be blessed" (Gen. 12:3 NRSV). Departure does not always mean actually physically leaving. It is first a spiritual exodus from false securities. Departure from human securities in response to God's call requires faith that we will arrive at an unknown destination that is nothing less than a "conviction of things not seen (Heb. 11:1). While departure puts us to a greater or lesser degree in the company of disenfranchised "strangers and aliens," we at the same time are assured of a home in the new heaven and new earth:

> All of these died in faith without having received the promises, but from a distance they saw and greeted them. They confessed that they were strangers and foreigners on the earth, for people who speak in this way make it clear that they are seeking a homeland. If they had been thinking of the land that they had left behind, they would have had opportunity to return. But as it is, they desire a better country, that is, a heavenly one. Therefore God is not ashamed to be called their God; indeed, he has prepared a city for them. (Heb. 11:13–16 NRSV)

Growing into a secure identity as members of God's heavenly kingdom will cause us to become effective advocates and defenders in the ministry of the Holy Spirit. At the same time, we will become healthier recruiters as we enter into our vocation to make disciples of all nations, inviting people into a kingdom that is "not of this world."

Chapter 6

Reentering the Promised Land

The Gospel accounts show us in different ways that as we follow Jesus from the wilderness back into the land and begin announcing the kingdom of God, we will experience social, religious, and other dislocations. As we shift our allegiance more and more from the dominant competing mind-sets toward Jesus and the kingdom of God, we may find ourselves moving increasingly "outside the camp"—alongside society's outcasts and sinners. The closer we move toward Jesus, the greater our intimacy with the "friend of sinners," the more we will find ourselves drawn to those God longs to seek and find through us.

Simultaneously, as outcasts and sinners become convinced that our attraction to and interest in them is genuine, they will be attracted to Jesus—in us, in Scripture, and as one who draws them to himself, from wherever he meets and calls them. As they respond to love, they will find themselves wanting to follow, engaging themselves in turn in his ministry to befriend, heal, deliver, and call sinners. Reconciliation between insiders and outsiders, the "saved" and the "damned," will happen as both are drawn to Jesus. Together we will find ourselves at the margins of Israel, there on the mountain in Galilee designated by Jesus where we will hear together: "All authority has been given to Me in heaven and on earth. Go therefore and make disciples of all the nations, baptizing them in the name of the

Father and the Son and the Holy Spirit, teaching them to observe all that I commanded you; and lo, I am with you always, even to the end of the age" (Matt. 28:18–20 NASB).

Jesus' commissioning word to his disciples in Galilee brings to mind the beginning of his ministry, when he first traveled to Galilee. In Matthew's Gospel Jesus' ministry in Galilee begins with a citation from Isaiah 9:1–2, reminding readers that Jesus began his ministry at the margins, where some of the first tribes to be exiled by the Assyrians are evoked: "Land of Zebulun, land of Naphtali, on the road by the sea, across the Jordan, Galilee of the Gentiles—the people who sat in darkness have seen a great light, and for those who sat in the region and shadow of death light has dawned" (Matt. 4:15–16 NRSV).

Jesus begins his ministry in Galilee proclaiming "repent, for the kingdom of heaven has come near" (Matt. 4:17 NRSV). He then immediately calls ordinary fishermen as his disciples (4:18ff.) and travels throughout Galilee "proclaiming the good news of the kingdom and curing every disease and every sickness among the people" (Matt. 4:23 NRSV). Disciples are called into a life of high adventure and risk that never ceases to pique the interest of inmates and Latino gangsters when I point it out. Jesus' proclamation that the kingdom of heaven "has come near" (NRSV), "is near" (NIV), or "is at hand" (RSV) is in full alignment with Matthew's version of the Lord's Prayer: "Your kingdom come, your will be done, on earth as in heaven." Real freedom from spiritual oppression and sickness is anticipated here and now by crowds and witnessed by new disciples and us as readers. "So his fame spread throughout all Syria, and they brought to him all the sick, those who were afflicted with various diseases and pains, demoniacs, epileptics, and paralytics, and he cured them. And great crowds followed him from Galilee, the Decapolis, Jerusalem, Judea, and from beyond the Jordan" (Matt. 4:24–25 NRSV).

Core discipleship training materials known as the Sermon on the Mount (Matt. 5–7) are inserted into Matthew's Gospel right at this point, breaking the momentum of the narrative and suggesting that Matthew's community understood Jesus to be a recruiter and movement builder. These teachings are immediately followed by accounts of Jesus healing a leper (8:1–4), a Roman centurion's servant (8:5–13), Peter's mother-in-law, and masses of demonized and sick (8:14–17). Jesus then casts out demons from a violent demoniac in Gadara (8:28–9:1) and heals a paralytic (9:2–9) before calling Matthew the tax collector (9:9). Calling ordinary people, healing the most excluded and despised, casting out demons from the most difficult people, and healing the masses are immediately followed with some of Jesus' clearest words to the religious authorities about his mission to recruit and empower sinners. In response to the Pharisees' judgment of him for sitting and eating with tax collectors and sinners Jesus says, "Those who are well have no need of a physician, but those who are sick. Go and learn what this means, 'I desire mercy, not sacrifice.' For I have come to call not the righteous but sinners" (Matt. 9:12–13 NRSV).

Jesus' ministry to a wide diversity of people continues: healing a hemorrhaging woman, raising the dead daughter of a synagogue leader (9:18–26), restoring the sight of two blind men (9:27–31), healing a man who is mute (9:32–34). Jesus' ministry in Galilee is summarized powerfully in Matthew 9:35–37 (NRSV):

> Then Jesus went about all the cities and villages, teaching in their synagogues, and proclaiming the good news of the kingdom, and curing every disease and every sickness. When he saw the crowds, he had compassion for them, because they were harassed and helpless, like sheep without a shepherd. Then he said to his disciples, "The harvest is plentiful, but the laborers are few; therefore ask the Lord of the harvest to send out laborers into his harvest."

Jesus then gives authority to his disciples "over unclean spirits, to cast them out, and to cure every disease and every sickness" (10:1 NRSV). While Jesus' focus according to Matthew is not yet to the non-Jews or even to the Samaritans, Jesus calls and sends his recruited fishermen, tax collector, and betrayer to the "lost sheep of the house of Israel" (10:6 NRSV) with hugely challenging orders: "As you go, proclaim the good news, 'The kingdom of heaven has come near.' Cure the sick, raise the dead, cleanse the lepers, cast out demons" (10:7–8a NRSV).

I am convinced that "a life of Jesus" is the only thing that competes with a life of crime. Recruiters into active service of Jesus need to themselves be embodying or at least be moving toward experiencing this life of Jesus. We must do everything possible to lower the bar of requirements, refusing to be intimidated by insignificant obstacles. Apparently lack of funding or long-range planning did not disqualify impoverished disciples. The Jesus movement is not dependent upon external funding but is an invitation to live by gift, trusting in the provision of the sender: "You received without payment; give without payment. Take no gold, or silver, or copper in your belts, no bag for your journey, or two tunics, or sandals, or a staff; for laborers deserve their food" (10:8b–10 NRSV).

When I taught a group of several hundred ragged peasants recruited as pastors in Pemba, Mozambique, the mobilizing power of Jesus' imperative to take no money, bag, extra clothes, or staff hit me in a new way. Most of the men were barefoot, had no money, and were wearing the only clothes they owned. They could easily point to their extreme lack as an understandable excuse for not going out in mission. The Mozambican church had no way of paying them. They had no constituency from which to raise their own support and no boards of directors to help them launch their ministries. This word from Jesus immediately qualified them, removing any barriers that would keep a poor person from ministry, since they already lacked that which they were told not to take.

When I read Luke 10:4–16 with men in the jail and we talk through what it would actually look like to follow Jesus' step-by-step instructions to the seventy, they see it as doable and attractive. They like envisioning themselves as being needed for an important mission—in this case laboring in an abundant harvest where there are not enough workers (10:2). They like the risk and adventure involved in going out with no money, provisions, or shoes and are glad they don't have to do it alone but are sent out with a partner. They are intrigued that saying "peace be to this house" (10:5–6) could actually make a positive impact if received and can imagine feeling welcomed and valued by whomever would show them hospitality as wages for ministry (10:7–8), which happens right there in the house: "And heal those in it who are sick, and say to them, 'the kingdom of God has come near to you'" (10:9). I regularly hear people on the streets and in jail express a longing for direct engagement in a positive movement of healing and transformation that goes beyond themselves. Many begin right there in the jail praying for fellow inmates' healing, court cases, family problems, and spiritual struggles. Some actually report back in ways similar to Jesus' happy returnees, "Lord, even the demons are subject to us in your name" (10:17). Jesus' high regard for his disciples to the point that he identifies himself with them as in Luke 10:16 feels like something better than family by gang membership. "The one who listens to you listens to me, and the one who rejects you rejects me; and he who rejects me rejects the one who sent me."

In Mark's Gospel account Jesus appears and speaks his final words to his disciples not in a religious location like a synagogue but as they sit around a table (Mark 16:14). He calls them to radical faith in the testimony of those who had seen him after he'd risen from the dead and scolds them for their unbelief and hardness of heart. This very lack of faith and stubbornness is once again surprisingly inclusive—Jesus' very disciples were not known for their high level of faith but were still qualified to be sent out. Jesus calls them to a stunningly universal mission: to proclaim good news to everyone and everything everywhere.

"Go into all the world and proclaim the good news to the whole creation," commands Jesus. Those who believe are to be baptized. Jesus' recruits are assured that as they step out in radical faith, they will be backed up, even in the face of terrible opposition. Jesus tells them that signs of their authority over creation through his name will be evident: "And these signs will accompany those who believe: by using my name they will cast out demons; they will speak in new tongues; they will pick up snakes in their hands, and if they drink any deadly thing, it will not hurt them; they will lay their hands on the sick, and they will recover" (Mark 16:17–18 NRSV).

Mark's Gospel ends with a statement confirming that the first disciples in fact experienced this, encouraging future followers that they are not going alone: "And they went out and proclaimed the good news everywhere, while the Lord worked with them and confirmed the message by the signs that accompanied it" (Mark 16:20 NRSV).

In May 2006, my then thirteen-year-old son Luke and I traveled to Pemba, Mozambique, to teach in Iris Ministries' pastors' training school. There in Mozambique I witnessed the empowering effect of this word on an ordinary man who serves as pastor in a village dominated by a mixture of Islam and witchcraft. On our first village outreach Iris leader Heidi Baker warned my son Luke and me and the others in her truck as we headed out to the village of Maranganya that she couldn't guarantee our security. "The last five or six times we've gone out to this village, people have thrown stones at us," she said. "If you're not willing to risk this, now's the time to tell me so I can let you off."

Not wanting people to throw rocks at him, my son Luke hesitated. Heidi went on to tell us that the previous pastor had been driven out by men wielding machetes. She pointed out that the best way to prepare is praying in the Spirit, as the little orphan children were already doing. Sure enough, the little girl on my lap in the front seat was praying fervently in some foreign tongue. The other children from the orphanage on the ministry team were praying like this too, and Heidi joined in. We arrived in the village as the Jesus film was starting. Heidi introduced us to the new pastor, who told us how he'd lived a wild life of drinking and fighting before coming to faith. A big scar across his face lent authenticity to his claims. Crowds of children and women gathered around the big screen to watch the film. Some agitated-looking men hung out around the edges, trouble in their eyes.

Under a big eucalyptus tree beside the screen, Pastor Chico told us story after story of conversions of local people, due to signs similar to Mark 16:18–19. He told how a notorious witch doctor had served him food spiked with a deadly poison. Villagers who knew were astounded that he didn't drop dead, but experienced only minor stomach pains. He described curse-bearing fetishes being buried in front of their church and home, the exact locations revealed in dreams to his wife so they could unearth and destroy them. He told us about God empowering them to kill deadly snakes that were sent to disrupt meetings and intimidate him and his leaders. He recounted how they had waded across a river full of aggressive crocodiles in front of unbelieving villagers who were awed when they successfully ordered the attacking beasts to turn around and go away. That night when the film ended, Heidi began to preach, inviting people who were deaf, blind, or lame to come up to receive their healing. We all laid hands on the many impoverished people suffering from ailments and witnessed God's healing presence at work.

Jesus' first public reading of Scripture in Nazareth, recorded in Luke 4:14–21, sets the stage for his strong ministry to tax collectors, sinners, the lame, the sick, and the excluded. His strong words to the religious insiders in his hometown synagogue in Nazareth and the people's subsequent attempt to throw him off a cliff show the consequences of choosing to be empowered on behalf of the poor.

Luke 4:14–20 is a foundational text for me personally and for Tierra Nueva. Though I've read these verses hundreds, even thousands of times, fresh revelation shone out more brightly on a recent Sunday as I moved through two bilingual jail services into our Tierra Nueva English and Spanish services—bringing all of us greater clarity on the path to greater empowerment for life and ministry.

I begin each Bible study by introducing Jesus as a fellow human like us. People look surprised when I point out that when Jesus began his ministry in Nazareth, he hadn't done any miracles yet and he was already thirty—older than most of the inmates present in the jail's multipurpose room. Now he's officially starting to minister as he returns from the wilderness to Galilee. I describe Galilee as an isolated place like the upriver communities of Skagit Valley—a place where outsiders and outlaws hang out. Today's Galilee would have its share of meth labs and fugitive hideouts. Four or five of the tougher-looking men in one of my jail gatherings give, "Oh no, I'm busted," looks and then get smiley—and I recognize that they are in fact some of the major upriver dealers.

"So how did Jesus come to Galilee? What does the verse say again?" I ask.

"In the power of the Spirit," someone notes, and rereads Luke 4:14. We agree that maybe he needed special empowerment to minister in such a dark place. I point out that Jesus in fact was about to begin ministering in powerful ways—loving people by healing them, casting out their evil spirits, and defending them from legalists.

"What about you?" I ask. "Do you need more power? What are some of the areas of your life where you could use more power for breakthrough?"

Every man in the jail gatherings agrees he needs more power—power to overcome their addictions, to change, to love, to follow through with their deepest desires. All of us at Tierra Nueva feel as if we too need more power—power to resist temptation, to persevere, to love, to minister healing and deliverance, to believe.

"So where did Jesus get the power of the Spirit in the first place?" I ask people in each group— hoping this will give us a helpful clue leading us to greater levels of empowerment.

Some think he must have had it from birth, or even from the foundation of the world. Others aren't sure, awaiting an explanation.

"At his baptism?" someone asks, hesitatingly.

Sure enough, after a volunteer reads Luke 3:21–22, we all see that the Holy Spirit descended upon Jesus in bodily form like a dove. We overhear the voice from heaven that could come only from a Father say, "You are my beloved Son, in you I am well pleased" (au. trans.).

"What had Jesus done to get the Spirit and God's favor?" "What was he doing when the heavens were opened?"

"He'd just been baptized, and he was praying," someone rightly observes.

We talk about how prayer to God pierces through to heaven, creating an open heaven through which God's Spirit comes down upon Jesus (and us) in the gentle but real (bodily) form and God reveals himself as adoring parent, father of unconditional love. I remind people that these prayers can be cries or groanings that rise to God, piercing heaven—like those of Israelite slaves in Egyptian bondage that rose up to God (Exod. 2:23–24; 3:7–9).

Next we read Luke 4:1–2 and see how Jesus is described as full of the Holy Spirit, who leads him about in the wilderness, where he is tempted by the devil for forty days: "And Jesus, full of the Holy Spirit, returned from the Jordan and was led about by the Spirit in the wilderness for forty days, while tempted by the devil. And He ate nothing during those days; and when they had ended, He became hungry" (4:1–2 NASB).

"Do any of you experience temptation?" I ask people in each group, knowing that it's an easy question for everyone to answer.

"Yeah, all of us do, all the time," a guy responds, and people nod or raise their eyebrows.

The men in the jail tell me that drugs, alcohol, sex, and money are areas where they experience regular temptation. Outside the jail people add other temptations to this list: greed, getting too busy with nonessentials, putting security first, letting themselves be overcome with worry, anger, sadness, or other emotions.

We can see that Jesus' being full of the Holy Spirit did not make him immune to temptations—especially when he was hungry. In fact, the Spirit takes him into places where he experiences direct confrontations with the tempter. If this is true for Jesus, we should expect this for ourselves too. Nearly everyone appears to agree that temptations abound when you are pursuing God. We also decide that Jesus shows us that we need to be *full of the Holy Spirit* in order to face temptations without being crushed!

I point out that Jesus goes from being full of the Holy Spirit to returning to Galilee, this time to minister *in the power* of the Spirit.

"Could the move from 'full' to 'in the power' between Luke 4:1–14 be showing us that empowerment comes to Jesus, and us, as we face the devil's provocations and overcome temptation?" I ask.

Men in the jail and we too are excited about this idea—that we all can receive more power and spiritual strength as we face and overcome temptation. In Luke's temptation narrative we have noticed together that the devil's strategy is to undermine the basis of Jesus and our empowerment by specifically calling into question our identities as God's children with his "*If* you are the son of God" in the first and third temptations (4:3, 9). The devil's temptations seek also to usurp the Father's place by tempting Jesus and us to serve him in exchange for power and control and heed his provocations to fruitless action. Jesus' empowerment increases as he exercises authority over the enemy. Jesus' empowerment and ours increase as we exercise authority over the enemy, ordering the devil not to tempt us and to worship and serve God alone.

We at Tierra Nueva find it encouraging to learn that as we clarify our identities as God's beloved daughters, learn to hear God's voice and exercise authority over spiritual enemies through resisting temptations, our empowerment increases. The example of Jesus of moving from being full of the Spirit to "in the power"offers an attractive incentive to resist.

"What is the reason for receiving more power?" I ask each group.

"Is this power just for Jesus and us to use for our own interests?" These questions bring us to the heart of Sunday's reading:

"The Spirit of the Lord is upon me because he has anointed me," reads Jesus (Luke 4:18 NRSV). For what purpose did the Spirit anoint him, I ask.

"To preach Good News to the poor!" is Jesus' first priority, someone observes.

The Mexican farm workers in our Tierra Nueva Spanish service look delighted as they see that Jesus uses his power from the Spirit *on behalf of the poor*—and not for the amassing of more power and wealth for the already powerful. And the news gets better and better.

- "He has sent me to proclaim release to the prisoners"
- "recovery of sight to the blind"
- "to set free those who are downtrodden"
- "to proclaim the favorable year of the Lord."

I ask people in each of our services if they are attracted to this way of Jesus: of being full of the Spirit to face temptation, of growing in the power of the Spirit through facing and overcoming temptation in the name of Jesus, of having the Spirit upon them to engage in the ministry of Jesus.

We read together Jesus' final words to his disciples before he ascended to heaven, recorded in Luke 24:49 (NRSV), where he stresses the need to wait for the Spirit: "And see, I am sending upon you what my Father promised; so stay here in the city until you have been clothed with power from on high."

I tell the men about Pentecost, fifty days after Jesus' resurrection, when the Holy Spirit came upon all those that were "constantly devoting themselves to prayer" (Acts 1:14 NRSV). The disciples went from being fearful, disempowered men to bold communicators of the good news, who themselves performed the same sorts of signs and wonders as Jesus in the face of terrible persecution.

In the jail my colleague Chris and I invite three young men to pray for more of the Spirit. A heavily tattooed gang member we've known for years laughs as God's presence envelops him. The hands of the young man to my right burn on my back—telling me he too is receiving and giving. We soak up waves of love that seem to flood over us in the few minutes before the guards come. In our last two services at Tierra Nueva, Gracie, my Honduran colleague Lolito, and I follow the person serving communion wine, anointing each communicant with oil and praying for greater fullness of the Spirit.

Epifania, a beloved farm worker and member of our fellowship who a few years before had experienced the miraculous cancellation of a removal order, mentioned at the end of chapter 4, asks if we can pray for the pain in her wrist and shoulder to go away. Troy and Roger excitedly tell us how when they laid hands on her, Epifania's arm become hot and all the pain left. The kingdom of God seems to be coming as we await and receive more of God's anointing through the Holy Spirit—freely given from an open heaven as we pray and receive our inheritance as adopted children of God.

For years I have understood that we, like Jesus, are invited to read and appropriate Isaiah 61:1–3 as our mission statement, affirming in our own contexts that "today this Scripture has been fulfilled in your hearing." This notion is supported by the genealogy between Jesus' baptism and his temptation, where he is depicted as the prototype descendant of Adam and Son of God (Luke 3:23–38). We enter into our spiritual inheritance as children of Adam, children of God by adoption through baptism—growing into our identity and authority as children of God as we follow Jesus. Luke also warns future disciples that while this may sound nice and easy at the beginning, trouble will come as we recognize that our spiritual family is universal—transcending barriers of nationality, ethnicity, gender, religion, and economic class.

Luke 4:22 suggests that we can expect today's religious insider equivalents of Jesus' nodding hometown synagogue attendees to find a radical Scripture like Isaiah 61:1–3 initially agreeable. The problem comes for Jesus and for us when we resist religious insider expectations that he use his power mainly for them and begin to define who the poor, blind, prisoners, and oppressed really are.

Jesus recognizes that religious insiders love signs and wonders of God's favor and expect him to perform. He directly confronts people's desire to see power exercised on their behalf when he says, "No doubt you will quote this proverb to Me, 'Physician, heal yourself! Whatever we heard was done at Capernaum, do here in your home town as well'" (Luke 4:23 NASB).

Jesus shows he knows his application of Isaiah 61 will not be welcome among those who have not departed from the land of slavery (Egypt) through the killing and purifying waters of baptism: "No prophet is welcome in his home town" (4:24).

Jesus invites his Jewish compatriots in Nazareth to remember that Israel was not a beneficiary of two of the biggest miracles done by the famous prophets Elijah and Elisha. Both prophets were rejected by Israel's leadership and worked miracles instead for people deemed completely unworthy of God's care and attention: a widow from the land of Sidon and a military commander of Israel's archenemy Syria. Jesus identifies with these prophets and shows his people that nothing had changed. The power will be used on behalf of the excluded and despised, while religious insiders remain outside the kingdom. "But I say to you in truth, there were many widows in Israel in the days of Elijah, when the sky was shut up for three years and six months, when a great famine came over all the land; and yet Elijah was sent to none of them, but only to Zarephath, in the land of Sidon, to a woman who was a widow" (4:25–26 NASB).

We are invited to notice, along with the people of Nazareth, that Elijah was ministered to by the Sidonian woman who received God's miraculous provision and the raising of her son from the dead. These events happened just after Elijah himself fled the persecution of Jezebel and Ahab after the confrontation with the prophets of Baal on Mount Carmel. Elijah had fled as an outlaw into the wilderness east of the Jordan (1 Kgs. 17:5)—the very wilderness Jesus has just returned from "in the power of the Spirit."

The Lord's command to Elijah to go to Zarephath in Sidon and receive provision from an impoverished Gentile widow (1 Kgs. 17:9) invites the people of Nazareth to embrace Jesus—following the example of an unclean Gentile woman. Jesus points the people from his hometown to Elijah's and his own openness to foreigners, women, and widows—people viewed as unclean and unworthy of God's attention and their attention. Jesus suggests that following the example of the Gentile widow's openness to the prophet and faith in his word may lead to miraculous provision and even raisings from the dead—as they did for the Sidonian woman (17:17–24). Jesus shows that God's call extends to the marginalized, who are included as ministers in the kingdom of God.

Jesus follows up his first offensive word with one that stings his hearers even more—inviting them and us to include even the worst of our national enemies as beneficiaries of the best of God's care: "And there were many lepers in Israel in the time of Elisha the prophet; and none of them was cleansed, but only Naaman the Syrian" (4:27).

Jesus invites the people in his hometown to remember how God healed a military commander of one of Israel's archenemies of his leprosy (2 Kgs. 5:1–14). Jesus' example suggests that Israelite insiders should look to the example of both unclean Gentile enemies like Naaman and the prophet Elisha. Naaman humbles himself by listening to the word of God through Elisha's servant Gehazi and through his own servants. Jesus invites his villagers and us into Elisha's openness to minister outside the borders. Modern equivalents for Americans to Naaman could easily include national enemies like notorious Islamic extremist Osama bin Laden.

Jesus' listeners in the synagogue in Nazareth are enraged to the point that they cast him out of the city and attempt to throw him off a cliff. The ethnic and religious insiders cast Jesus out into his mission based in Capernaum, in ways that are highly suggestive of how people may need to be launched into ministry among the marginalized today. Later, when Jesus recruits and appoints seventy others to go out ahead of him to every city where he plans to go, he tells them: "The harvest is plentiful, but the laborers are few; therefore beseech the Lord of the harvest to send out [literally, cast out] laborers into His harvest" (Luke 10:2 NASB).

In the book of Acts, Paul and Barnabas are cast out of Antioch's synagogues and entire region by persecutors (Acts 13:50). This is how they end up in Iconium, where they minister with signs and wonders before having to flee to Lystra and Derbe, where they keep proclaiming the good news (Acts 14:6–7). Paul and Silas are cast into prison in Philippi (Acts 16:23, 37), where miraculous events take place that lead to the conversion of the jailer and his entire household (16:25–34). Perhaps Jesus urges the workers to beg the Lord of the harvest to cast workers out because he prefers they are sent out by faith communities as willing harvesters. In Matthew's account, Jesus' compassion for the masses and his awareness of their distress and sadness is behind this urgent plea for workers to be cast out: "And seeing the multitudes, He felt compassion for them, because they were distressed and downcast like sheep without a shepherd. Then He said to His disciples, 'The harvest is plentiful . . .'" (Matt. 9:36 NASB).

In Luke the actions of the people of Nazareth—violently casting Jesus out and attempting to throw him off a cliff—propel him to Capernaum. There, as in Mark's Gospel (Mark 1:21ff.), his mission begins in earnest with his first miracle. He casts out an unclean spirit from someone inside the synagogue before ministering healing outside to Simon's mother-in-law (Luke 4:38–39) and to others.

> While the sun was setting, all who had any sick with various diseases brought them to Him; and laying His hands on every one of them, He was healing them. And demons also were coming out of many, crying out and saying, "You are the Son of God!" And rebuking them, He would not allow them to speak, because they knew Him to be the Christ. And when day came, He departed and went to a lonely place; and the multitudes were searching for Him, and came to Him, and tried to keep Him from going away from them. But He said to them, "I must preach the kingdom of God to the other cities also, for I was sent for this purpose." (4:40–43 NASB)

We see from this scripture that "all who had any sick with various diseases brought them to him." The power of the Spirit in Jesus attracted people who needed relief. Multitudes searched for him, showing how the masses of poor found Jesus attractive. What might this look like today?

By looking carefully at the beneficiaries of Jesus' ministry in the Gospels, we can see more clearly who today's most likely equivalents might be. Undocumented immigrant women and violent offender men would clearly be candidates to receive ministry from Jesus' followers for the purpose of themselves ministering.

The county jail where I minister was built to house 85 people. Until recently Skagit County has had the highest crime rate in Washington State. There are currently around 5,000 active warrants for people's arrest in Skagit County—requiring law-enforcement officers to enforce selectively based on a triage approach. The average number of men and women housed in the jail in 2006 was 185. The courts release (PR) most inmates charged with misdemeanors on their own recognizance to make room for people charged with felonies—with a priority on detaining those charged with violent crimes. Many of the men with whom I read Scripture are "violent offenders" with past convictions and current charges such as assault, armed robbery, rape, and murder.

Outside the jail violent men make the headlines daily, and many people consider them deserving of banishment or death. Yet so many people in North America today resort to violent responses to problems that the category "violent offenders" is rapidly growing to include a significant percentage of the population. God has called me and many at Tierra Nueva to seek, find, bind up, love, pray for, and in various ways minister to violent men and women—both inside jail and outside jail. God is calling the entire church to reach out in love to men and women prone to violence, inviting them into a life filled with adventure, love, and meaning as agents of transformation in the company of Jesus.

Every week I have the privilege of seeing hardened, violent men profoundly touched by God's affectionate embrace. When people in our weekly jail Bible studies come to realize truly that God adores them, they respond to God's call and become disciples—often twelve to fifteen at a time.

Sinners' attraction to Jesus should come as no surprise. In Luke 15:1 (NASB) "all the tax-gatherers and [all] the sinners were coming near Him to listen to Him." Jesus was known as a "friend of sinners" (Matt. 11:19). "The Son of Man has come to save that which was lost. . . . It is not the will of your father who is in heaven that one of these little ones [lost sheep] perish" (Matt 18:11, 14 NASB).

I often say to people in our jail Bible studies, "Take it as a compliment that you are harassed and targeted by the Enemy. He's trying to take you down because he knows what a threat you'd be if you were an agent of love for the kingdom of God." This is not empty flattery, but a conviction repeatedly supported by Scripture.

I point out to men in the jail and people in the churches on a regular basis that throughout Scripture we see God highly valuing violent men, calling them as God's choice ministers. Moses was called, after murdering an Egyptian, to be Israel's liberator. David was anointed after years of violence defending sheep and attacking Philistines, and became the author of our psalms of worship. Jesus met the apostle Paul in the midst of his violent campaign against the first Christians. Paul writes powerfully about God's choice of himself:

> I thank Christ Jesus our Lord, who has strengthened me, because He considered me faithful, putting me into service; even though I was formerly a blasphemer and a persecutor and a violent aggressor. And yet I was shown mercy, because I acted ignorantly in unbelief; and the grace of our Lord was more than abundant, with the faith and love which are found in Christ Jesus. It is a trustworthy statement, deserving full acceptance, that Christ Jesus came into the world to save sinners, among whom I am foremost of all. And yet for this reason I found mercy, in order that in me as the foremost, Jesus Christ might demonstrate His perfect patience, as an example for those who would believe in Him for eternal life. (1 Tim. 1:12–16 NASB)

Violent offender types like Paul and many others were targeted and attacked by both flesh-and-blood enemies and spiritual enemies. I believe that those most involved in violence today are at the top of God's list of people whom God is seeking and calling—and should be our highest priority in a different kind of Jesus-inspired war on terror. God calls the worst as an example for those who would believe. So who and where might these big, bad "little ones" be?

County jails across North America are filled with people charged with violent crimes, as well as others labeled "felons" with violent convictions. Rather than demanding harsher prison sentences and fines that increase shame and violence, our incarcerated neighbors need much more love, respect, and the honor of being invited to follow Jesus to bring life and liberation to the world.

Al-Qaeda and Taliban combatants and people who strap explosives to their bodies need to placed at the top of our prayer and outreach priorities, and certainly not destroyed. We must stop excluding enemy combatants from those for whom we grieve, as if their deaths are less important than those of innocent civilians or U.S. troops. This grieves the Holy Spirit, who comes to comfort and defend.

The world's many orphans definitely need to be sponsored so their needs are provided for. But let us not forget that most violent men are grown-up neglected and abused children or orphans in need of love, healing, and spiritual adoption—which includes a calling. Rather than letting them be easy prey for the military recruiters, drug dealers, and other forces that would rob, kill, and destroy, join us in recruiting them as workers in God's harvest fields.

Loving enemies is not an easy or natural task—but it is at the heart of our calling. This kind of extreme love can come only directly from God. I have been constantly humbled both by my weakness before the powers of violence, addictions, and death and by the bigness of God's love. Saying yes to the call to seek lost sheep until we find them requires more of God's abundant love and the anointing of the Holy Spirit than we yet have. I am thankful that God is rich in mercy, full of love and goodness, and eager to fill us so we can "not be overcome by evil, but overcome evil with good" (Rom. 12:21).

Jesus invites disciples to join with him in his agenda, clearly articulated when he says, "I did not come to call the righteous, but sinners" (Mark 2:17 NASB). As more and more "violent aggressors" are recruited into God's service as agents of love, the kingdom of God will certainly be drawing closer. This happens as we go out to where people are, sharing about a God who is so good that people will find themselves naturally attracted.

After our first village outreach in Mozambique, followed by a week of teaching a group of two hundred Mozambican pastors, Iris leader Heidi Baker arranged for us to go out into the bush to minister alongside a Macua-speaking pastor. Two young men who had grown up in Iris's orphanage in Maputo, Jose and Elvis, accompanied us to the home of Pastor Juma, where we pitched our tent. I was surprised to learn that Pastor Juma had been a Christian for only six years and a pastor for five. Already he had founded twenty-five churches. Like all Iris pastors, Pastor Juma receives no salary but works his land and lives by faith— following literally Jesus' teaching in Matthew 10:9–10 and Luke 9:3 and 10:4 about freely giving what you have freely received and carrying no purse, bag, or shoes. When I asked him how he starts churches, he told me that he begins by gathering those in his faith community willing to pray with him and fasts breakfast and lunch for ten days in preparation for going into a new community, praying and studying the Bible throughout the day, breaking each day's fast in the style of the Muslim Ramadan with a dinner.

"If it is a particularly hard village, we go on a total fast of no food or water for three days," he specified. "By the time we enter the village, the hard work has already been done. God shows us the homes where people are ready to receive. People come to faith, and we begin meeting in their homes."

Pastor Juma did not even mention the many healings that accompany the proclamation of him and other Iris Ministries pastors—to avoid falling into spiritual pride. I asked him if he practiced Jesus' commands in Matthew 10, even the one about raising the dead. Indeed he had seen two people raised from the dead, beginning with his own daughter, who after a long illness died of cerebral malaria while bundled to her mother's back in the marketplace.

"We placed her on our bed and gathered the community around her to pray. After several hours, she defecated and then began to cry. She was immediately healed and has not had malaria for five years since that happened," he told me. Many neighbors believed as a result of this miracle and began attending the church that gathers in a mud and stick building beside his hut.

After conversing I learned to my dismay that I was expected to preach that night from the back of a flatbed after showing the Macua version of the Jesus film in the village of Miessi. After dark we piled into the back of a flatbed truck full of villagers from his church, singing worship songs as we bumped along a potholed dirt road into the town square of a village of mud huts. Jose and Elvis quickly set out huge speakers and a massive screen, fired up the gas generator and hooked up the PowerPoint projector to a DVD player that began playing clips of African villagers dancing to lively worship music. People began to appear from every corner of the village, attracted to rare evening entertainment in a region with no electricity. By the time the Jesus film was showing, some 1,200 were gathered to watch the movie. After Pastor Juma and I prayed together, Luke and I walked the periphery of the crowd, amazed at the masses of impoverished villagers, men, women, and children. Throughout the hour-and-a-half film I found myself walking the periphery of the crowd under an awe-inspiring canopy of stars, crying out to God for wisdom and direction for my talk. What was I to say to these Macua-speaking Mozambican villagers—most of whom were devoted to a mix of traditional African religion and Islam? Luke and I both felt that Jesus wanted to bring healing to people's backs, necks, and feet—so they could farm and carry water and firewood without pain. I also felt compelled to share about God's love for criminals and violent men—sharing some stories from Skagit County jail.

As soon as the film ended, I was introduced in Portuguese and in Macua and given a microphone. I had been warned by Pastor Juma that many people would likely leave for their homes as soon as the film was over—not wanting to be preached to. Just as I was about to speak, something quite unexpected happened. A man found a snake in the middle of the crowd, which he flung with a stick onto the ground lit by the PowerPoint projector. He then proceeded to stomp it to death before the crowd. I later learned that the crowd had viewed this snake as having been sent by the witch doctor to disrupt the meeting. The discovery and killing of this poisonous serpent in the middle of a crowd in the darkness was viewed as a sign of the superior power of the God who had sent us. Most of the people stayed to hear me speak on God's affection for the poor and God's longing to embrace and recruit into his service people afflicted by addictions and prone to violence. Many people apparently were healed of pain in their necks, backs, and feet when I stopped in the middle of my preaching to invite people in the crowd to raise their hands and receive prayer for healing if they were suffering. When I called for men who felt attracted to Jesus' love and pursuit of them to respond by coming forward to give their lives over to Jesus and receive prayer, many ragged, violent-looking men streamed forward. One man with fetishes draped around his neck, who claimed he had been living in the cemetery, gave his life over to become a disciple of Jesus. Before a crowd of onlookers he removed the fetishes he'd received from the witch doctor from around his neck and handed them to Pastor Juma, asking him to destroy them.

After returning to Pemba from the village Luke and I walked along the beaches of the Indian Ocean. Orphaned children not yet adopted by Iris tried to sell us carvings, artwork, musical instruments, bartering for shirts, shampoo. Luke wanted to adopt some kids, give away his clothes, buy whatever we could to help these entrepreneurial street kids.

One night we talked with Shara Pradhan, a woman in her mid-twenties who serves as Heidi's personal assistant. Shara told me how inspired she was working with Rolland and Heidi Baker, who had worked as missionaries for over twenty-five years without making formal fund-raising appeals. They practiced literally Philippians 4:6 "Be anxious for nothing, but in everything by prayer and supplication with thanksgiving let your requests be made known to God." God has consistently supplied their needs and caused their ministry to grow into some 24 countries. God also supplies the needs of their thousands of village pastors, who receive no salary but depend on subsistence farming and God's provision. Shara told how she too had been living by faith, making her needs known only to God, and how God has been taking care of her in miraculous ways. She, the Bakers, and many of the Western missionaries serving with Iris are convinced that Jesus' words to carry no money, extra coat, etc. apply to them as well—even though their expenses far exceed those of subsistence farmer pastors. As Shara told her stories I felt God nudging me to give her every dollar that I had in our possession.

The next day Luke and I flew down to Maputo, where we were picked up and driven out to Xai Xai, where I was to participate in a regional conference for Mozambican pastors and leaders. The conference started with an outreach in a nearby village, where the Jesus film was to be shown, followed by preaching and prayer for healing. We putted along a dirt road behind Heidi and Rolland and other Iris leaders trying to find that evening's village. When we arrived, we discovered that our baggage had been stolen from the back of the canopied truck somewhere along that road. So there we were without money and without clothes.

That night for some reason, men like those I work with in the jail were drawn to me as I stood in a crowd of African villagers. One by one they began asking me how they could get free from addictions and from troubles with the police. I offered to pray for them and soon had seven or eight men around me. Heidi came over, and we prayed together for these men. That night Heidi had to return to Pemba and came to say good-bye to Luke and me. She handed me an envelope with an unexpected gift of cash that was nearly three times what I had given away the night before. The next day the Mozambican leaders Jose and Supresa took us shopping in the poverty-stricken center of Xai Xai, insisting on buying our clothes! This humbling experience has increased my faith and expectation of God's provision.

Right now at New Earth–Tierra Nueva we are being blessed by a growing number of young men and women who are feeling called to join us in ministry to inmates, ex-offenders, immigrants, and the homeless. None of them is getting a salary. People are working odd jobs to survive and pouring out their lives in service, seeking first the kingdom of God and God's righteousness. God is inviting us to step into the kingdom of heaven and its economy of grace and inclusion. "On earth as in heaven" does not have to wait for perfected lives, organized boards of directors, or funding. Jesus is inviting us here and now into a movement with unlimited potential.

Recently, seventy-five Skagit County jail inmates in five groups participated in a study on Psalm 23 and Luke 15:1–7. Before reading, I point out that this psalm is spoken by a sheep with an ideal shepherd, unlike my family's llama shepherd, who loses our sheep to coyotes that scatter them and nab the easiest prey. We start with verses 4–5, which are easiest for people in crisis to hear: "Even though I walk through the valley of the shadow of death, I fear no evil; for Thou art with me; Thy rod and Thy staff, they comfort me. Thou dost prepare a table before me in the presence of my enemies" (NASB).

The men assume the shepherd's rod and staff are for correction, to hit or snag the straying sheep. I often ask men in jail, "How many of you have been beaten by a stick or club?" Nearly everyone always raises their hand. In Mozambique, on a second trip, in June 2007, I bring a thick stick of bamboo and a long piece of firewood to a teaching session and ask several hundred pastors in training how many of them had been beaten with a rod or staff like these. Nearly everyone had. I tell the men in jail and the Mozambican pastors that I know from experience that sheep only run farther away when threatened or struck. I point out that the rod and staff are weapons the shepherd used to fend off predators.

"What forces prey on you?" I ask men gathered in the jail.

"The police," one says, eliciting laughs from everyone. Others name emotions, drugs, addictions, obligations, the court system, jealousy, and anger. We might add pressure to perform, busyness, stress, resentment, and media bombardment. The African pastors mention malaria, HIV/AIDS, poverty, witchcraft, and thieves.

The psalmist's description of the shepherd who brings comfort through protection and sets a table in the presence of enemies is appealing. Everyone finds the images in the psalm highly desirable—lying down beside still waters, having your soul restored, being guided, not fearing evil, God's continual presence, dwelling in the house of the Lord.

"If we're not experiencing the Shepherd's presence, how do we come into the sheep herd?" I ask.

"Praying and reading the Bible?" someone asks, assuming these to be right answers. I agree in part, but invite the men to check out the parable in Luke 15:1–7 to see how one lost sheep got connected.

First, I introduce the tax gatherers in the passage as bottom feeders, disliked because of illicit gains at the people's expense. The men identify some modern equivalents: loan sharks, undercover drug task force agents, and telephone solicitors. I encourage them to identify equivalents to tax collectors and sinners from a mainstream perspective—to prepare them better to understand the scribes' and Pharisees' reaction. People settle on "meth-cooks" for tax collectors and "felons" for sinners. We choose religious people for Pharisees, and law enforcers for scribes.

Then someone reads Luke 15:1–2 like this: "Now all the meth-cooks and felons were coming near him to listen to him. And both the religious people and the law enforcers began to grumble, saying, 'This man receives felons and eats with them.'"

The men laugh at the reader's contemporary version. I ask them what kind of person Jesus would have to be to attract meth-cooks and felons to himself.

"He'd have to be on the side of the people and not the system," a man says.

"He must have been viewed as safe—not a snitch," someone else says.

Everyone agrees that Jesus must have been well known as someone who clearly sided with the bad guys. After all, the text says that *all* the tax collectors and *all* the sinners were attracted to him.

"It seems that Jesus' identification with those whom society rejected was total and obvious, leading to judgments from the authorities," I summarize. "Why do you think the scribes and Pharisees reacted to Jesus the way he did?" I ask.

"They thought of themselves as better than everyone else—like they were the only ones who deserved Jesus' attention," someone says.

In Bible study after Bible study on this text with inmates, undocumented immigrants, and impoverished Honduran campesinos, I have seen people clearly identify the contemporary equivalents of the scribes and Pharisees—the "them" who exclude the "us bad-guys" who are reading together about the attractive, inclusive, embracing Jesus. Lots of pain and bitterness gets expressed as people identify prosecutors, judges, priests, pastors, religious people, and family members who have wounded them through excluding, shaming, blaming, judging, despising them. I ask a volunteer to read the story Jesus tells to the scribes and Pharisees to move the study in the direction of more good news.

> And he told them this parable, saying, "What man among you, if he has a hundred sheep and has lost one of them, does not leave the ninety-nine in the open pasture, and go after the one which is lost, until he finds it? And when he has found it, he lays it on his shoulders, rejoicing. And when he comes home, he calls together his friends and his neighbors, saying to them, 'Rejoice with me, for I have found my sheep which was lost!' I tell you that in the same way, there will be more joy in heaven over one sinner who repents, than over ninety-nine righteous persons who need no repentance." (Luke 15:3–7 NASB)

"What did the lost sheep have to do to get connected to the shepherd?" I ask.

"Wander off," says one man, intrigued.

"Get lost," another says.

"Nothing," says someone else with a smile.

I look around and see the men looking surprised or happy.

"So what does the pastor do when he finds the sheep?" I ask. "Does he scold it? Does he punish it?"

"No," someone responds. "He takes it on his shoulders and rejoices."

"Where does he bring it?" I ask. "To the jail?" "To church?"

"No," someone says with a big smile. "He brings it home. He throws a party for his friends and family."

Everyone agrees that they'd want to be found if they would be taken home to a party thrown in their honor.

I then ask what they think Jesus means when he says, "There will be more joy in heaven over one sinner who repents." I know that this final word appears to snatch away the good news that's just beginning to dawn on people used to resigning themselves to their habitual sinner status. I know that most people on the streets and in the church understand repentance as being sorry for your sin, requiring heartfelt contrition and change. I point out that "repentance" in Greek literally means having an after-mind, or another mind—thinking differently.

We return to verses 1–2, and I ask what image of God is visible through the attitude of the Pharisees and scribes. People note that this God looks judgmental, grumbling, uncaring, exclusive, legalistic. Nobody feels attraction to this God. In contrast, God revealed through Jesus is compassionate, a friend of sinners, pursuing, finding, inclusive, loving.

"Are you attracted to Jesus?" I ask, and I hear nothing but "Yes" and "Sí."

"Then if you—like the tax-collectors and sinners—feel attracted right now, you are repenting. You are drawing near to Jesus to listen to him. Your mind is changing regarding who God really is. You like what you see and want more." The men agree.

We reread the psalm and note that we can experience union with the Shepherd—receiving all the benefits—because this Shepherd is seeking and finding us and we are attracted. Jesus receives us at his table, even though we're surrounded by enemies.

I end by pointing out that the Shepherd wants to anoint our heads with oil, which equals sharing with us his anointing as Messiah. When we receive his anointing, he gives us authority over God's enemies, much as ancient Israelite kings were empowered to exercise dominion over the enemies of God's kingdom. I offer to anoint with oil anyone desirous of being united and empowered by Jesus. Nobody refuses. They appear eager to be recruited and empowered to engage in something that is both adventurous and of eternal significance. We end the study with prayers for families, courts, and physical ailments.

The growing delinquency in our communities in North America and throughout the world is fueled largely by a crisis in meaning and purpose. Many young people see no place they can make a difference in the world. While immigrants straight from Mexico are willing to do stoop labor harvesting strawberries and cucumbers or working long hours in meatpacking and fish-processing plants, their children growing up in a culture of affluence usually won't. Joining a gang, dealing drugs, and partying offer far more excitement, sense of belonging, and meaning than a life struggling to survive on low-paying work.

The riots of immigrant youth in France in February 2006 deeply upset the French people and leaders throughout Europe. Gangs of angry young people took to the streets burning cars, breaking windows, vandalizing everything in their paths in ways that looked senseless and chaotic but were at the same time organized and widespread, happening simultaneously in cities across the nation.

These riots reflect a crisis of meaning and purpose at the heart of Western society. Young people throughout the world are desperate for a legitimate and sustainable way to live out their lives. They are ready and willing to give their lives to something worth dying for, but it is not being offered to them. The parable of the laborers in the vineyard is prophetic for our time.

In this parable Jesus says the kingdom of heaven is like a landowner who goes out early in the morning to hire workers for his vineyard. He agrees to pay people a denarius for the day and sends them out. Apparently his need for more and more workers compels him to keep returning to the marketplace, where he recruits groups of idle workers at the third hour, the sixth hour, and the ninth hour. Finally, near the end of the day, at the eleventh hour he returns again to find people idle. The vineyardist's question and their response highlight Jesus' assessment of the problem then and now. Isabelle Rivière's powerful commentary on Matthew 20:7 speaks prophetically into our time.

> "Why have you been standing here idle all day long?" They said to him, "Because no one hired us." He said to them, "You also go into the vineyard" (Matt. 20:7).
>
> And so, that which is good for nothing for the world is always good for the Lord. Those whom the human masters have disdained as unusable, the divine Master, he would always have a job to offer them, because the only work that he demands of us is to love him, and since he makes humans expressly for this, there is not one who has not received from him the capacity to love. Everyone, consequently, is adequate all the time, in every place, and in every case, to there agree to do [this work].
>
> Let us rejoice then, the incapable, the little, the disabled, the unfortunate, the worn out, the awkward, the ignorant, the defeated, those who are too ugly for one to love, and those who are not rich enough for someone to marry, those who are not gifted like those who have not known what to do with their gifts, all those who have not succeeded, all those who are without a "situation," without hopes, and without occupation, those that the world has rejected, and those that it has broken; take up courage, take up life: if men do not want us any more, God, he, the universal Master and the perfect patron, God does want us.
>
> And he even wants us, he desires us, he searches for us! At every hour of the day he goes out to search for the left-behind ones and the strays, and, without worrying about references or certificates, antecedents or aptitudes, he gathers uncritically, without distinction all those who let themselves be gathered.
>
> However radically inept that we have been recognized according to human judgment, failed by them (to all the candidates) small and big, you find us always capable enough for you, oh inexhaustible Master. And you do not fail one of those who take the exam of love, because infallibly you fill with yourself the difference between that which we value and that which we should value to be worthy to serve you. And if we have no available inheritance, or the least amount of money available as we pass through this mortal life, we always have the hope—that by our simple agreement it becomes certainty and even fulfillment—to possess today, and forever if we want it, the salary guaranteed to each of God's workers: God himself, the God apart from whom there is no other.

. . . That is why it doesn't matter in the end for the worker the hour in which he enters into his employment; the position is always vacant, the position claims him always; in God nobody, ever shows up in excess, since the positions/spaces are infinite.[1]

I was speaking in Paris at the ecumenical conference Embrasse Nos Coeurs, shortly after the youth riots in France, on Jesus as recruiter of harvesters, who are themselves recruiters for a growing movement to advance the kingdom of God throughout the world. At the end of my talk I invited people who felt called enough to give the Lord of the harvest permission to cast them out into the harvest to stand and come forward for prayer. I was surprised and deeply moved to see what looked like the whole assembly of several hundred people rise to their feet and stream forward, themselves clearly longing to join Jesus, the disciples, the Samaritan woman, and countless later followers to go out to wherever people are idle, to recruit them into the adventure of faith. I have since given similar talks and had similar responses from more mainstream audiences in Europe and North America.

At the same time, however, it is clear from the parable, the Gospel accounts, and the current experience of believers throughout the world that resistance to total inclusion of the poor and the excluded can be expected. As the kingdom of God advances, those currently holding power will become unsettled and oppose the movement of the Spirit. Jesus was resisted and finally crucified, as were the apostles then and now. As the kingdom advances, we are reminded that though we can expect it here and now, his kingdom is not of this world.

Chapter 7

Announcing the Victory of the Cross

Jesus is depicted throughout the Gospels as Israel's awaited Messiah, the Savior of the world. The Gospel writers also present Jesus as establishing the new covenant in a way that completely breaks with the old covenant in his proclamation and embodiment of the kingdom of God. The newness, otherness, and demanding nature of Jesus' way of being the Messiah are often missed or rejected today by those claiming to be Christians. Jesus' way of redemptive suffering on the cross must be recovered and intentionally and explicitly embraced if we're to see and enter the kingdom of God.

We have seen in chapter 2 how Jesus begins his ministry by first himself entering into the waters of a baptism of repentance for the forgiveness of sins—symbolically dying under water along with the enemies of his kingdom and rising filled with the Spirit to demonstrate a new way: embodying God's will, on earth as in heaven. His ministry is made complete when he goes to the cross. There he willingly embraces weakness and apparent defeat, dying as God's beloved Son and the lamb slain for the sins of the world. On the cross Jesus shows how far God himself will go in taking upon himself humanity's hatred, violence, guilt, shame, and sin. Jesus lays down his life into the hands of sinners in total trust before the Father. Jesus the Messiah, the anointed one, embodies the only effective way of combating and defeating evil in this world: he steps toward his enemies who oppose his anointing and his kingdom. He allows himself to be delivered into the hands of sinners and forgives them all as they put him to death. "Father, forgive them; for they know not what they do" (Luke 23:34 RSV). Jesus defeats the power of the Evil One in the most unexpected of ways, and invites his church to follow. "Then Jesus said to His disciples, 'If any one wishes to come after Me, let him deny himself, and take up his cross, and follow Me. For whoever wishes to save his life shall lose it; but whoever loses his life for My sake shall find it'" (Matt. 16:24–25 NASB). Jesus' way of forgiveness and love of enemy to the point of death creates a scandal and division for some. It is welcomed by the desperate, beaten down, and tired—who seek relief from human justice, vengeance, and hate—as the following story of three Honduran enemies, Julian, Ernesto, and Lolito, illustrates.

Julian and the two Cruz brothers, Ernesto and Lolito, live in the remote mountain village of Guachiplin in the Wild West–like center of Honduras. During a break while I was there to give a four-day course, I visit Julian, a farmer then fifty-three years old, whose body and face are crisscrossed with long scars from machete wounds. Julian plants corn and beans and makes sugar from sugar cane. He is working on his ox-driven "trapiche," a device used to squeeze the juice out of sugar cane so he can boil it down into raw sugar. Julian tells me how he has finally come to the point of forgiving Ernesto and Lolito, the brothers who nearly killed him years before.

Ernesto and Lolito tell me their version of the conflict and reconciliation with Julian, which began years before. Julian was at that time serving his term as his village's civilian police liaison. Julian had a disagreement with Ostilio, the father of Ernesto and Lolito, that led him to report to the nearest Honduran army commander that Ostilio owned firearms that he was using to threaten people. Soldiers came to Ostilio's house in the middle of the night. They beat him and confiscated his hunting rifle and revolver. In another incident, after a cow had died giving birth, Ostilio had removed the hide so it wouldn't go to waste. Julian falsely accused him before the authorities of slaughtering a cow without a permit, which led to his arrest, jailing, and heavy fine. Other incidents between the families kept tensions alive. Then four or five years later at a fiesta Julian showed up very drunk.

"I was dancing with my wife-to-be," recounts Lolito. "Julian came after me, body slamming me and mocking me. He continued to bother me. I was angry, pulled out my gun, and got it ready to use. My wife and cousin didn't let me, they pulled me away. He laughed and hit my cousin on the back, taunting him with 'We'll see who's a man.' He then left the fiesta for his house, returning with a machete in his right hand and a revolver in his left. He stood at the door and shot at my brother Ernesto, who put out his hand with a flashlight in it just in time. The bullet hit the flashlight and ricocheted onto his back, causing him to fall to the ground wounded. Our older brother Eduardo then jumped in, saying, 'Now you're going to have to kill me.' Eduardo cut up Julian all over his body with his machete."

Julian's family rushed him to the hospital hours away by nearly impassible dirt roads. That night Julian's family members stalked the Cruz family, seeking revenge. Meanwhile Julian hovered for many days at the point of death. Finally he recovered enough to return home, where he began plotting vengeance against the brothers.

"Our brother Eduardo was arrested and sentenced to four years in prison," recounts Lolito. "Julian's cousins from outside the area were coming and going, looking for us to get revenge. Ernesto and I carried our machetes around for the next year, ready for a fight."

"For years I had been planning my revenge," says Julian as we stand under the tile roof covering his sugar cane mill, scars cutting through his lips, like stitches dividing baffles in a down comforter. "Now I have left all that in God's hands," he continues. "I know that my part is to forgive. God will take care of the rest."

Ramiro, the Tierra Nueva promoter who visited impoverished subsistence farmers in Guachipilin, brokered the reconciliation. He invited Ernesto to attend Bible study and conflict-resolution courses at the University of the Countryside in Minas de Oro. Ernesto says that it was there that for the first time in his life he read the Bible and began to develop a faith in God.

Ernesto received a course I gave on conflict resolution,[1] where he participated in Bible studies on loving enemies.[2] He was deeply challenged by Jesus' words in Matthew 5:43–48 (NASB): "You have heard that it was said, 'You shall love your neighbor and hate your enemy.' But I say to you, love your enemies, and pray for those who persecute you, so that you may be children of your Father in heaven. . . . For if you love those who love you, what reward have you? Do not even the tax-gatherers do the same? . . . Be perfect, therefore, as your heavenly Father is perfect."

Ernesto asked Tierra Nueva promoters Ramiro and Saul to act as intermediaries to initiate a dialogue and possible reconciliation with his enemy Julian.

Meanwhile, Julian received our first three-day course the year before, and was inspired to study the Bible every night in his home. The Scripture that most impacted Julian was Romans 12:17–21 (NASB), which reads:

> Do not repay anyone evil for evil, but take thought for what is noble in the sight of all. If it is possible, so far as it depends on you, live peaceably with all. Beloved, never avenge yourselves, but leave room for the wrath of God; for it is written, "Vengeance is mine, I will repay, says the Lord." No, "if your enemies are hungry, feed them; if they are thirsty, give them something to drink; for by doing this you will heap burning coals on their heads." Do not be overcome by evil, but overcome evil with good.

Ernesto eventually became an agricultural promoter with Tierra Nueva, and before giving his first soil and water conservation course to new farmers in his village, he publicly told his community of his change of heart and asked forgiveness from Julian.

"From that time on, we have been at peace," says Julian, smiling.

"And let me tell you something, Roberto. It was not I and not Ernesto that did this. This was a miracle from God. God did this work in both of us."

I believe him as I look at his face; a deep scar runs from his forehead through his nose and upper lip into his cheek.

Julian's forgiveness of Ernesto and Lolito inspired me. I too struggled with hatred I felt toward people I viewed as enemies of the people of Central America. My own government's history of funding and arming powerful minorities that oppressed the poor made me feel particularly responsible. People whom I identified as enemies at that time included CIA director William Casey, Presidents Ronald Reagan and George Bush, Assistant Secretary of State for Inter-American Affairs Elliott Abrams, U.S. Ambassador to Honduras John Negroponte, and two notorious Central American death-squad masterminds, Roberto D'Aubuisson of El Salvador and Honduran general Gustavo Alvarez Martinez.[3] The anger and hatred I felt toward these people and what they represented at times nearly overcame me. Though I had come to Central America as a committed pacifist, I found myself increasingly sympathizing with regional guerrilla movements that claimed to be fighting for liberation and justice for the poor.

I often read and prayed the psalms against enemies. I tried slipping in the names of notorious individuals, but at times found this difficult due to the harshness of some of these psalms:[4]

> Let ruin come on them unawares. And let the net that they hid ensnare them; let them fall in it—to their ruin. (Ps. 35:8 NRSV).

> Let their table be a trap for them, a snare for their allies. Let their eyes be darkened so that they cannot see. . . . Pour out your indignation upon them, and let your burning anger overtake them. . . . Add guilt to their guilt; may they have no acquittal from you. Let them be blotted out of the book of the living; let them not be enrolled among the righteous. (Ps. 69:22–24, 27–28 NRSV)

Praying these psalms and others against people clearly contradicted the admonitions of Jesus and the apostle Paul to love enemies and pray for those who persecute. Finally I ended up praying these psalms against detested institutions which I distinguished from the individuals within them: Reagan administration, Pentagon, Salvadoran army, CIA, DIN (Honduran secret police), the contras, USAID, and so forth. I felt powerless to stop these forces myself and wanted to see God intervene in some way to stop the injustices.

Julian's scriptural basis for his reconciliation with the two brothers both intrigued and bothered me. Julian's visible relief at having dropped his plans for vengeance resulted from something he heard from a text that had always troubled me: "Beloved, never avenge yourselves, but leave room for the wrath of God; for it is written, 'Vengeance is mine, I will repay, says the Lord'" (Rom. 12:19 NRSV).

I struggled with the image of God as wrathful and avenging. These images offended my grace-focused theology. Language about a God who repays appeared to reinforce a theology of divine retribution and judgment that I was not ready to embrace—except when it came to God stopping the notorious offenders in Central America. My dilemmas came to a head on a family vacation to a resort on the Bay Islands, a tropical paradise in the Caribbean on the north coast of Honduras.

We sat one afternoon together on the veranda of a diving resort with my in-laws and a young American journalist eating shrimp and tropical fruits. A middle-aged Latino couple sat at a table just in front of us, conversing quietly. Suddenly the journalist gasped as she recognized the man as Roberto D'Aubuisson, the dreaded organizer of some of El Salvador's most brutal death squads and suspected mastermind of Archbishop Oscar Romero's assassination.[5] She quickly excused herself and came back a few minutes later to tell us that the resort receptionist had confirmed the couple to be the D'Aubuissons.

For the next few days I found myself obsessed with thoughts that ranged from trying to make contact with the Salvadoran guerrillas to let them know that D'Aubuisson was there, to confronting him or even killing him myself, to trying to pray for him and love him though he was an enemy. I wondered how many Salvadoran lives I might save by ending this killer's life. I struggled to pray for him, even as I looked for signs that one of my heroes, Dietrich Bonhoeffer, might have discerned before he became involved in a plot against Hitler.

One morning, as I snorkeled along a coral reef, I came around a corner to find myself some ten feet away from D'Aubuisson, who was struggling to cut off a piece of coral with a big knife. Was this an opportunity that God had given me to stop an evil man? Later in the afternoon, when Gracie fell off the end of a boat that had taken a group from the resort to a hot diving spot, Roberto D'Aubuisson reached down and quickly helped her back into the boat. I talked with him and his wife briefly about El Salvador, and came to see him as a human being that I did not want to kill, but felt compelled to pray for.

Years of ministering to people who have suffered from sexual and physical abuse and injustices of every kind have helped me understand people's need to see God defend, judge, and even punish. Scriptures that emphasize apocalyptic divine intervention and retribution come out of situations of desperation and violence, where evil appears all-powerful and people long for and anticipate God's intervention and righting of the wrongs. Oppressed people or victims of brutality need assurances that God will deal with the enemy. Lack of belief that God is for justice and will finally bring relief from oppression drives people to take justice and struggles for economic and political liberation into their own hands. Faith that God will repay frees the offended one from the burden of vengeance. Once freed from this heavy load, the offended one or victim can do the work of loving and praying for the persecutor as one who is not all-powerful, but a finite human being. This work of love is the only alternative to being overcome by evil and is the way Julian, Ernesto, and Lolito chose to overcome evil with good.

Several years after my encounter with Roberto D'Aubuisson, I came across an article stating he had died of throat cancer in a Houston hospital in 1992. General Alvarez-Martinez was shot down in the streets of Tegucigalpa in 1989. William Casey, the CIA chief under Reagan, died of brain cancer, and Ronald Reagan too has died. I do not attribute these deaths to God. Rather, I have come to recognize that oppressors who had once appeared unstoppable are finite.

Faith that God is both sovereign and good includes coming to believe God not only opposes evil in the world but will stand with the oppressed and accompany them in their liberation process, however long it takes. Jesus' call to "stand with" may appear powerless and ineffective, much like his hanging crucified between the two dying thieves. Yet on the cross Jesus embodies Paul's imperative, "Do not be overcome by evil, but overcome evil with good," to the final, scandalous extreme.

Jesus invites his followers and all humanity to receive his love and follow in his way, embracing the scandal of the cross. Today followers of Jesus must recognize and embrace anew, over and over, Jesus, the crucified one, remembering and affirming that his particular life and death, and ours as his followers, embodies the only effective way of defeating evil and advancing the kingdom of God. Jesus calls us to renounce all other ways, take up our crosses, and follow him. Embracing Jesus' life and his death most certainly includes associating ourselves directly and entirely with a scandal that will lead to offense, rejection, division, and persecution—even as we witness and experience signs of the coming kingdom.

As we follow Jesus through the Gospels, we hear the kingdom announced and see in many stories concrete signs of his victory over sickness, evil spirits, sin, and death. John the Baptist sent disciples to ask Jesus whether he was the awaited Messiah. John the Baptist's possible location in Herod's prison would understandably cause him to question whether Jesus was indeed the awaited liberator. According to Luke's account, "Jesus had just then cured many people of diseases, plagues, and evil spirits, and had given sight to many who were blind" (Luke 7:21 NRSV). Jesus answered John's disciples in ways that affirm clearly that the kingdom of God can be expected here and now, on earth as in heaven: "Go and tell John what you have seen and heard: the blind receive their sight, the lame walk, the lepers are cleansed, the deaf hear, the dead are raised, the poor have good news brought to them. And blessed is anyone who takes no offense at me" (Luke 7:22–23 NRSV).

Yet Jesus' presence as Messiah does not keep the enemies of his advancing kingdom from persecuting, pursuing, and taking offense. In Matthew's Gospel he is born in a scandalous way and is rushed away from Herod's murderous plot as a refugee to Egypt. In Mark's Gospel Jesus' cousin and forerunner is imprisoned and beheaded (6:14–32). In Luke's Gospel, Mary and Joseph present Jesus to the Lord at the temple in Jerusalem, where Simon blesses them and prophesies to Mary people's opposition to Jesus: "This child is destined for the falling and the rising of many in Israel, and to be a sign that will be opposed so that the inner thoughts of many will be revealed—and a sword will pierce your own soul too" (Luke 2:34–35 NRSV).

In Matthew's Gospel and elsewhere in the New Testament,[6] Psalm 118:22 is quoted regarding people's rejection of Jesus and his particular way of being Messiah. Jesus says to the Pharisees who oppose him:

> "Have you never read in the scriptures: 'The stone that the builders rejected has become the cornerstone; this was the Lord's doing, and it is amazing in our eyes'? Therefore I tell you, the kingdom of God will be taken away from

you and given to a people that produces the fruits of the kingdom. The one
who falls on this stone will be broken to pieces; and it will crush anyone on
whom it falls." (Matt. 21:43–44 NRSV)

In Mark's Gospel, just after Peter confesses Jesus to be the Christ (Mark 8:29),
Peter rebukes Jesus after he tells his disciples that "the Son of Man must suffer many
things and be rejected by the elders and the chief priests and the scribes, and be
killed, and after three days rise again" (Mark 8:31 NASB). This leads Jesus to rebuke
Peter: "Get behind Me, Satan; for you are not setting your mind on God's interests, but man's" (Mark 8:33 NASB). Jesus is subsequently resisted, persecuted, and
finally betrayed, arrested, imprisoned, tortured, and killed. Later in Luke's Gospel
the resurrected Jesus comes alongside disillusioned disciples to show them a new
way of thinking about a suffering Messiah, who brings about the kingdom through
suffering love. Jesus expects the disciples to understand that suffering is redemptive: "'O foolish men and slow of heart to believe in all that the prophets have spoken! Was it not necessary for the Christ to suffer these things and to enter into His
glory?' And beginning with Moses and with all the prophets, He explained to them
the things concerning himself in all the Scriptures" (Luke 24:25–27 NASB).

Following Jesus means embracing him as the anointed one who did in fact
come to redeem Israel (Luke 24:21). Jesus' way of redeeming is supported by a
particular way of interpreting the Torah (Moses) and the Prophets that requires
his coming alongside us as rabbi and interpreter—or receiving divine revelation
somehow. The transfiguration is highly important in showing that Jesus is greater
than the fulfillment of the Law and the Prophets. When Jesus is transfigured, his
way of love, characterized by suffering and compassionate presence, is highlighted above and beyond the Law and the Prophets, even as it fulfills and exceeds
their expectations. Matthew and Luke present the Father as instituting a superior way of redemption that bypasses the Old Testament.

There on the mountain, before Jesus' inner circle of disciples, while Jesus is
praying his appearance changes, "His face became different, and His clothing
became white and gleaming" (Luke 9:29 NASB), reminiscent of Moses after his
face-to-face with God on Mount Sinai. The disciples see Moses and Elijah, representatives of the Torah and the Prophets, talking with Jesus. Had Peter's desire
to make separate and apparently equal tabernacles for Jesus, Moses, and Elijah
been accepted, it would have represented an affirmation that Jesus was on par
with the Torah and the Prophets' teaching. God's very presence, depicted by the
overshadowing cloud and voice, comes bringing precise correction to Peter and
all future disciples right at this point. The Father himself elevates Jesus as Son,
chosen as a new way and as the highest revealer—the one to be listened to over
and above anything taught by Moses (the Torah) and Elijah (the Prophets):
"While [Peter] was saying this, a cloud came and overshadowed them; and they
were terrified as they entered the cloud. Then from the cloud came a voice that
said, '*This is my Son, my Chosen; listen to him!*' And when the voice had spoken,
Jesus was found *alone*" (Luke 9:34–36a NRSV, emphasis added).

Jesus' way of nonviolent redemption is crystal clear when he enters Jerusalem.

Jesus does not come to overthrow the Romans, religious leaders, or any other human enemies through expected messianic violence.[7] When he approaches Jerusalem on his donkey and first sees it, Luke tells us he weeps over it and says, "If you, even you, had only recognized on this day the things that make for peace! But now they are hidden from your eyes" (Luke 19:42–44 NRSV).

Jesus laments his own people's inability to see and embrace his way of being the Messiah as the only way that makes for peace. That lamentation is not followed by a firm commitment to defend Israel against enemies using whatever means necessary. Rather, Jesus weeps and speaks prophetically as the bearer of the new covenant, announcing the destruction of even the holiest of cities, should they reject him and his way of being the Messiah: "Indeed, the days will come upon you, when your enemies will set up ramparts around you and surround you, and hem you in on every side. They will crush you to the ground, you and your children within you, and they will not leave within you one stone upon another; because you did not recognize the time of your visitation from God" (Luke 19:42–44 NRSV).

You would think that if Jesus affirmed theories of just war and defense of the modern state of Israel through any means necessary, he would have been more nuanced here. Jesus does not even call for the use of violence in defense of children or of oneself. Rather, Jesus laments his people's ignorance of the true way of peace and invites them and us to break with just war theories not in keeping with the way of suffering love. Today Christian witness should be informed and affected by Jesus' attitude of mourning and lamentation for impasses in the Middle East, and holding closely to Jesus' way of dealing with conflict. Later in Luke, instead of calling for people to defend Jerusalem from her enemies, Jesus calls followers to abandon it to its destroyers:

> "When you see Jerusalem surrounded by armies, then know that its desolation has come near. Then those in Judea must flee to the mountains, and those inside the city must leave it, and those out in the country must not enter it; for these are days of vengeance, as a fulfillment of all that is written. Woe to those who are pregnant and to those who are nursing infants in those days! For there will be great distress on the earth and wrath against this people; they will fall by the edge of the sword and be taken away as captives among all nations; and Jerusalem will be trampled on by the Gentiles, until the times of the Gentiles are fulfilled." (Luke 21:20–24 NRSV)

Apocalyptic Christian writers today see this message as referring strictly to the fall of Jerusalem in AD 70, which it does—but not exclusively. It is also true that strategically Jesus is recommending flight to preserve the lives of his followers, who were most certainly a small minority who would have been crushed along with everyone else by the advancing Roman soldiers. However, the fact that the writer of Luke locates this call to flee right before verses describing Jesus' second coming suggests that readers should not limit the application of this passage to first-century Christians in Jerusalem.

Jesus' call for disciples not to defend Jerusalem but to flee, followed immediately by Luke 21:25ff. depicting his second coming suggests that Jesus' refusal to call his followers to war continues to be in effect until he returns. Even the holy city of Jerusalem has become a principality not to be defended, but allowed to be destroyed. In the Synoptic Gospels Jesus' first move upon entering Jerusalem is to go right to the core of holiness, the temple itself. There he functions as exorcist, casting out the money changers from this house of prayer. Mark's Gospel emphasizes that the temple is a "house of prayer for all the nations" (Mark 11:17 NRSV), emphasizing Jesus' and Israel's universal mission. His earlier words, "destroy this temple and in three days I will rebuild it," point to the future destruction of the temple itself, and to his own death at the hands of sinners.

Throughout the Synoptic Gospels and John, Jesus consistently renounces the use of violence against human enemies, permitting only violence against oneself as a manifestation of love. Jesus' deliberate embracing of the cross invites all future disciples into his way of self-sacrificing love, clearly articulated by John's Gospel in numerous places: "I am the good shepherd. The good shepherd lays down his life for the sheep. . . . I am the good shepherd. I know my own and my own know me, just as the Father knows me and I know the Father. And I lay down my life for the sheep" (John 10:11, 14–15 NRSV). "No one has greater love than this, to lay down one's life for one's friends" (John 15:13 NRSV).

Archbishop Oscar Romero of El Salvador understood this well. Weeks before he was assassinated while serving the Eucharist in the cathedral in San Salvador, he said during his radio messages the following:

> The only violence that the gospel admits is violence to oneself. When Christ lets himself be killed, that is violence—letting oneself be killed. Violence to oneself is more effective than violence to others. It is very easy to kill, especially when one has weapons, but how hard it is to let oneself be killed for love of the people![8]

> We have never preached violence, except the violence of love, which left Christ nailed to a cross, the violence that we must each do to ourselves to overcome our selfishness and such cruel inequalities among us. The violence we preach is not the violence of the sword, the violence of hatred. It is the violence of love, of brotherhood, the violence that wills to beat weapons into sickles of work.[9]

Jesus' willingness to step toward violence against himself for love is visible in the lives of many martyrs in Central America and throughout the world.[10] A recent story from Honduras illustrates the power of redemptive suffering.

Lolito once led a group of seventy poor families from his village that sought to recuperate[11] 59 hectares of prime farmland in the fertile valley below Guachipilin from a wealthy cattle rancher. The landowner had paid the local military squadron to forcibly evict the families from the land, destroying their shacks and jailing their leaders, including Lolito. Fear of violence and persecution caused the group to diminish to twenty-seven families. These families persisted, rebuilding their shacks and planting their crops. The soldiers continued to be paid to evict them, and Lolito and others were jailed three more times for a month at a time. Finally the landowner, who was a physician and Christian and owned hundreds of acres throughout the valley, acquiesced, giving in to the persistent campesino group Vecino de las Vegas, who called their settlement La Catorce.

Five years later another group, Quatro de Marzo, comprising some forty landless peasant families from the neighboring villages, formally requested from the government 111 hectares of prime farmland that already belonged to the Instituto Nacional Agraria (INA). This land had been taken over and fenced by two wealthy landowners who were cattle ranchers, one of whom had thousands of acres in many places. The rich landowners had not been paying the taxes, and INA officials had agreed to grant the peasant group the land. The cattle ranchers kept paying bribes to keep things from happening, frustrating the group to the point that they decided to seize the land by force.

The campesino group Quatro de Marzo occupied the land and began to cultivate it and built their houses. As in the case of the neighboring La Catorce group, the landowners paid the soldiers to come and destroy everything. The landowners waited for the harvest, descending on the field with a cattle truck full of poor peasants whom they hired to harvest and take away all the campesino group's corn. They took everything they could and then set the cows onto the land.

"All of us from La Catorce—men, women and children went to help the group, chasing the cows off," recounts Lolito. "And then the soldiers and workers began to shoot at us, wounding two of our group members."

Lolito goes on to tell how the campesino group returned to the land, and how soldiers returned with poor workers recruited by the mayor of the nearby municipality and with men hired by the landowners to kill.

"This time they came armed with AK-47s and cast the group out, shooting over the heads of the workers," recounts Lolito. "Then the soldiers left, and the hired campesinos camped out on the land. Eight days later they hid, pretending to have left. When the land reform group returned, the ambushers attacked and killed one of the members, named Cecilio, and captured thirty-two-year-old Eulices."

Eulices' father Teofilo, age 55, a delegate of the Word in the Catholic Church and longtime member of Tierra Nueva's agricultural committee in Zapote, happened to be headed on foot to his field, where he was cutting grass to feed his horses. When he saw the men beating his son, he went and begged them to leave him alone.

"They grabbed him after he said, 'Leave my son, please, and take me, you take me,'" recounts Lolito. "They beat him, shot him in his hip, and then told him to go. He began to drag himself along when they grabbed him and drug him into the disputed property by one of his legs. He tried to crawl away toward the barbed wire to get out, but they kept dragging him back in. Finally they pulled his pants off, cut off his testicles and penis, opened his stomach up, and continued to drag him, his guts twisted in the grass. They buried his members by a tree. That night they left, leaving his body behind. Meanwhile some of the workers employed by the landowners, who knew Teofilo's son Eulices, convinced the others not to kill him. The next morning the bodies of Cecilio and Teofilo mysteriously appeared laid out in front of the municipality of Victoria." Five of the men who killed him were arrested, and imprisoned while the main organizer remains free.

Lolito tells how the brutality of Teofilo's death and his offering himself up in place of his son deeply moved his son's campesino group. Lolito himself carefully washed his friend Teofilo's body, cleaning the wounds and preparing him for burial. The shed blood of an innocent one on the land strengthened the group's resolve. After the community buried and mourned Cecilio and Teofilo, the group Quatro de Marzo reclaimed the land. Another peasant group from the same organization, Comité Nacional de Trabajadores del Campo (CNTC) from the north coast, which had faced similar violence from landowners, sent more than twenty men armed with AK-47s to help the group. Finally the military authorities refused to work for the landowners when they saw the resolve of the campesinos and when INA measured the land and granted it to the group. They have built houses on the land and continue to farm without problems, experiencing at least one part of Isaiah 65's vision: "They shall not build and another inhabit; they shall not plant and another eat; for like the days of a tree shall the days of my people be, and my chosen shall long enjoy the work of their hands" (Isa. 65:22 NRSV).

"Eulices and his three brothers and three sisters never sought vengeance for his father's death," recounts Lolito. "He and his family are very humble and good Christians. They followed the path of Jesus and forgave those who killed their father."

In John's Gospel, Jesus tells his disciples of the hour when he will be glorified, referring to his death: "The hour has come for the Son of Man to be glorified. Very truly, I tell you, unless a grain of wheat falls into the earth and dies, it remains just a single grain; but if it dies, it bears much fruit" (John 12:23–24 NRSV).

Jesus talks about death as redemptive, bringing a harvest of life, much as Teofilo's death saved his son and led to the campesino land-reforms resolve. "Those who love their life lose it, and those who hate their life in this world will keep it for eternal life. Whoever serves me must follow me, and where I am, there will my servant be also. Whoever serves me, the Father will honor" (John 12:25–26 NRSV).

More recently I led a series of courses on the ministry of Jesus and kingdom of God for a group of North Americans and Venezuelans living among and ministering to the urban poor in the impoverished barrios of Caracas. In the days before we left, National Public Radio had labeled Caracas the most violent city in the world, due to the high number of robberies and murders in the lawless, drug-infested barrios carved into the mountainsides surrounding the city, where more than half the city's five million people reside. On my way to the airport a friend prayed for me over the cell phone. He told me he saw a picture of a rusty lock that looked as if it could never open. Then he saw a rusty key inserted and the apparently impossible happened—the padlock opened.

My colleague Chris and I stayed with InnerCHANGE workers John and Birgit Shorack and their three children and ministry worker Ryan Mathis in their home and ministry center, perched high in the heart of a maze of winding roads, alleys, and paths amid the ramshackle brick cubes and tin roofs of barrio Pedro Camejo. The Shoracks are veteran ministry workers in dark and difficult places. They began their ministry to Caracas's impoverished barrio dwellers five years ago after serving over twelve years in inner-city Los Angeles. I counseled, prayed, and taught their staff in the mornings. We led Bible studies and prayed with families and walked the streets where muggings and killings are commonplace in the afternoons and early evenings. We were all delighted to see Jesus free people from pain in every home we visited, as we gathered family members, ministry workers, and neighbors around whoever needed relief and invited God's kingdom to come, right where we were, as in heaven.

Ryan, a twenty-four-year-old American living and working there with InnerCHANGE, was attracted to the "bad guys" in a special Jesus-like way. Though he had been traumatized by numerous muggings and encounters with dead bodies on the streets, his love led him boldly and respectfully to reach out to the hated *malandros* (hoodlums, thieves, scum), who terrorize the barrios with constant muggings, even in broad daylight, at gunpoint and in taxi jeeps that come through.

Even though Ryan had nearly left due to the trauma of these holdups, he had been pressing in and interceding for the *malandros* and trying to make connections. Reaching out to the barrio outlaws is a particularly risky venture. Not only are they themselves armed and dangerous, but they have enemies seeking to kill them at all times, making you a potential target as their associate or a victim caught in the crossfire. Ryan invited Chris to go visit two of the most infamous guys he had befriended, hoping to find the worst of them, David, known as Calimero.

Calimero was a nineteen-year-old man caught up in drugs, thievery, and violence. He had on different occasions robbed nearly every one of the ministry staff and their children. He and his fellow bandits had held up taxi drivers and busloads of people and likely had been involved in the killings that have been claiming growing numbers of victims every month.

Ryan took Chris with him to seek out and find Calimero. He had felt inspired to give something special to this guy who was always taking, offering him a prized poster of Jesus' face made up of verses from the Gospels. Calimero received Ryan and Chris into his tin-roofed shack hide-out, where he had lived alone since he was orphaned years before. Chris told about their meeting and the aftermath.

"We blessed Calimero straight out, while most of the neighborhood wanted him dead, and he received it. I started getting (prophetic) images[12] and tentatively went for it, sharing them right there outside his shack. I hesitantly shared with him the image I had of hands pressed over his ears and felt prompted to ask, 'Are you tormented by hearing screams at night?' I thought it might be a problem with his neighbors, but he immediately responded that yes, he hears terrifying shrieks every night. He understood them as coming from ghosts. I explained that as children of God we can receive greater authority from God and command evil spirits to leave. Without question he held out his palms with us and seemed to receive like a child this possible authority. The three of us then held out our hands toward his shack and took authority over the oppressive forces tormenting him. Then his friend showed up, and I immediately got an image of his wrist being yanked. Thinking maybe the police had grabbed him, I asked. Yep, the police had tugged him by the wrist for blocks this week. I asked if I could pray for him. When he agreed to let me pray, I put my hand on his wrist and prayed for God to restore the respect the cops stole, and thanked Jesus that he's about restoring the things the enemy steals and how God respects him and adores him, and knows these details in their lives and sends us to tell them because he is a good papi and cares a lot."

Calimero then invited Ryan and Chris into his house, something unheard of, as most people in the barrio didn't know where he lives and even "friends" didn't go in. When Ryan suggested that he wanted to bless his place, Calimero shyly agreed. His ear was torn like a scrappy dog's off the streets from a fight.

"He is dark, wearing nylon shorts," recounted Chris, "old basketball shoes, a tank top, and cap. Very shy, quiet. I would even say sweet. But I hear he is the most feared around here. Kids with guns, man, not terrorists. We spend over an hour in this empty shack of rusted metal sheets nailed to scrap two-by-fours, with the back wall blown out and a great view of all the valley's barrios. We silence the voices. Even his hand is extended. We talk about how God is pursuing him, not to hurt him like others in the barrio, but to embrace him. God knows that hurting people who aren't doing good is like burning down a house that has trash in it, instead of just taking out the trash. God knows how to take the bad stuff out of us and cast it out, burn it like the trash around here. He likes this. Then Ryan gives him a really cool poster of Jesus' face made from scribbled words, passages." That night, on a risky beer run Chris sees Calimero on the corner. He smiles and the first thing he says is that the poster is up.

The next day Chris and I led the staff in a session of prophetic worship and listening prayer, where we sought to come into God's presence as a group to discern what God was doing in our lives and in their ministry. The Spirit was present powerfully, touching everyone in different ways that they hadn't experienced. One got hit with uncontrollable laughter, another with weeping; another began speaking in tongues for the first time; someone ended up on the ground, hands and feet burning up as God's presence came with a feeling of weightiness. Birgit, the mother of the team, who said she does get prophetic words or feel God, said she had a vision where she saw Calimero's body wrapped in the Jesus poster. Not wanting to affirm this after the breakthroughs with Calimero the day before, I awkwardly underplayed it.

The next morning the whole team headed out of town with leaders of the house churches for a two-day retreat in the mountains. Nearly all of the thirty-five or so who attended the retreat live in impoverished barrios where violence is rampant. I taught on the ministry of Jesus and the kingdom of God. At one point Chris sang a song he wrote in Skagit County jail—based on Luke 7:34, where

Jesus is judged by his enemies as "a gluttonous man, and a drunkard, a friend of tax collectors and sinners"—that simply repeats the Spanish version of the refrain: "Jesus, friend of sinners, we love you." After a few lines he replaced the Spanish word for sinners, *pecadores*, with *malandros*, causing some to visibly wince. I decided to lead a session on the relationship between forgiveness and deliverance from evil spirits, based on the parable of the debtor who is forgiven and then refuses himself to forgive.

According to Jesus' parable, a slave owing ten thousand talents begs a king to forgive him his debt rather than selling his wife, children, and all he has. The king feels compassion and releases him, forgiving his debt. The slave in turn seizes and chokes a fellow slave owing only a hundred denarii, throwing him in prison rather than forgiving him. When the king hears about this, he calls him in and asks, "Should you not have had mercy on your fellow slave, as I had mercy on you?" (Matt. 18:33 NRSV). He then hands him over to the torturers until he repays all that was owed him (18:34). Jesus ends his teaching with a stern warning: "So my heavenly Father will also do to every one of you, if you do not forgive your brother or sister from your heart" (18:35 NRSV).

We discussed how living according to human justice rather than in the mercy of God leads to being delivered over to the accuser, who torments and tortures us, requiring us to live according to the harsh demands of human justice: demanding that we pay back everything we owe. I reminded people of the prayer that Jesus taught his disciples, "Forgive us our debts, as we also have forgiven our debtors" (Matt. 6:12 NRSV). I briefly presented Leviticus 19:17 (NRSV): "You shall not hate in your heart anyone of your kin; you shall reprove your neighbor, or you will incur guilt yourself." I pointed out that the Septuagint version translates the end of this verse fittingly with "so thou shalt not bear sin on his account." When we hold judgments against people in our hearts, we are allowing their sin to infect us. We are carrying their sin, rather than letting Jesus bear it.

I suggested that as we drop our judgments against people that are based on justice, we will become free from any of their guilt or sin that we bear due to our resentment and bitterness. When we confess our sin of judging and drop charges against others, the legal right for the torturers (evil spirits) to torment us disappears. I invited people to confess their bitterness, hatred, and judgments and to drop their charges against enemies and others who have offended them. I insisted that our forgiveness has nothing to do with our offenders' confessing, asking for forgiveness, or deserving our pardon. This is about extending the grace that has been offered freely to us by God in Jesus on the cross. I passed out paper and pencils and invited people to list names of people against whom they hold judgments, writing the specific offenses beside their names. We invited the Holy Spirit to come, bringing to memory people whom God is calling us to forgive. For the next twenty minutes or so, people reflected and wrote. Some cried as they wrote. I am sure that many *malandros* stalking their barrios received pardon, as did people's neighbors who were known *santeros, spiritistas,* and others practicing witchcraft.

We ended that session with a corporate prayer where we dropped our charges against people who have offended us, forgiving them and blessing them in Jesus' name. I placed a big cast iron frying pan in the middle of the circle and invited people to crumple up their papers and place them in the pan. We burned the papers and invited God's Spirit to fill us with love and the strength to live in a place of mercy rather than judgment.

The retreat ended and the bus arrived, driving us down from the mountain paradise and back to the barrios of Caracas. People seemed full of joy, singing and chatting as we bumped down the mountain road. I wondered what sorts of break-throughs awaited us all as we reentered the violent streets of the city. As we descended toward a nearby town, a man stopped our bus, warning us there had been a *tiroteo* (shootout) just ahead. He suggested we go down the mountain a different way. The bus driver obliged, but after heading down another road he stopped, realizing he was completely lost. He decided to turn around and head down where the shootout happened. People in our bus were visibly agitated. Though they live with violence every day, someone began vomiting and others were crying. We headed past several groups of people where the shootout took place. They were visibly rattled: traumatized and angry-looking. We made it back to Caracas fine and took a jeep taxi back up to the barrio. Then we heard the bad news. An hour after we'd left, Calimero had been stabbed repeatedly by someone just around the corner from the Shoracks' home. He'd staggered down the road, where he fell and slowly bled to death below the corner of his most recent crimes.

We prayed for Ryan, shocked and sobbing. The next day we had a final ses-sion and ended with worship. We remembered Birgit's vision and were perplexed. We decided to embrace it as a sign of this community's newfound ability to hear from God. We agreed that Birgit's picture of Calimero wrapped in a poster of Jesus' face was an image of a certain kind of victory. Calimero "died not wrapped in hate," reflected Chris, "but in so little time knowing Ryan, died with the one thing given to him that he didn't have to steal. This gift was a picture of Jesus' face, the only thing on his wall he eagerly put up, symbolically now wrapping him in the friendship of Jesus in a world that doesn't love orphans-gone-thieves like that." I saw Ryan's gift to Calimero as preparing him for his burial, as the woman's pouring perfume on Jesus' feet prepared Jesus for his. We wondered if Calimero's death would be the key to the rusty padlocked neighborhood where this team had been ministering for four years with little fruit.

This seemed confirmed that night as Ryan and John headed off to attend the wake. Ryan returned late, sobered and more hopeful. He told of hanging around Calimero's still body with other young men, *malandros* like Calimero, who smoked a concoction of heroin and other drugs together in Ryan's presence in memory of their fallen companion. Ryan's deeper rapport with the *malandros* was certainly hopeful. He and the other house church members were visible signs of forgiveness, freely offered, lives poured out. Ryan's calling was deepened now and the stakes were getting higher. The need was certainly clearer and more urgent than ever to live out an embrace of these kids like Calimero, whose blood was call-ing from the street like an invitation to Ryan and others to seek a gospel that has the power to truly save, heal, and liberate the most broken and violent ones—who rob by day and can trust no one. The team was pondering a vigil through the barrio for Calimero and all those dying in the streets, both innocent and perpetrators. Upon returning from the retreat, one of the house-church families found bullet holes across the front of their home. Others witnessed a woman shot and killed when she threw herself in front of her son's assailants, taking the bullets.

Chris, who had weeks before hung with murderous gangster *mareros* sentenced to life in prison in Guatemala's gang prisons, summed up the heightened sense of calling he himself felt after this experience:

> As in Guatemala, where I just was with the gangsters in the prisons, it is common for the community who feels understandably paralyzed in fear at the spread of such youth in their neighborhood to just wish these *mareros* and *malandros* dead. To wait silently, lock your doors, and hope that either the police lock them away somewhere darker or their own cohorts get to them first and kill them directly makes a kind of sense. But when you get to know one or two, the mention of a dead *malandro* that has the name of the one you saw with God's eyes hurts. It makes you weep and come together in prayer and feel like you want to do this for the rest of your life with Jesus, even if you catch a knife or bullet yourself. It's funny how love works, and how Jesus gives it so heavily and points us with it in the oddest directions.

"Very truly, I tell you," says Jesus, "unless a grain of wheat falls into the earth and dies, it remains just a single grain; but if it dies, it bears much fruit" (John 12:24 NRSV). The worst that the enemy can throw at us, death, is paradoxically the very thing that emboldens the campesino community in the aftermath of Teofilo's death and Ryan, Chris, and the InnerCHANGE team following Calimero's murder. God turns the enemy's weapon into a catalyst for fruitfulness and victory as new disciples find themselves unable to resist the call. This is because the Spirit works in the midst of dark and difficult situations, calling and empowering us.

Epifania showed up in July 2007 to speak at a Tierra Nueva "Open Your Eyes" evening on Mexican farm workers in the Skagit Valley. She spoke passionately about her life as a farm laborer and cried as she shared her heartache about her son Juan who died of cirrhosis of the liver several years before and her other son who is heading for prison. She told how God has accompanied her, liberated her, and healed her. The next day when she went to an appointment at the Department of Probation, the Internal Customs Enforcement (ICE) agents were waiting. They arrested her and transfered her to a privately run federal immigration detention center in Tacoma. She was once again in deportation proceedings for felony criminal convictions since her cancellation of removal victory in 2000. Everyone at Tierra Nueva was shocked and dismayed by this major setback. Roger and Rocio immediately went to work investigating how we could defend her. We learned that she was no longer eligible for cancellation of removal and there were no legal channels available to rescue her from deportation. Our only hope was to marshal everyone we could find who supported her to attend her deportation hearing. Maybe the judge would let us speak on her behalf and show mercy.

Six of us and her son Jessie drove two hours to Tacoma to attend her 8:30 hearing. A young woman guard ushered us into a courtroom where we sat on wooden church pews beside 12–15 brown-skinned, blue-uniformed male detainees awaiting their hearings. The guard told us in advance that the immigration judge hearing Epifania's case is especially demanding, requiring her defense to be presented in military order. The judge was not physically present, but was visible and audible via a video monitor far above us all where the altar would be. He was speaking from his 25th floor courtroom of the federal building in Seattle. He did not allow her to tell her story or any of us to speak on her behalf. When she didn't answer his questions clearly and directly he berated her with increasing rage. He insisted on the court proceedings going in such a rigid order that Epifania was only allowed to answer "yes," "no," and other short, precise answers. He stated that there was no relief for her and ordered her deported, offering her the right to appeal. Epifania turned her ashen face to us all and raised her eyebrows, desperate for advice. We didn't know what to tell her, and there was nothing we could do but watch and pray.

The guard ushered us out and told us she would put her immediately in a visiting booth so we could meet with her. Epifania told us through the glass that she was at peace. "I have totally given myself over to Jesus. I am no longer the Epifania who came her two months ago. I am another Epifania." She told us how there in detention she had been praying for fellow women detainees, for their healing. "Many women come to me for prayer," she told us, delighted. She told us how one wheel-chair bound detainee asked her to pray for her healing. Epifania prayed for her and nothing happened. The woman came to her a second time for prayer and once again experienced no physical relief. The third time Epifania prayed for her, she got up out of her wheelchair and began to walk. Epifania was in awe. She told us how the same woman guard who had ushered us into the courtroom and arranged our visit had witnessed the woman getting up out of her wheelchair after the prayer and began weeping. Epifania went on to tell us how the woman who was healed wanted to give her the golden ring she was wearing. Epifania told us that she insisted: "No, no, I can't charge for healing you. This is Jesus doing this for you. No, I cannot take anything from you. This is God doing this for you." Finally after the woman kept insisting, begging her to take the ring as a token of her thankfulness, she received it.

"I am just totally given over to Jesus now," says Epifania. "It doesn't matter to me if I lose my Mica (legal permanent residency card). It's okay if they keep detaining me here. I will just continue to pray for the women. Let them deport me to Mexico. God will help me."

Epifania's children and grandchildren are all U.S. citizens living in the United States. She has no remaining family in Mexico after having lived over 40 years in the United States. Should she return illegally and be apprehended, she could face federal prison time for illegal reentry. Yet Epifania is free to pursue her higher calling as an agent of transformation in the borderless kingdom of God.

Jesus' way of being the Messiah was not easy for even him to accept, yet it was difficult if not impossible to resist. He asked his Father to save him from the cross. Yet he fully embraced it (John 12:27), unable to keep from loving and forgiving his enemies and his friends to the bitter end. Jesus understood his own death as the judgment of this world that would alone drive out the ruler of this world: "Now is the judgment of this world; now the ruler of this world will be driven out. And I, when I am lifted up from the earth, will draw all people to myself" (John 12:31–32 NRSV).

Jesus acknowledged and accepted his betrayer Judas's plan to deliver him over to the authorities, offering him bread, dipped possibly in wine,[13] in John's version of the Lord's Supper (John 13:26–30)—where only Judas gets served. Jesus' giving himself over to his enemies revealed his glory in a way that is certainly foreign while at the same time welcomed: "When [Judas] had gone out, Jesus said, 'Now the Son of Man has been glorified, and God has been glorified in him. If God has been glorified in him, God will also glorify him in himself and will glorify him at once'" (John 13:31–32 NRSV).

Jesus' glory is the love of God made visible through the giving of his life in love for others, the love that Teofilo demonstrated in offering his life in the place of his son and that Ryan and Chris are now feeling in their call to ministry among violent offenders. "I give you a new commandment, that you love one another. Just as I have loved you, you also should love one another. By this everyone will know that you are my disciples, if you have love for one another" (John 13:34–35 NRSV).

Jesus understood clearly that his followers are called to a similar path. He also warned his disciples that the world may well hate Jesus' way of embodying his anointing Messiah in them, much as it hated him (John 15:18–19). Jesus recognized clearly that his having chosen his disciples out of the world set them and us apart, associating us with his scandalous way of dealing with evil—the cross. In Jesus' high-priestly prayer to the Father he emphasized this: "I have given them your word, and the world has hated them because they do not belong to the world, just as I do not belong to the world. I am not asking you to take them out of the world, but I ask you to protect them from the evil one" (John 17:14–15 NRSV).

Jesus did not pray that the Father would keep them out of the world, but that they would be kept from the evil one (17:15). Apparently, Jesus recognized here that the battle being waged was "not against enemies of blood and flesh, but against the rulers, against the authorities, against the cosmic powers of this present darkness, against the spiritual forces of evil in the heavenly places" (Eph. 6:12 NRSV). The evil one is apparently most threatened by Jesus' way of bearing God's anointing, as it is the only effective way of expelling him from the world. Before looking directly at how Jesus' death brings judgment on this world and casts out the evil one, let's look briefly at how Satan returns to tempt Jesus away from his particular way of being the Messiah.

According to Luke's account of the temptation narrative, after "the devil had finished every test, he departed from him until an opportune time" (Luke 4:13 NRSV). Satan is mentioned as returning only as he enters Judas to betray Jesus

(Luke 22:3), which Jesus consciously acknowledges and does not avoid. Judas's betrayal into the hands of the chief priests and scribes who are already looking for ways to put him to death (22:2) is directly linked to Passover through a verse that invites readers to connect Jesus' death to that of the Passover lamb: "Then came the day of Unleavened Bread, on which the Passover lamb had to be sacrificed" (Luke 22:7 NRSV).

There are also signs of a certain repeat of the temptations in the passion narratives. Jesus resists Peter's attempt to protect him with the sword from the multitude coming to arrest him, led by Judas. "No more of this!" (Luke 22:51 NRSV), he tells Peter after he cuts off the ear of the high priest's slave. He then touches his ear and heals him. The men who hold him in custody provoke him as they mock and beat him, blindfolding him and saying: "Prophesy, who is the one who hit You?" (Luke 22:64 NASB). Jesus is silent in response to his accusers, yet responds affirmatively when Pilate asks him if he is the King of the Jews (Luke 23:2–3). Jesus is silent before Herod's questions and the accusations of the chief priests and scribes (Luke 23:8–12). In the passion narratives Jesus' longest statement is in response to the women who mourn and lament as he heads to the cross. In keeping with Jesus' refusal to defend Israel as her Messiah, Jesus calls them to lament for themselves, saying: "Daughters of Jerusalem, do not weep for me, but weep for yourselves and for your children. For the days are surely coming when they will say, 'Blessed are the barren, and the wombs that never bore, and the breasts that never nursed'" (Luke 23:28–29 NRSV).

While Jesus refuses to defend himself or his people using violence, he does invite them into a posture of lamentation. He also offers forgiveness to his enemies while he hangs on the cross, without their confessing or asking for it and before he even dies. "Father forgive them, for they do not know what they are doing" (Luke 23:34 NRSV).

The clearest parallels to the temptation narratives are words spoken to Jesus while he is on the cross. The rulers speak their own version of Satan's "if you are the Son of God" challenges in the desert with their mocking "He saved others; let Him save Himself if this is the Christ of God, His Chosen One" (Luke 23:35 NASB). One of the thieves in turn cries out his challenge: "Are You not the Christ? Save Yourself and us!" (Luke 23:39 NASB). Between these two challenges Luke inserts the verse describing the inscription hung above him: "This is the King of the Jews" (Luke 23:38). Jesus resists the temptation to use his authority as Messiah to avoid suffering and death. What is the meaning of this death and path of redemptive suffering? How is the ruler of this world cast out so that all are drawn to Jesus?

In each of the Synoptic Gospel accounts of Jesus' last Passover meal with his disciples, Jesus is presented as offering his own body and blood in place of that of the ceremonial lamb.[14] Under the old covenant, the blood of the ceremonial lamb would normally be sprinkled around the altar[15] or poured out at the base[16] as an offering to God. Blood was necessary for the forgiveness of sins to be effective, as Hebrews 9:22 emphasizes. "Indeed, under the law almost everything is purified with blood, and without the shedding of blood there is no forgiveness of sins" (Heb. 9:22 NRSV).

While the roasted lamb would be eaten by the people and other animal sacrifices by the priests, blood would never be eaten, "for the life of the flesh is in the blood; and I have given it to you for making atonement for your lives on the altar; for, as life, it is the blood that makes atonement" (Lev. 17:11 NRSV). "For as for the life of all flesh, its blood is identified with its life" (Lev. 17:14 NASB).

Under the new covenant in Jesus' blood, there is a complete reversal of movement. Rather than humans sacrificing to God, God sends his Son, delivering him over into the hands of sinners as an offer of radical love. Yet Jesus is no victim. He too offers himself in love without resistance to his enemies and his friends. Jesus offers his body and blood to us, giving us his very life as food and drink. "Take, eat, this is my body" (Matt. 26:26 NRSV). Jesus offers his disciples his very life. "Drink from it, all of you; for this is my blood of the covenant, which is poured out for many for the forgiveness of sins" (Matt. 26:28 NRSV). "This is my blood of the covenant, which is poured out for many (Mark 14:24 NRSV). John's Gospel is especially clear regarding God's offering his son from heaven to the world: "I am the living bread that came down from heaven. Whoever eats of this bread will live forever; and the bread that I will give for the life of the world is my flesh" (John 6:51 NRSV).

Rather than seeing Jesus as a sacrifice to God to appease his wrath or need for justice, the Synoptic Gospels show Jesus' offering himself to us in intimate communion, and as God's meal offering of reconciliation.

> "Very truly, I tell you, unless you eat the flesh of the Son of Man and drink his blood, you have no life in you. Those who eat my flesh and drink my blood have eternal life, and I will raise them up on the last day; for my flesh is true food and my blood is true drink. Those who eat my flesh and drink my blood abide in me, and I in them. Just as the living Father sent me, and I live because of the Father, so whoever eats me will live because of me." (John 6:53–57 NRSV)

This life through Jesus' blood has become particularly real and practical to us in an unprecedented series of healings at Tierra Nueva during Lent 2007. Two men were healed from work-related accidents as we celebrated communion during our Spanish service. Around these healings the Holy Spirit has worked as helper, advocate, and provider.

Bonifacio, known affectionately as Boni, a laborer from Mexico in his mid-30s, showed up at our service three weeks ago, complaining of intense pain in his finger after he'd shot a staple into it on a construction job. He'd pulled the staple, deeply embedded in the bone of his index finger, with a pair of pliers. Gracie and others prayed for him. The next week he came to tell us that just after he'd received prayer, communion wine had accidentally spilled from his bread onto the spot on his finger where the hole was. "All the pain went away right then and has not come back," he told us. This sounds almost magical, but then it happened again.

Two weeks ago Boni's friend from California, Victor, showed up. He'd come up for a court hearing regarding custody of his two daughters, whom child protective services (CPS) had taken away from his ex-partner. He hobbled into the service and responded at the end when we invited anyone with pain to come up for prayer. Victor had caught his booted foot in a ladder on a roofing job and twisted his knee a week before.

"I could hardly walk," he told me. "The whole way up in the car from California I was wincing, and often felt like crying from the pain," he said.

After praying for Victor, we moved into a circle and into our communion service. As we were serving communion, Sara, who had not been present the week before, came to me with what she called a strange idea. "I don't know what to do with this, but I just had a vision in my mind's eye of wiping Victor's knee with communion wine. What do you think?"

Since Boni had recently shared how the pain in his finger had left, I was open to trying this. I had also been reflecting on how Isaiah 53 was appropriated in the New Testament to suggest that healing is tied to Jesus' passion. The Greek version of Isaiah 53:5, which says that "by his bruises we ourselves were healed," is cited by 1 Peter 2:23–24 (NASB), which links Jesus' vulnerable suffering with forgiveness, healing, and reconciliation with God as our shepherd:

> And while being reviled, He did not revile in return; while suffering, He uttered no threats, but kept entrusting Himself to Him who judges righteously; and He Himself bore our sins in His body on the cross, that we might die to sin and live to righteousness; for by His wounds you were healed. For you were continually straying like sheep, but now you have returned to the Shepherd and Guardian of your souls.

I approached Victor with Sara after everyone had taken communion and asked him if he was open to us wiping down his knee with communion wine. "Sure," he said, desperate for relief. He pulled up his trousers to reveal a swollen knee, and Sara applied a liberal dousing of the blood of Christ.

"The next day I woke up and there was no more pain," said Victor, in amazement. That day he also went to court with Roger and had a positive outcome.

We had wanted to interview Victor about his healing and follow up with his court case, but couldn't track him down until another day. That morning I took my 16-year-old son Isaac down to the Department of Licensing to get his driver's license. As we awaited the examiner whom Isaac would take for a spin, there was Victor parked beside me, waiting for his wife to take her exam. The examiner stood behind the car and called out to Isaac to turn his right and left turn indicators on and to step on the brakes to test the brake lights. She called me over to tell me that Isaac couldn't take the test because the third brake light didn't work. Isaac was really disappointed. "Wait!" yelled Victor, running toward us. "Here, you can use my truck." Isaac was able to borrow Victor's truck, which had insurance and all indicator lights in working order. Isaac passed his test, and I was able to interview Victor.

For the past nearly thirteen years we at Tierra Nueva have loaned our personal cars to countless Mexicans in need of a car with insurance and everything in order so they could take their driver's tests. Then this day, Tierra Nueva's director got some timely advocacy from an immigrant worker for his son, so he could get his license. Healing and advocacy are both linked to the cross in ways that are becoming increasingly clear in our lives and in the Scriptures.

Jesus' death as a righteous one for sinners undoes any legal right of the accuser, Satan, to level charges. In the book of Revelation, John of Patmos describes Jesus' blood as purchasing people for God (Rev. 14:4 NRSV). Humans are purchased not from God, but from among men,[17] from the ruler of this world who functions as a prosecutor requiring and meting out punishments for crimes committed. Jesus subverts the evil empire by offering his body and blood not to Satan, or to the rulers and authorities, but to humans, before they actually take him and crucify him. In giving his disciples his body and blood, he makes them and us all priests who benefit directly from the offering.[18] He then is delivered over to death, where his blood is poured out as ransom. This is an accomplished victory which is celebrated in heaven. "They sing a new song: 'You are worthy to take the scroll and to open its seals, for you were slaughtered and by your blood you ransomed for God saints from every tribe and language and people and nation; you have made them to be a kingdom and priests serving our God, and they will reign on earth'" (Rev. 5:9–10 NRSV).

In this way the ruler of this world is thrown down, according to Revelation 12:10–11 (NRSV):

> Then I heard a loud voice in heaven, proclaiming, "Now have come the salvation and the power and the kingdom of our God and the authority of his Messiah, for the accuser of our comrades has been thrown down, who accuses them day and night before our God. But they have conquered him by the blood of the Lamb and by the word of their testimony, for they did not cling to life even in the face of death."

Luke's account of the Passover meal is distinct from that of Matthew and Mark, and is closer to that of John of Patmos. In Luke, Jesus offers his disciples two cups rather than one. Jesus invites his disciples to share the first cup among themselves (Luke 22:17). He then goes on to break the bread and give it to them, saying, "This is My body which is given for you; do this in remembrance of Me" (Luke 22:17 NASB). Jesus then takes the second cup, saying, "This cup that is poured out for you is the new covenant in my blood" (Luke 22:20 NRSV). There is no mention of the disciples drinking this second cup, which is described as being poured out. The meaning of these two cups becomes somewhat clearer in the garden of Gethsemane.

There in the garden Jesus appears to refer to the first cup he told his disciples to share, a cup of suffering, when he says to his Father, "Father, if you are willing, remove this cup from me; yet, not my will but yours be done" (Luke 22:42 NRSV).[19] The second cup, which only Jesus can drink, appears to be referred to in

Jesus' subsequent anguish when "he prayed more earnestly, and his sweat became like great drops of blood falling down on the ground" (Luke 22:44 NRSV).[20]

Jesus mentions his own suffering as distinct from that of his disciples directly in Luke 17:25 (NRSV), which states that before his second coming "he must endure much suffering and be rejected by this generation" and after his Last Supper when he says, "I have eagerly desired to eat this Passover with you before I suffer" (Luke 22:15 NRSV). The resurrected Jesus later emphasizes to his disciples that his suffering as Messiah was in keeping with an understanding of redemptive suffering present throughout the Scriptures, the Torah, and the Prophets of that time (Luke 24:25–27, 46). Later, in the Acts of the Apostles, Peter reaffirms this same understanding of a suffering Christ, calling his hearers to repent in response: "In this way God fulfilled what he had foretold through all the prophets, that his Messiah would suffer. Repent therefore, and turn to God so that your sins may be wiped out, so that times of refreshing may come from the presence of the Lord, and that he may send the Messiah appointed for you, that is, Jesus" (Acts 3:18–20 NRSV).

Later the apostle Paul continued this tradition, "proving that it was necessary for the Messiah to suffer and to rise from the dead, and saying, 'This is the Messiah, Jesus whom I am proclaiming to you'" (Acts 17:3 NRSV). The cup of Jesus' blood "poured out for you" appears to refer to Jesus' own suffering, which releases the Holy Spirit and God's love into the followers and empowers them to share the first cup. The link between Jesus' blood, the Holy Spirit, and God's love is visible in two key scriptures. In Acts 10:45 circumcised Jewish believers are astounded and decide to include Gentiles after they see the gift of the Holy Spirit poured out upon them. In Romans 5:5 (NRSV) the apostle Paul affirms that "God's love has been poured into our hearts through the Holy Spirit that has been given to us." Christ's blood, his very life poured out upon the disciples, is certainly intimately linked to the Holy Spirit and God's love.

Jesus speaks to his disciples in Jerusalem at the end of Luke's Gospel, calling them and us his readers back to images of baptism, through language evoking John's baptism of repentance for the forgiveness of sins (Luke 3:3). Jesus' words invite disciples into deeper understanding of the Scriptures, the suffering related to his way of being Messiah, and the need for them to receive greater empowerment by the Holy Spirit:

> Then he opened their minds to understand the scriptures, and he said to them, "Thus it is written, that the Messiah is to suffer and to rise from dead on the third day, and that repentance and forgiveness of sins is to be proclaimed in his name to all nations, beginning from Jerusalem. You are witnesses of these things. And see, I am sending upon you what my Father promised; so stay here in the city until you have been clothed with power from on high." (Luke 24:45–49 NRSV)

In Acts 5:27–32 we see how Peter and the apostles proclaimed repentance and forgiveness of sins in the face of extreme opposition. A recent Bible study in Skagit County jail proved the ongoing fruitfulness of Luke's version of the Great

Commission. Before inmates read the text aloud in Spanish and English, I give everyone the background.

I first remind the inmates that when Jesus himself was under arrest, Peter had denied him three times, and the other disciples had fled the scene. Jesus had told them to wait in Jerusalem until they were clothed with power from on high. Then, fifty days after Jesus' resurrection, on the day of Pentecost, the Spirit had come upon them. A new boldness is evident in Peter and the other apostles after Pentecost, which is visible in their willingness to preach Jesus openly in the temple. Peter and the apostles are thrown in prison by the temple police for preaching about Jesus. An angel of the Lord opens the prison doors and leads them out. The next day when the guards go to fetch them for court, they discover the jail break. Soon they learn that the apostles are back in the temple preaching about Jesus. When the temple police arrest them again and the high priest confronts them with their lawbreaking, they say: "We must obey God rather than any human authority" (Acts 5:29 NRSV).

"So whom are we to obey first and foremost, according to this scripture?" I ask the inmates.

"God," everyone responds enthusiastically. I tell them that it's important to obey the laws too, whenever they don't go against what God is calling us into. The men smile and appear to agree.

"What's God like and what does God do, according to verse 30?" I ask.

"He raises Jesus from the dead," someone says. Others mention how the angel had just released them from prison.

"What about human authorities, what do they do?" I ask.

"They killed Jesus by nailing him to a cross," someone reads.

"So whom would you rather obey, a God who raises you from the dead or authorities who can kill you by giving you the death penalty?" I ask.

At first everyone says, "God"—until Rickie, a young veteran of gangs and the prison system, says something very true and sobering.

"It's not that easy. The people with the guns can be pretty intimidating, as they have the power. God did resurrect Jesus, but you have to believe in him enough to trust your life to him, because you have to die before you can be resurrected, and you can't know for sure you'll be resurrected. And nobody wants to die. You might obey men to avoid getting killed."

I invite people to read the next verse, looking deeper into what God does for Jesus and for us. We hope that people see that the benefits to receiving from God outweigh simple compliance with rules or going along with the pressures of the crowd. We read in Acts 5:31 how God exalts Jesus to his right hand—the place of power and authority. The men are encouraged to learn that God has made him the ultimate authority and Savior. We talk about how Jesus gives repentance (understood as a new way of thinking) and forgiveness of sins. I ask the men if they feel as if they need someone to lead them and save them, someone who offers to give them a new way of thinking and forgiveness of all their sins. Everyone appears to want to receive God's gift of Jesus and all he offers. We read Acts 5:32, where the Holy Spirit is described as a witness to these things. I ask the men if they are willing to let me pray for the Holy Spirit to show them whether God has truly made Jesus their leader and Savior and is offering them a new way of thinking and forgiveness of sins. Everyone agrees, and we pray for the Holy Spirit to come.

I then ask the men if they feel attracted enough to Jesus and what he offers to welcome Jesus as their leader and Savior and to give them a new mind and forgiveness. When I begin praying and invite people to pray along, men begin agreeing out loud, in their own words, saying yes to Jesus, accepting his offer to be their Savior with a new way of thinking and forgiveness.

After each Bible study, I suggest that God longs for each one of them to become witnesses to God's acts of liberation. We pray for two men in the first study who are healed of pain, one in his heart and another in his side. I tell the inmates in the second Bible study that I believe Jesus wants to free them from their pain. I invite them to place their hands on parts of their body where they have pain or know they need healing. Nearly everyone places one or both hands somewhere—on their neck, knees, lower back, heads, hearts, shoulders. After praying for God's healing presence to come, the men tell the group one after another that their pain immediately has left. Nine or ten men experience immediate healing! They are joyful and visibly pleased.

I notice that a big, tall guy, probably 6'7", who stands right across from me in the circle, removes his hand from his right shoulder and lower back after a few seconds. He looks discouraged and says he feels no relief when I ask him about his pain. "Do you mind if I pray for you some more?" I ask. "Yeah, I guess," he responds.

When I ask him how it happened, he tells me the police wrenched his shoulder when they pulled his arm behind his back to handcuff him. The handcuffs dug into his back as they drove him to the jail.

"Do you think you might need to forgive those officers for anything?" I ask.

"No, they were just doing their job. I'm a big dude," he responds.

I place one hand on his shoulder and another on his lower back and start praying: "Jesus, we thank you for your huge love for this guy. Show him that you had nothing to do with the use of force that damaged his shoulder and back. I ask that you reverse the damages done by the police. Thank you that your call on his life is still there, and that nothing he's done has made you give up on him."

After praying I step back to where I've been standing. I ask him if he notices any improvement.

"Well, it doesn't hurt right now," he says. "But I'm sure that when I pull my arm behind my back the pain will still be there."

He moves his arm behind his back, and I watch surprise fill his face. He tries it a few more times and looks up astonished and says, "Well, I grant you this one, I'll grant this to you. There's no more pain."

As the reality that Jesus actually touched him and healed him dawns on him, I watch a wave of emotion flow over him. His face flushes red, his eyes fill with tears. He sits down, head bowed and slowly shaking back and forth. Manny, another inmate, encourages him. "That's okay, man. You're a good dude." I leave giving thanks to God for seventeen to twenty men who responded to Jesus' offer of love and the signs that confirmed the word.

Empowerment by the Spirit is necessary if Jesus' followers are to enter into his way of redemptive suffering—which is certainly what the apostles experienced and invited others into. When the Lord appeared to Ananias in a vision, telling him to pray for Saul after Saul's encounter with Jesus, God told Ananias that the apostle Paul (Saul with a new name) would suffer greatly "for the sake of my name" (Acts 9:16 NRSV). Ananias then prayed for Saul to receive his sight and to be filled with the Holy Spirit (Acts 9:17).

Paul and many others in the early church did in fact experience suffering similar to that of Jesus, as is evident from 1 Thessalonians 2:14–15 (NRSV): "For you, brothers and sisters, became imitators of the churches of God in Christ Jesus that are in Judea, for you suffered the same things from your own compatriots as they did from the Jews, who killed both the Lord Jesus and the prophets, and drove us out; they displease God and oppose everyone."

The first Christians experienced their suffering for Christ as a great privilege, as is evident in Philippians 1:29 NRSV, where Paul writes that God "has graciously granted you the privilege not only of believing in Christ, but of suffering for him as well."

This suffering is not an individualistic experience, nor is it continuous. Jesus gives his followers a cup to divide among themselves, sharing together in the joy, comfort, and suffering that come as we move forward as a united body of Christ. "If we are being afflicted, it is for your consolation and salvation; if we are being consoled, it is for your consolation, which you experience when you patiently endure the same sufferings that we are also suffering. Our hope for you is unshaken; for we know that as you share in our sufferings, so also you share in our consolation" (2 Cor. 1:6–7 NRSV).

The disciples' sharing in the cup of his suffering is only possible because of the breakthrough occasioned by Jesus' own suffering and death. In Luke's account of Jesus' passion, right after he is crucified between two robbers he says: "Father, forgive them; for they do not know what they are doing" (Luke 23:34 NRSV). This is immediately followed by descriptions of suffering, including sneering and mocking challenges by the rulers (23:35), the soldiers (23:36), and one of the criminals (23:39).[21] Apparently Jesus' act of forgiveness, together with his suffering, occasions the darkness and obscuring of the sun and culminates in the tearing of the temple curtain from top to bottom, removing the separation, before he even dies. While Jesus' blood is poured out for the disciples as Jesus' body, empowered to advance his kingdom through redemptive suffering, we see in Jesus' final cry and death God's solidarity with Egyptian oppressors, Roman occupiers, and other visible flesh-and-blood enemies of the kingdom of God.

Jesus cries out with a loud voice. Could his cry here be evoking the great cry in Egypt at the death of the firstborn (Exod. 12:30)?[22] Jesus' death between two criminals and his words "Father, into your hands I commend my spirit" (Luke 23:46 NRSV) show how the death of God's only Son brings Jesus full circle in his communion with the flesh-and-blood enemies of the kingdom of God. Finally Jesus' expiring leads the Gentile centurion to begin praising God, saying, "Certainly this man was innocent" (Luke 23:47 NRSV). The centurion literally recognizes here that Jesus is *dikaios*, best translated "righteous" or "just." The centurion gives glory (*doxazō*) to God, using the same language as in the Septuagint of Exodus 15:1–2, where Moses and the Israelites rejoice at the destruction of the powers of enslavement and death, represented by God's victory over Pharaoh and his army. Luke here may well be suggesting an interpretation of Jesus' death similar to that in 1 Peter 3:18–19 (NRSV): "For Christ also suffered for sins once for all, the righteous [*dikaios*] for the unrighteous, in order to bring you to God. He was put to death in the flesh, but made alive in the spirit, in which also he went and made a proclamation to the spirits in prison."

Might the Roman centurion be a stand-in for the Egyptians and anyone who opposes the reign of God? In response to Jesus' loud cry as God's firstborn Son and righteous sacrificial lamb, the executioner glorifies God that the righteous one has suffered for the sins of the unrighteous. A strange reversal is evident as the Jewish multitudes return "beating their breasts" (Luke 23:49 NRSV). Might Luke be suggesting that they are suddenly aware that they have sacrificed their own righteous Messiah to the powers? And yet this is exactly the time bomb that explodes from within the beast of death at the moment of apparent victory.

The apostle Paul writes in 1 Corinthians 1 that Christ crucified, the weakness of the cross, is what brings down the strongholds of this world. I often begin teaching on Jesus' two final loud shouts from the cross in Matthew's Gospel by reading 1 Corinthians 1:18, 21–25 (NRSV):

> For the message about the cross is foolishness to those who are perishing, but to us who are being saved it is the power of God. . . . For since, in the wisdom of God, the world did not know God through wisdom, God decided, through the foolishness of our proclamation, to save those who believe. For Jews demand signs and Greeks desire wisdom, but we proclaim Christ crucified, a stumbling block to Jews and foolishness to Gentiles, but to those who are the called, both Jews and Greeks, Christ the power of God and the wisdom of God. For God's foolishness is wiser than human wisdom, and God's weakness is stronger than human strength.

Jesus' death on the cross is hailed by Paul as itself unleashing the power of God. Jesus exercised his authority as the Son of God in a way that made him free from the constraints put on him by the official authorities. This threatened the authorities, leading them (high priests, scribes, and Pharisees) to do everything possible to crush and in every way repress this announcer of the kingdom of God.

The religious authorities accused, denounced, arrested, charged, convicted, handed over, and condemned Jesus to the death penalty. We see them going to extreme measures to do away with Jesus' threat. They even put his tortured, dead body in a prison cave, sealing it and leaving armed guards:

> The next day, that is, after the day of Preparation, the chief priests and the Pharisees gathered before Pilate and said, "Sir, we remember what that impostor said while he was still alive, 'After three days I will rise again.' Therefore command the tomb to be made secure until the third day; otherwise his disciples may go and steal him away, and tell the people, 'He has been raised from the dead,' and the last deception would be worse than the first." Pilate said to them, "You have a guard of soldiers; go, make it as secure as you can." So they went with the guard and made the tomb secure by sealing the stone. (Matt. 27:62–66 NRSV)

After reading these verses, I ask the group to name situations they are facing in their lives, ministries, or in the world that seem like no-exit situations—like this heavily guarded tomb. People mention crack and methamphetamine addictions, debt, HIV/AIDS, the global economic systems, the legal and prison systems, the war in Iraq, the Israeli-Palestinian conflict, racism, relationship problems, and other things. I then invite someone to read Matthew 28:1 (NRSV): "After the sabbath, as the first day of the week was dawning, Mary Magdalene and the other Mary went to see the tomb."

I suggest that this is like us when we go and face problems that appear insurmountable. For some people involved in ministry in the face of the powers, going out to the drug corner, the jail, or their parish is analogous to the women's going to see the tomb. Despair before the obstacles to life and ministry overcomes any reasons to hope. Yet what they find at the tomb leads to a surprising event. I invite someone to read Matthew 28:2–4 (NRSV): "And suddenly there was a great earthquake; for an angel of the Lord, descending from heaven, came and rolled back the stone and sat on it. His appearance was like lightning, and his clothing white as snow. For fear of him the guards shook and became like dead men."

Despair before death is interrupted by a great earthquake. Help from heaven in the form of an angel descends to overcome all human attempts to keep Jesus dead and in every way repressed. These happenings strike fear into the guards assigned to guard the dead man to such an extent that they themselves become "like dead men." The angel makes sure that the women know that the event is not to terrify them but rather to fill them with joy. I invite a reader to continue reading Matthew 28:5–10 (NRSV):

> But the angel said to the women, "Do not be afraid; I know that you are looking for Jesus who was crucified. He is not here; for he has been raised, as he said. Come, see the place where he lay. Then go quickly and tell his disciples, 'He has been raised from the dead, and indeed he is going ahead of you to Galilee; there you will see him.' This is my message for you."

The women respond to the good news by running away from the grave to announce to the disciples the incredible news. Then they themselves are met, encouraged not to be afraid, and sent off to tell the disciples to go back to the place in Galilee where they had first experienced good news, expectant of an encounter with someone on the other side of death. "So they left the tomb quickly with fear and great joy, and ran to tell his disciples. Suddenly Jesus met them and said, 'Greetings!' And they came to him, took hold of his feet, and worshiped him. Then Jesus said to them, 'Do not be afraid; go and tell my brothers to go to Galilee, there they will see me'" (Matt. 28:8–10 NRSV).

"When was this power unleashed that led to the earthquake and opening of the tomb?" I ask. I suggest that at Jesus' moment of greatest weakness, on the cross, power was released. This is when Jesus cried out with a loud voice, which actually happened two different times. This loud voice is in Greek a *phone megale* (megaphone), which could be translated "a great or big voice or noise." Each cry is important, reflecting two distinct symbolic actions on the part of Jesus. The first cry happens in Matthew 27:46 (NRSV): "And about three o'clock Jesus cried with a loud voice, '*Eli, Eli, lema sabachthani?*' that is, 'My God, my God, why have you forsaken me?'"

This cry represents Jesus' total solidarity in weakness with human beings who feel God's distance in their suffering. In this case, his cry in Aramaic shows his identification with the common people under Roman occupation, who were oppressed by the very ones who were crucifying him. This cry shows Jesus as humanly present, suffering alongside them. God's suffering presence in Jesus brings comfort to sufferers, much like ministries of presence and solidarity among the marginalized.

I invite the group to consider joining with Jesus in his shout, "My God, my God, why have you forsaken me?" in solidarity with all who feel God's distance and even abandonment in the midst of suffering. People are in agreement that we should cry out together with Jesus. Before we cry out, I ask them silently to ponder Jesus' anguish and that of others today who suffer from depression, anguish, loneliness, grief, or similar sentiments. Together we cry out with Jesus. The shout feels almost blasphemous, but potent.

After another moment of silence, I suggest that this cry alone is not enough. People in bleak, no-exit situations also need God to come in power. Ministries emphasizing solidarity and presence alongside those who are suffering are essential, but must also come to appreciate and embrace Jesus' second cry, which releases power. After a period of silence in Matthew's Gospel as people try in vain to bring relief by offering the dying Jesus sour wine, Jesus cries out with a loud voice a second time and releases his spirit: "Then Jesus cried again with a loud voice and breathed his last [literally, released his spirit]" (Matt. 27:50 NRSV).

Jesus' second cry is followed by his releasing of his spirit. The Greek term here, a form of *aphiemi* (to forgive, let go, release, drop), can be interpreted as a loud cry of victory or possibly even a war cry—but different from a triumphalistic cry. Jesus' loud cry and release of his spirit accomplishes many powerful things on behalf of people. I invite a reader to read Matthew 27:51–54 (NRSV):

At that moment the curtain of the temple was torn in two, from top to bot-tom. The earth shook, and the rocks were split. The tombs also were opened, and many bodies of the saints who had fallen asleep were raised. After his resurrection they came out of the tombs and entered the holy city and appeared to many. Now when the centurion and those with him, who were keeping watch over Jesus, saw the earthquake and what took place, they were terrified and said, "Truly this man was God's Son!"

Jesus loud cry achieves five significant liberations:

1. The veil in the temple is torn in two from top to bottom (27:51), show-ing God's removal of the separation between the clergy and the laity, the religion leaders and the masses, the holy God and the profane peo-ple, heaven and earth. God rips the curtain from top to bottom, show-ing that this separation can be lifted only as a divine act.
2. The earth shakes (27:51), showing how Jesus' cry, like God's revelation of his power at Sinai in Exodus 19, unsettles creation itself, and how God is more powerful than the visible world.
3. Rocks are split, showing that some of the hardest elements of this world are broken at this moment of God's total weakness.
4. Tombs are opened, and many bodies of the saints that had fallen asleep are raised.
5. Finally, the centurion and others keeping watch, the executioners who work for the powers, are terrified and come to recognize Jesus' true iden-tity as the Son of God, as they recognize the power of Jesus' loud cry.

I invite people to look at other scriptures that support this reading of the loud cry as a victory cry. A volunteer reads Joshua 6:20 (NRSV): "So the people shouted, and the trumpets were blown. As soon as the people heard the sound of the trumpets, they raised a great shout, and the wall fell down flat; so the people charged straight ahead into the city and captured it."

In John's Gospel Jesus, after being deeply disturbed in his spirit (John 11:38) at the death of his friend Lazarus, cries with a loud voice, "'Lazarus come out!' And the dead man came out" (John 11:43–44 NRSV).

I invite someone to read the account of Paul's healing of a man crippled from birth, which illustrates how crying out with a loud voice releases physical heal-ing: "In Lystra there was a man sitting who could not use his feet and had never walked, for he had been crippled from birth. He listened to Paul as he was speak-ing. And Paul, looking at him intently and seeing that he had faith to be healed, said in a loud voice, 'Stand upright on your feet.' And the man sprang up and began to walk" (Acts 14:8–10 NRSV).

Crying out with a loud voice represents pledging a counterallegiance to Jesus: away from the powers and principalities.

After this I looked, and there was a great multitude that no one could count, from every nation, from all tribes and peoples and languages, standing before

> the throne and before the Lamb, robed in white, with palm branches in their hands. They cried out in a loud voice, saying, "Salvation belongs to our God who is seated on the throne, and to the Lamb!" And all the angels stood around the throne and around the elders and the four living creatures, and they fell on their faces before the throne and worshiped God, singing, "Amen! Blessing and glory and wisdom and thanksgiving and honor and power and might be to our God forever and ever! Amen." (Rev. 7:9–12 NRSV)

A loud voice is heard from heaven announcing Jesus' victory over death and all the powers in Revelation 12:10–12 (NRSV):

> Then I heard a loud voice in heaven, proclaiming, "Now have come the salvation and the power and the kingdom of our God and the authority of his Messiah, for the accuser of our comrades has been thrown down, who accuses them day and night before our God. But they have conquered him by the blood of the Lamb and by the word of their testimony, for they did not cling to life even in the face of death. Rejoice then, you heavens and those who dwell in them! But woe to the earth and the sea, for the devil has come down to you with great wrath, because he knows that his time is short!"

A multitude in heaven echo this voice, celebrating the judgment of the great whore Babylon: "After this I heard what seemed to be the loud voice of a great multitude in heaven, saying, 'Hallelujah! Salvation and glory and power to our God, for his judgments are true and just; he has judged the great whore who corrupted the earth with her fornication, and he has avenged on her the blood of his servants'" (Rev. 19:1–2 NRSV).

Finally, the loud cry is associated directly with a roar, which unleashes God's work in the world in Revelation 10:3 (NRSV): "He gave a great shout, like a lion roaring. And when he shouted, the seven thunders sounded."

After we complete the above readings, I invite the group once again to name all the obstacles to life and liberation that they are confronting. At first, people resist getting personal, mentioning only the larger structural obstacles: indebtedness, the war in Iraq, racism, HIV/AIDS, global warming, poverty. Then people begin to share obstacles to healing and liberation that are closer to home. People mention cancer and addiction to methamphetamines, alcohol, painkillers, and other drugs. Depression, addiction to pornography, jealousy, anger, hatred, and lust are also vocalized, along with many other things.

I invite people to imagine setting themselves against these things as we prepare to join Jesus in his final shout. I suggest that our shout, like Joshua's before the walls of Jericho and Jesus' before the tomb of Lazarus, is powerful because of the Spirit of God that is released. Together we shout, many as loud as they are able. Some shudder and even cry after this shout. The shout breaks a dam, opening people in extraordinary ways. People report emotional release and even healing. Others experience a revival of hope. The shout is an act of radical faith in God's superior power, released in the moment of greatest weakness and vulnerability. The kingdom of God is released as the Holy Spirit is released over the earth, where it hovers over the darkness and chaos, awaiting the word: "Let there be light" and God's response: "There was light!" Life from the dead.

The Scream

There is the scream. The scream so loud it will be the last word. The scream so loud it will render the man mute. The scream so loud the man will die. You cannot release such a cry and survive. You can release such a cry only if it is the last thing you do. You can release such a cry only if all things are done.

It is the cry of death.

It fills the whole earth. The very earth shudders. The very earth splits. The very earth might not survive. The very earth tears.

The very rocks tear.

And history tears. And all stories tear. My story tears.

And the cry is more than volume, more than decibels, more than sound. The cry is the power of death. The cry is the power of life. The cry releases power.

There is the moment of the cry. There is the moment the man dies. But what is released in his cry and what is released in his death is life.

The dead rise.

The dead walk.

The dead are given a way through.

Because his spirit, which exits his body, fills the very earth. And the earth cannot hold still. And the dead spill out like salt, like salt pouring out through the millions of tiny holes torn in the earth. The dead spill. They rush back into life like children into their mothers' arms, like babies carried by a river, like an infant sailing through the air. His exiled spirit fills this earth with life.

Life.
Like bread.
Like wine.
Like what you always longed to ingest.

Life.
Like hope.
Like a future.
Like a meaning you always wished to believe.

Life.
Like jumping.
Like floating.
Like a body you actually belong in.

Life.
Like peace.
Like grace.
Like everything old and stupid and done being forgotten.

Life.
Like joy.

In response to this teaching, Brita Miko wrote this poem, which is from her forthcoming book *Nailed*.

Like laughter.
Like children climbing into your heart.

Life.
Like energy.
Like voltage.
Like light so comforting you don't miss the dark.

Life.
Like miracles.
Like magic.
Like fairytales becoming truth.

Life.
Like blood.
Like water.
Like all that flows within you.

Life.
Like breath.
Like spirit.
Like inhaling the love of God.

And in the scream, life left his body and entered ours. And in the scream, one boy with black hair dies and another boy with black hair comes back to life.

Life.
Like change.
Like difference.
Like your dead son returning home.

When we cry out with Jesus, "Kingdom of God come, will of God be done, on earth as in heaven," we must expect the presence of the future now possible because of Jesus' suffering, death, and resurrection. At the same time we are painfully aware that we are strangers and sojourners. While we can expect and celebrate concrete signs of Christ's victory over the powers, the more I see, the more I long for God's kingdom to break in completely. In Hebrews we are reminded that "faith is the assurance of things hoped for, the conviction of things not seen" (Heb. 11:1 NRSV). In the midst of a description of the faith of patriarchs, the writer reminds us: "All of these died in faith without having received the promises, but from a distance they saw and greeted them. They confessed that they were strangers and foreigners on the earth. . . . They desire a better country, that is, a heavenly one. Therefore God is not ashamed to be called their God; indeed, he has prepared a city for them" (Heb. 11:13, 16 NRSV).

Hebrews 11 ends powerfully with examples of God's victory over the powers (11:32–34), followed by verses that describe terrible suffering (11:36–38). The simultaneous reality of victory and suffering is visible in Hebrews 11:35: "Women received their dead by resurrection. Others were tortured, refusing to accept release, in order to obtain a better resurrection." Romans 8:18–25 (NRSV) expresses well the expectancy and hope for redemption in the midst of suffering:

> I consider that the sufferings of this present time are not worth comparing with the glory about to be revealed to us. For the creation waits with eager longing for the revealing of the children of God; for the creation was subjected to futility, not of its own will but by the will of the one who subjected it, in hope that the creation itself will be set free from its bondage to decay and will obtain the freedom of the glory of the children of God. We know that the whole creation has been groaning in labor pains until now; and not only the creation, but we ourselves, who have the first fruits of the Spirit, groan inwardly while we wait for adoption, the redemption of our bodies. For in hope we were saved. Now hope that is seen is not hope. For who hopes for what is seen? But if we hope for what we do not see, we wait for it with patience.

Finally, John of Patmos invites us into his vision of the new heaven and the new earth that is replacing the old in Revelation 21. Contemplating the "holy city, the new Jerusalem, coming down out of heaven from God" allows us to envision and welcome the future into the present. We learn from this vision what we can know only through divine revelation. A loud voice from God's throne declares what is not yet evident: "See, the home of God is among mortals. He will dwell with them; they will be his peoples, and God himself will be with them; he will wipe every tear from their eyes. Death will be no more; mourning and crying and pain will be no more, for the first things have passed away" (Rev. 21:3–4 NRSV).

John's vision invites us to anticipate in the now what is not yet evident, much as Jesus, in the first and last beatitudes of Matthew's Gospel, calls blessed the poor in spirit and those who are persecuted for the sake of righteousness "because theirs *is* the kingdom of God," now in the present. All who are not yet experiencing the fullness of the new heaven and the new earth are invited to wait expectantly for God to come and satisfy our deepest longings. Those who mourn are blessed here and now because "they will be comforted." The meek can be assured that in spite of the appearance, they are blessed because "they will inherit the earth." Those who hunger and thirst for righteousness in the present can anticipate the banqueting table of the kingdom of God, where "they will be filled." The merciful and pure in heart are already blessed in the present because they will most certainly receive mercy and see God. Finally, the peacemakers too are declared by Jesus already blessed because one day they will be called sons and daughters of God (Matt. 5:3–12).

In the midst of our struggle to see the kingdom of God come, we need to hear directly from the one who sits on the throne, who says: "See, I am making all things new" (Rev. 21:5 NRSV). Jesus here speaks as commander and chief about the present reality that he is here and now, already in the process of making all things new. The future reality of the new heaven and the new earth is already accomplished and now must be lived into, as if it were more real than the darkness of our present age.

"Also he said, 'Write this, for these words are trustworthy and true.' Then he said to me, 'It is done! I am the Alpha and the Omega, the beginning and the end'" (Rev. 21:5–6a NRSV).

As we welcome and live into God's future in the midst of the crumbling of empires as the old passes away, our thirst will increase to the point of desperation. Jesus anticipates this, offering us the gift of living water to empower us and true words of life to remind us of our victory, inheritance, and true identity.

"To the thirsty I will give water as a gift from the spring of the water of life. Those who conquer will inherit these things, and I will be their God and they will be my children" (Rev. 21:6b–7 NRSV). So we drink deeply from God's presence, continually being filled with the Holy Spirit as we contemplate God's Word, welcoming new birth as the word becomes flesh in us, through us, and around us, full of grace and truth. And we will see his glory as the children of God awaken to satisfy the anxious longing of all creation.

Notes

Introduction

1. Matt. 4:17; Mark 1:14–15; Luke 4:43; 16:16.
2. The sending of the Twelve suggests the reconstitution of Israel, and the seventy or seventy-two suggests the universal mission of the nations. The Hebrew text of Genesis 10 lists seventy nations, whereas the Septuagint lists seventy-two.
3. The NRSV's "I am about to create" does not adequately translate the Hebrew imperfect tense, which suggests the present ("I create") and permits my own translation here—"I am creating."
4. See Tierra Nueva's Web site www.tierra-nueva.org and my own www.bobekblad .com.
5. See Heidi Baker's forthcoming book *Compelled by Love*.
6. See William Stringfellow, *An Ethic for Christians and Other Aliens in a Strange Land* (Eugene, OR: Wipf and Stock, 2004), 67ff.
7. These three pairs of powers (money/materialism, laws/legalism, and patriotism/ flag) appear to me as near the top of today's North American "high places" before which people are tempted to offer sacrifices. The refusal of Israel and Judah's kings (Messiah/anointed ones) to tear down their high places directly limited the positive impact and led to the eventual downfall of each Anointed One's reign. Sacrifices offered at these high places were tempting as they appeared to guarantee economic success. In like manner the lifespan and fruitfulness of today's movements of spiritual renewal will depend in part on Christians' willingness to turn away from idols and be faithful to God alone: Father, Son, and Holy Spirit. I intend to deal with this in more detail in a future book.

Chapter 1

1. See the School of the Americas Witness Web site for the full list of names and informative articles, www.soaw.org.
2. A whole other model exists for prophetic ministry to those already in exile. I recognize that Isa. 40–66 offers an empowering image of ministry that recruits the downtrodden as God's change agents and begin to think on this.
3. Gospel Outreach of Eureka, California, established Verbo Church in Guatemala, supporting then President Rios Montt with help from Pat Robertson's *700 Club* during one of the bloodiest, most oppressive periods of Guatemala's history. See Sara Diamond, *Spiritual Warfare: The Politics of the Christian Right* (Boston: South End Press, 1990), 167–81.
4. Peter had also benefited from other renewal centers like Brownsville, Florida; the International House of Prayer in Kansas City; Morningstar Ministries in North Carolina.

5. The ministry of Rolland and Heidi Baker is well documented in Rolland and Heidi Baker, *There's Always Enough* (Tonbridge: Sovereign Word, 2002), and Guy Chevreau's *Turnings: The Kingdom of God and the Western World* (Tonbridge: Sovereign Word, 2004). Also check out Iris Ministries' Web site at www.irismin.org.

6. There are some good books that describe the gifts of the Spirit released by the anointing of the Holy Spirit. See Mark Stibbe, *Know Your Spiritual Gifts: Practicing the Presents of God* (Grand Rapids: Zondervan, 1997); Francis MacNutt, *Healing* (Notre Dame, IN: Ave Maria Press, 1974, reprint 1999); *The Healing Reawakening: Reclaiming our Lost Inheritance* (Grand Rapids: Chosen, 2005).

7. For more information on Toronto Airport Christian Fellowship, see John Arnott, *The Father's Blessing* (Lake Mary, FL: Karisma House, 1995); John Arnott, *Experience the Blessing: Testimonies from Toronto* (Ventura, CA: Renew, 2000). See also www.tacf.org.

8. While there were not overt verbal links between Zack's actions and our Bible study on Luke 15, I believe that Zack saw himself both as one of the sinners with whom Jesus ate and as a discriminatory Pharisee to whom he addressed the parable. In any case, Zack exercised a bold freedom, much like Jesus, in response to the reading of Scripture and the presence of the Spirit in our Bible study.

9. Maximilien Mission, *Le Théâtre Sacré des Cévennes,* ed. Jean-Pierre Richardot (Paris: Les Éditions de Paris, 1996).

Chapter 2

1. In Matt. 3:5 and Luke 3:3 John is described as ministering in the district around the Jordan.

2. Matt. 4:1–2; Mark 1:12–13; Luke 4:1–2.

3. Matthew and Mark emphasize Jesus' coming up out of the water (Matt. 3:16; Mark 1:10), which Luke does not mention.

4. Though the word "baptism" signifies immersion, pictures of Jesus' baptism from around 85 CE show Jesus up to his waist in water, with John the Baptist pouring water over his head. In Rome the earliest surviving baptismal fonts are in the shape of coffins in which the baptized were immersed.

5. Luke's Gospel alludes to this with the addition of the detail surrounding Jesus' baptism, "when all the people were baptized, that Jesus also was baptized" (Luke 3:21 NASB).

6. In the light of New Testament teaching on the principalities and powers as spiritual enemies that are distinct but linked to actual human institutions, institutions, and passions I believe that categories like "Egyptians," "chariots and horsemen," and "army" should be viewed as spiritual enemies that God opposes, that God has finally stripped of their power through Jesus' victory on the cross, and that must be resisted. In the same way, the Canaanite, Hittite, Hivite, Perizzite, Girgashite, Amorite, and Jebusite, whom Joshua (3:10) says the Lord will dispossess before the advancing Israelites as they enter Canaan, must be read as spiritual enemies of the kingdom of God, as the early church fathers do. (See Bob Ekblad, *Reading the Bible with the Damned* [Louisville, KY: Westminister John Knox, 2005], 133–41.)

7. See also Pss. 78:53; 106:11.

8. I understand repentance to signify more a change of mind than feeling sorry for sin. Jesus' acceptance of John's baptism of repentance for the forgiveness of sins begs the question, what sins was Jesus repenting of? If Jesus was without sin, then Jesus' repentance could be interpreted as "identificational"—an act of repentance on behalf of the people of Israel, his ancestors, and his contemporaries. Jesus' will-

ingness to enter into the consequences of his people's sins at the beginning of his ministry is certainly played out throughout his life and in his death "for sinners."

9. See my chapter "Following Jesus the Good Coyote," in Bob Ekblad, *Reading the Bible with the Damned*, 179–96.

10. See also Col. 3:11; Rom. 3:22; 1 Cor. 12:13.

11. Some would argue that our status as children of God through adoption is not illegal, as Jesus posted bail to the powers through giving over his very life "in exchange" for ours. Paul speaks of this in a different way in Gal. 3:13, where he describes Jesus as redeeming us from the curse of the law by becoming a curse for us. In becoming a curse Jesus, as the descendant of Abraham par excellence, reaches out to cursed ones, including the nations in the promise given to Abraham, which he received by faith before he was ever under the law. Since the promise was given before any law existed, the nations are in fact legally grandfathered into the family.

12. The scribes and Pharisees did not believe Jesus in a way that Moses expected the elders and people of Israel to receive him (Exod. 4:1). The people of Israel are described as believing after Moses and Aaron tell them their mission and perform the signs (Exod. 4:29–31).

13. The Pharisees' inability to perform the signs that Jesus did parallels Pharaoh's magicians' final awareness that they could not compete with the "finger of God" (Exod. 8:19; 9:11).

14. At this point in John's Gospel, the only public signs Jesus has performed are the turning of water into wine (2:1–12) and the overturning of the money changers' tables when he cleansed the temple (2:13–17). When the Jews asked him for a sign as a mark of his authority, he responded cryptically: "Destroy this temple, and in three days I will raise it up" (2:19).

15. Some inmates and other Bible study participants in mainstream groups see water birth as referring to the actual physical birth event, when the woman's water breaks preceding the birth. However, in the context of John's Gospel, "born of water" refers most clearly to John the Baptist's baptism (see John 1:26).

16. "Renewal of the mind" is another way of talking about repentance. The Greek word underlying "repentance," *metanoia*, literally means having another mind or after-mind (*meta* = after or other and *noia* = mind or heart).

Chapter 3

1. Systems of this world also include religious institutions like churches and their belief systems. People who have not "left" these worlds may be those who perceive that they are successfully complying with the demands or membership or have not yet given up trying. People who have repeatedly failed to comply with the perceived demands of God and find themselves outside the group have left the world. Alcoholics Anonymous (AA) elevates departure from a belief system that emphasizes reliance on willpower as the first step toward recovery. People must first recognize that they are incapable of stopping drinking or drugging as the first step, before they move to step two, which affirms that they can move toward recovery only with the help of a "higher power." While AA's approach can itself become legalistic, qualifying as "the world" that people may need to leave, the official 12 steps do in fact begin with departure as a basis for reentry into a new alcohol- or drug-free life.

2. See 1 Cor. 15:24–27 and Eph. 1:18–23.

3. See my chapter on the powers and principalities in *Reading the Bible with the Damned*, 133–53.

4. The term "fuck it" is often used as synonymous with "I give up," "forget it," or "screw it."

5. Fidelity to the gang or *clica* often appears to outsiders as extreme, as members will regularly risk their lives and long prison sentences to defend their own or comply with the demands of allegiance. The hardest "world" to leave for many Latino gang members is their gang, which functions as family/*familia* over and against the system.

6. The world's persecution of Jesus' followers is described as normal and expected by Jesus, who continues: "Remember the word that I said to you, 'A slave is not greater than his master.' If they persecuted Me, they will also persecute you; if they kept My word, they will keep yours also" (John 15:20 NASB).

7. See my detailed treatment of Jesus' death between criminals in *Reading the Bible with the Damned*, 172–78.

8. "Now we have received, not the spirit of the world, but the Spirit who is from God, that we might know the things freely given to us by God" (1 Cor. 2:12 NASB).

9. "Homies" is short for "homeboys," who are fellow members of a gang.

10. We need to expose injustices without fear of treason. If I am completely openly vocal about my identity as a citizen of the kingdom of God, then whom could I possibly be a traitor to? It isn't treason if my allegiance is to the ultimate victor—Jesus.

Chapter 4

1. John Cassian, *Conferences*, trans. Boniface Ramsey, O.P., Ancient Christian Writers #57 (New York/Mahwah: Newman Press, 1997); John Climacus, *The Ladder of Divine Ascent*, trans. Colm Luibheid and Norman Russel, Classics of Western Spirituality (New York: Paulist Press, 1982); Marva Dawn, *Powers, Weakness and the Tabernacling of God* (Grand Rapids: Eerdmans, 2001).

2. There is extensive literature on the topic of the powers. I list only the most important contributions here: Walter Wink, *Naming the Powers: The Language of Power in the New Testament* (Minneapolis: Fortress Press, 1984); *Unmasking the Powers: The Invisible Forces That Determine Human Existence* (Minneapolis: Fortress Press, 1986); *Engaging the Powers: Discernment and Resistance in a World of Domination* (Minneapolis: Fortress Press, 1992); Charles L. Campbell, *The Word before the Powers: An Ethic of Preaching* (Louisville, KY: Westminster John Knox Press, 2002); Dawn, *Powers, Weakness, and the Tabernacling of God*.

3. Social prophetic voices draw from Old Testament preexilic prophets who decry injustice committed against the poor and oppressed by the rich and powerful. They affirm the prophets of exile in their ministries alongside the marginalized and see Jesus as champion of the poor and announcer of a paradise on earth, the kingdom of God. They see oppressive institutions, ideologies, and policies of world governments and corporations as "principalities and powers" conquered by Jesus. Charismatic prophetic voices rightly emphasize the ability of everyone to hear God speak and guide today, calling people into vocations and directing healing and deliverance for oppressed individuals. They call everyone into the healing and deliverance ministry of Jesus seen in the Gospels through empowerment by the Holy Spirit, and they practice effective spiritual resistance/warfare in keeping with biblical teaching on intercession, fasting, and other worship.

4. In Matthew's account, the devil, also called "the tempter" (Matt. 4:3), tempts Jesus (Matt. 4:1, 5, 8, 11), who says, "Away with you Satan!" (Matt. 4:10 NRSV) in response to the final provocation. In Luke's account only the devil is mentioned (Luke 4:2, 3, 5, 6, 9, 13), while in Mark's Gospel it is only Satan who tempts (Mark 1:13).

5. In Exod. 17:1 (NASB) the congregation of Israel is described as journeying in stages from the wilderness of Sin "according to the command [literally, mouth] of the LORD."

6. Frank D. Hammond, *Demons and Deliverance in the Ministry of Jesus* (Kirkwood, MO: Impact Christian Books, 1991), 5.

7. "Methamphetamine," Wikipedia, the free encyclopedia, http://en.wikipedia.org/wiki/Methamphetamine, p. 2. "Chocolates dosed with methamphetamine were known as *Fliegerschokolade* ('flyer's chocolate') when given to pilots, or *Panzerschokolade* ('tanker's chocolate') when given to tank crews" (ibid.).

8. Wikipedia, ibid.

9. Methamphetamine is widely known "to increase the need and urgency for sex, the ability to have sex for extended periods of time" (Wikipedia, ibid., p. 5).

10. The Bible does in fact present humans and creation as very good. Humans are described as made in God's image and likeness. God is totally good, clean of violence, 100 percent about love, life, liberation, healing, and peace.

11. When I have more time I often read on with people, noting how the Paraclete comes to convict the world "about judgment, because the ruler of this world has been condemned" (John 16:11). This verse beautifully supports John's clear understanding that Jesus and the Holy Spirit consistently target the ruler of this world over humans, and reveal this truth to people in the trenches of spiritual resistance.

12. See my Bible study on this text in Bob Ekblad, *Reading the Bible with the Damned* (Louisville, KY: Westminster John Knox, 2005), 187ff.

13. Ibid., 6.

14. See also Rev. 20:10. The "one who deceives" is a present participle, indicating that this role is ongoing.

15. There are a number of very sensitive presentations of deliverance ministry. See Neal Lozano, *Unbound: A Practical Guide to Deliverance* (Grand Rapids: Chosen Books, 2003); Francis MacNutt, *Deliverance from Evil Spirits: A Practical Manual* (Grand Rapids: Chosen Books, 1995).

16. Jesus rejoices in the Holy Spirit that the Father had revealed to babes (*nepiois*) their authority (Luke 10:21) after the seventy-two return in joy, saying "Lord, even the demons are subject to us in Your name" (Luke 10:17 NASB). "And he said to them, 'I saw Satan fall like lightning from heaven. Behold, I have given you authority to tread upon serpents and scorpions, and over all the power of the enemy; and nothing shall hurt you'" (Luke 10:18–19 RSV).

17. See the Septuagint Version of Exod. 34:11, 24; Num. 21:32; Deut. 11:23; 33:27; and Josh. 24:12.

18. Lancelot C. L. Brenton, *The Septuagint with Apocrypha: Greek and English* (Peabody, MA: Hendrickson Publishers, 1986), 101.

19. John Cassian reflects this tendency to spiritualize Old Testament flesh-and-blood enemies when he writes: "I will go before you. I will humble the powerful of the earth, I will break the doors of bronze and shatter the bars of iron; I will open to you hidden treasures and the deepest secrets (Isa 45:2–3). We are guided by the word of God; let him first humble the powerful of the earth, that is, those evil passions against which we strive, which exercise their dominion and relentless hold over our mortal bodies; let the Lord make them bow before our searching gaze; let him burst the gates of our ignorance and shatter the bars of vice which exclude us from true knowledge; let him lead us to the deepest secrets, and as the Apostle says, (1 Cor 4:5) let him reveal to our enquiry things which are hidden in darkness, and make known the thoughts of our hearts. Thus may we with clean hearts penetrate the darkness of vice, open it up, and bring it out into the light. Let us be able to expound the roots and nature of sins, both to those who are free

from them and those still enchained. Thus may our minds according to the prophecy (Psalm 65/66:12) pass through the fire of sin which scorches them so sorely, and swiftly plunge on, unscathed, into the waters of virtue which will cool them. Sprinkled with holy remedies, may we be found worthy to emerge with purity of heart into the cool repose of perfection." John Cassian, *The Monastic Institutes: On the Training of a Monk and the Eight Deadly Sins,* trans. Jerome Bertram (London: The Saint Austin Press, 1999), 69–70.

20. One afternoon I get a surprise visit from the Border Patrol. They have unofficially decided to cooperate with us. There will be no more raids this season and maybe not next season.

Chapter 5

1. When Moses saw how he was perceived by his fellow Israelites when he sought to be their liberator, with their "who made you a prince and judge over us?" (Exod. 2:14), he knew he had to flee.

2. William Stringfellow, *An Ethic for Christians and Other Aliens in a Strange Land* (Eugene, OR: Wipf & Stock), 13–14.

3. Ibid., 77–78. Stringfellow unfortunately tends to confuse the biblical categories of the principalities and powers with Satan and the demons: "They are designated by such multifarious titles as powers, virtues, thrones, authorities, dominions, demons, princes, strongholds, lords, angels, gods, elements, spirits. Sometimes the names of other creatures are appropriated for them, such as serpent, dragon, lion, beast. . . . Terms which characterize are frequently used biblically in naming the principalities: 'tempter,' 'mocker,' 'foul spirit,' 'destroyer,' 'adversary,' 'the enemy.' And the privity of the principalities to the power of death incarnate is shown in mention of their agency to Beelzebub or Satan or the Devil or the Antichrist. Biblical language regarding authorities and powers is at times imprecise, resisting offering a detailed anatomy of the hierarchy of the demonic or the powers" (77–78).

4. Ibid.

5. I intentionally am using both these words, "creature" and "creation," as the Bible suggests that human institutions are at times linked to spiritual beings, as in Psalm 82, where they are described as gods (vv. 1, 6) who are not infinite but mortal, like people (6–7); cf. also Dan. 10:13, 20, 21.

6. An immigration hold allows immigration authorities to keep someone detained in jail until exonerated or deported.

7. Now the U.S. Border Patrol are called Immigration and Customs Enforcement (ICE) officials.

8. This seems accurate, as demons (also known in Scripture as evil spirits or unclean spirits), featured especially in the Gospels and Acts of the Apostles, are obviously in a lower category than Satan and his many designations (the Accuser, Adversary, Destroyer, Tempter, Thief, Father of Lies, Enemy, Evil One, Devil). Another category often called "principalities and powers" or "authorities and powers" comes from Paul's writings. The mix-up of all these categories leads to confusion.

9. John and Mark Sanford warn against identifying attitudes or emotions like anger, lust, greed, and fear as demons. They distinguish between things of the flesh that must be "crucified" and demons that need to be cast out; see *A Comprehensive Guide to Deliverance and Inner Healing* (Grand Rapids: Chosen Books, 1992), 40–41. However, more detailed discussion of deliverance and inner healing is already available elsewhere and goes beyond the scope of this book.

10. Charles H. Kraft, *Defeating Dark Angels: Breaking Demonic Oppression in the Believer's Life* (Ventura, CA: Regal Books, 1992), 123–25; and Frank and Ida Mae

Hammond, *Pigs in the Parlor: A Practical Guide to Deliverance* (Kirkwood, MO: Impact Christian Books, 1973).

11. Charles Kraft, *I Give You Authority* (Grand Rapids: Chosen Books, 1997), 147.
12. Ibid., 148.
13. Note: A big evil spirit (territorial spirit) can be brought in (attached) to calm other demons/passions like fear, anxiety. Dealing with fear, anxiety, unbelief could strip a territorial spirit of its footholds. Can people who are attached to these sorts of powers be negatively affected by curses, hexes, or other spiritual warfare actions directed against them? Can a person wearing sweatshop clothing or eating produce assembled or picked by exploited workers who curse the company be negatively affected by a curse attached to clothing or a food item?
14. Jesus' uniting of his will with that of his Father's allowed for miraculous deeds of power. The positive aspects of soul ties to territorial and ethnic spirits might be the need for cohesive, ordered human society and group unity around common background. "Relationship bonds establish a direct channel between two or more people and/or a person and an institution so that they can have a positive influence on each other." See "Toolbox for Ministry—Relationship Bonds and Bondages," Isaiah 61 Ministry School, Winter 2005 (Singing Waters Ministries), p. 1.
15. Soul ties are an ungodly covenant with another person (organization or thing) based on an unhealthy emotional and/or sexual relationship. This covenant binds the two people together. God "honors," or recognizes, these covenants. He leaves each of us free to decide when and if we will appropriate his provisions to break/cut the ties and release our self and the other person. Chester and Betsy Kylstra, *An Integrated Approach to Biblical Healing Ministry: A Guide to Receiving Healing and Deliverance from Past Sins, Hurts, Ungodly Mindsets, and Demonic Oppression* (Kent: Sovereign Word, 2003), 272.
16. Mark Virkler, *Prayers That Heal the Heart: Prayer Counseling That Breaks Every Yoke* (Gainesville, FL: Bridge-Logos Publishers, 2001), 31.
17. Ibid., 32.
18. The only exception I have found is a note in Singing Waters training materials that says: "We can have 'demonic linking' to inanimate objects, carved images, idols, buildings, etc., especially if false religions or the occult are involved (Ex 20:3–5; Jer 3:6, 8)" ("Toolbox for Ministry—Relationship Bonds and Bondages," 7).
19. INA: ACT 337—Oath of Renunciation and Allegiance (current law) Sec. 337. [8 U.S.C. 1448] US Code.
20. According to Webster's dictionary, abjure means "(1) to repudiate or recant solemnly, (2) to renounce under oath, forswear."
21. Soul ties with the global economic system are established through investing in the stock market, participating in pension plans, and a host of other activities. When we purchase and consume products from companies with oppressive labor practices, can consumers be adversely affected, perhaps even by curses workers place on their employers?
22. "Toolbox," 7. The following is another version of prayers to cut unhealthy soul ties: "Lord, I break my ungodly soul ties with .... I release myself from him/her/it and release him/her/it from me. As I do this, Lord, I pray that you would cause him/her/it to be all that you want him/her/it to be and me to be all that you want me to be. Lord, please cleanse my mind from all memories of ungodly unions so I am totally free to give myself to you and to my spouse. I renounce and cancel the assignments of all evil spirits attempting to maintain these ungodly soul ties. Lord, thank you for restoring my soul to wholeness. I choose to walk in holiness by your grace. In the name of Jesus Christ I pray,

amen" (Chester and Betsy Kylstra, *An Integrated Approach to Biblical Healing Ministry*, 273).

23. When Abraham's submission to Pharaoh in Gen. 12:12–20 and later Abimelech, king of Gerar, included lying about Sarai's being his sister, the Lord sent plagues against Pharaoh and his household and warned Abimelech in a dream that he would die if he didn't return Sarah (Gen. 20:1–18). Esther respectfully approaches the king to advocate for the Jewish people when they are threatened by Haman's murderous plot (Esth. 7).

24. In this story we see King Darius himself called to submit to the rule of law (Dan. 6:15), much like in a democracy. Daniel's resistance shows an understanding of allegiance to God taking precedence over allegiance to laws or governing authorities.

25. Mark 3:1–12; Luke 14:1–6; John 9:1–34.

26. Matt. 9:10–13; 11:19; Luke 7:39; 15:1–2.

27. Causes, ideologies, or principles can all fit under the designation principality or power or even idol, whenever they become elevated above, or are viewed as more important than, human life.

28. Territorial spirits and other spirits that are higher up in the demonic hierarchy (nationalism, racial pride) are parasitic on other lower-level spirits (e.g. fear, rejection, shame). These lower-level demons must first be cast out before the "open doors" to territorial spirits can be shut.

29. The rules for breaking the authority given by people through the dedication of territories, buildings, and organizations are parallel to those for breaking such authority over an individual. The dedication of such places or institutions to God or Satan can be weakened, sometimes broken, either through the opposite dedication or through usage for the opposite purpose (Kraft, *I Give You Authority*, 150).

30. According the Charles Kraft, "With individuals committed to Satan, we need to look for and clean out the garbage that gives satanic spirits rights in the individual. For territories, buildings and organizations, it is crucial to find and break the power of commitment, dedications, curse and sins that have been made on the land, as well as agreements forged consciously or unconsciously by those in authority over the land that gave legal rights to the enemy. . . . It is an important step in breaking the enemy's power for the people of an infested place (just as with individuals) to confess sin, repent and turn from their wicked ways (2 Chronicles 7:14). . . . In prayer we need to give attention to breaking all historical and contemporary commitments, curses and dedications holding a territory or organization in Satan's grip. We must repent of any sins committed in that territory. Next, in authoritative praying, we speak the power of God over 'the spiritual powers in space' (Eph 2:2), laying claim to the territory or organization in the name of Jesus" (Kraft, *I Give You Authority*, 151).

31. *The Book of Common Prayer* (New York: Seabury Press, 1979), 302–3.

Chapter 6

1. *A chaque jour suffit sa joie* (Paris: Emile-Paul frères, 1949), 368–69. Sister of the author of *Le Grand Meaulnes*, Alain-Fournier, Isabelle Rivière was born in 1888 and married the writer Jacques Rivière. In 1925, after becoming a widow, she retired close to a Benedictine monastery in Calcutta to dedicate herself to meditating on Scripture.

Chapter 7

1. Tierra Nueva's course on conflict resolution included a detailed discussion of the chain of violence, where a simple insult may lead to hidden resentment, gossip,

distrust, believing the worst, return of accusations, open conflict, total breaking of relations, and physical violence.

2. These Bible studies included Matt. 5:38–48; John 18:19–23; and Rom. 12:9–21.

3. http://ncronline.org/NCR_Online/archives/032103/032103h.htm; http://pangaea.org/street_children/latin/soa.htm.

4. See my treatment of praying psalms against enemies in *Reading the Bible with the Damned* (Louisville, KY: Westminster John Knox, 2005), 133–41.

5. See http://www.serendipity.li/cia/death_squads.htm; http://en.wikipedia.org/wiki/Roberto_D'Aubuisson; http://www.usip.org/library/tc/doc/reports/el_salvador/tc_es_03151993_casesD1_2.html.

6. Acts 4:11; Rom. 9:33; 1 Pet. 2:7.

7. The Gospels and the book of Revelation depict the fulfillment of messianic texts regarding Jesus' final victory and judgment as happening at his second coming (Matt. 24:36–51; Rev. 6:12–17; 18:1–24).

8. Oscar Romero, *The Violence of Love*, compiled and trans. James R. Brockman (Maryknoll, NY: Orbis, 1988), 152.

9. Ibid., 12.

10. Christians in China have suffered terribly for their faith, being imprisoned, tortured, and martyred by the state. Yet, in spite of the oppression, the underground church has grown. See Danyun, *Lilies amongst Thorns: Chinese Christians Tell Their Story through Blood and Tears* (Tonbridge: Sovereign Word, 1991); and Paul Hattaway, *The Heavenly Man: The Remarkable True Story of Christian Brother Yun* (Grand Rapids: Monarch Books, 2002).

11. Campesino groups use the term *recuperar* (take back, recuperate) when they solicit and often legally invade land that Honduran agrarian reform laws deem as available to landless peasants.

12. There are two helpful books on the use of the gift of prophesy in evangelism. See Mark Stibbe, *Prophetic Evangelism: When God Speaks to Those Who Do Not Know Him* (Milton Keynes, Bucks: Authentic Media, 2004), and Doug Addison, *Prophesy, Dreams and Evangelism: Revealing God's Love through Divine Encounters* (North Sutton, NH: Streams Publishing, 2005). Graham Cooke's *Developing Your Prophetic Gifting* (Grand Rapids: Chosen Books, 2003) is a good introduction to charismatic understanding of the prophetic. See Brad Jersak's excellent book *Can You Hear Me? Tuning In to the God Who Speaks* (Abbotsford: Fresh Wind Press, 2003) on hearing the voice of God.

13. In Matt. 26:23 and Mark 14:18–21, it appears that Jesus dips the bread he gives to Judas in the bowl of food, as distinct from in the cup. However, in both accounts Judas is served the bread and the wine.

14. Matt. 26:19, 26–29; Mark 14:12, 22–31.

15. Lev. 9:18.

16. Exod. 29:12; Lev. 9:9; Deut. 12:16.

17. The Greek genitive *apo ton anthropon* can be translated "from the men" but is best rendered "from among men." The saints are not purchased from men, but from the powers.

18. In the Old Testament, the priests would eat the meat of the offerings. Jesus includes us all in the priesthood and life by giving all of us his body and blood.

19. In Matthew, Jesus declares to the sons of Zebedee that they will drink the cup (Matt. 20:23). Yet in Gethsemane (Matt. 26:36–46), when he asks them to accompany him to stay with him and keep watch, he prays that the cup, referring to his death, could pass from him. Three times Jesus asks them to accompany him, and each time they are unable. In this way Matthew demonstrates that the disciples are unable to do what only Jesus does. The disciples do drink the cup of his blood poured out for many for the forgiveness of sins (Matt. 26:28).

20. Jesus' sweat falling to the ground like drops of blood evokes the sprinkling of blood around the altar according to the Levitical sacrificial system (Lev. 9:12, 19).
21. In Mark 9:12, suffering is linked to being treated with contempt. In Heb. 2:18, Jesus is described as being tested by what he suffered.
22. Jesus' cry in Luke differs from Matthew and Mark. While the Septuagint of Exod. 12:30 reads *kraugē megalē* (κραυγὴ μεγάλη) (great cry), Luke's *phonēsas phonē megalē* (φωνήσας φωνῇ μεγάλη) is a Greek equivalent to the Hebrew text of Exodus, possibly reflecting Luke's own unique translation, which continues to link Jesus' cry intertextually with other important O.T. references.